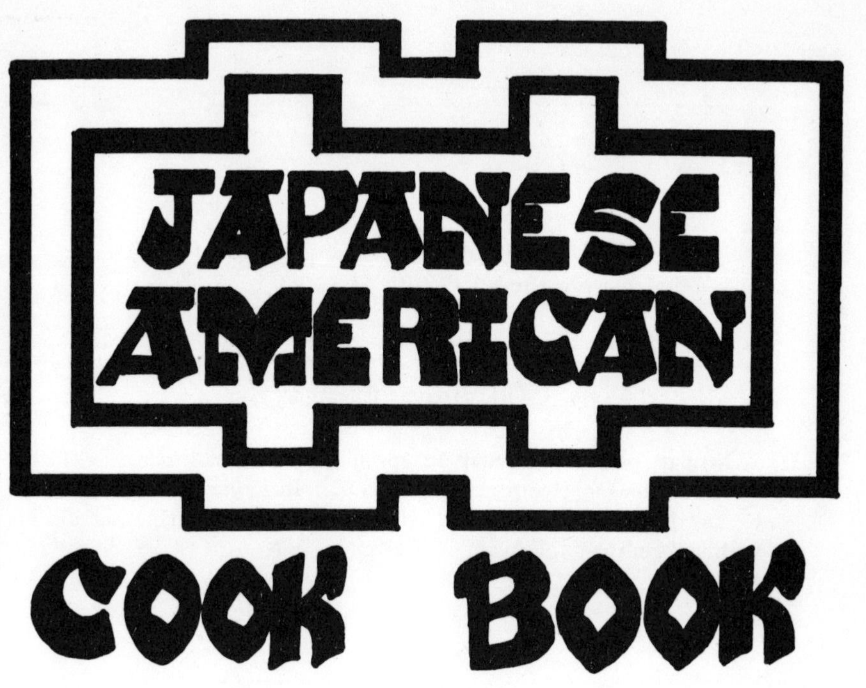

By Marjorie W. Young

Published By
DROKE HOUSE/HALLUX
Atlanta, Ga.

THE JAPANESE-AMERICAN COOKBOOK
Copyright© 1972 By Marjorie W. Young

FIRST EDITION

Standard Book Number: 8375-6750-5
Library of Congress Catalog Number: 74-120-297

Manufactured in The United States of America

Published By
DROKE HOUSE/HALLUX
116 West Orr Street
Anderson, S. C. 29621

INTRODUCTION

During my six years in Japan, I exchanged lessons in American cooking, table settings with silver, linens, dishes, guest seatings and menues with a small group of eight notable Japanese ladies, in return for proper chopstick maneuvering with types of porcelains and lacquer used at formal and informal dinners and luncheons.

Receipts were exchanged and tried in our respective home kitchens.

My dining table was properly set with silver, dishes and crystal. It took quite a few meals before the ladies learned how to pick up the proper fork until they learned the secret of eating from the outside silver first on down to the plate-side. They had difficulty in cutting meat with a knife and fork at first, and eating soup with a spoon instead of drinking from the bowl. Just as I had difficulty in learning to place my chopsticks properly on their resting pad and never holding them in my hand except to pick up food and to place it in my mouth. You do not hold chopsticks in your hand while chewing, any more than you would wave a knife or fork around while eating.

Japanese food is a true culinary art and equally as artistic and carefully prepared as Japanese flower-arranging, Japanese tea ceremonies or Japanese gardens.

Foods are tastefully prepared for visual as well as eating enjoyment and served in special porcelain or lacquer bowls and small dishes for special dipping sauces, all placed on individual lacquer trays.

Family style meals in Japanese homes are served on one large low table with side trays for the covered rice bucket and other main course foods.

A regular dinner would be served on trays raised on legs. It could consist of a dish of mixed foods on the far side of the tray, a bowl of soup with a lid and another bowl along with sake and tea cups. When being served you hold the bowl or cup in the right hand bracing the bottom with the left hand. Then the food or drink is placed on the tray before eating or sipping. Hot tea and boiled polished white rice are served with all meals.

Next served would be fish and broiled meat and a vegetable or green herb, a boiled fish, some steamed egg custard and a fried dish brought in, in this order and earlier dishes removed. At the end, rice and a bean-paste soup are served followed by hot tea.

Sometimes the tray is removed, and fruit served, such as giant strawberries in season, or cakes and tea.

There are many festival days in Japan each with special foods for the occasion. There are children's days, religious days, cultural days and calendar days.

Children's days consist of boys' celebrations when they are three and five years old; girls have a seventh year feast. There is flying of gigantic carp kites over the house for the boys in the family, one kite for each boy. The carp is used because it can swim upstream.

Girls celebrate with a formal obi or kimono sash gift and a doll festival. Special foods are prepared and enjoyed after which the family walks to the temple with offerings of thanks.

There are religious festivals of Shinto and Buddhist and Western Christmas with trees and ancestor worship holidays.

Weddings are great events and the bride wears a tri-cornered hat to keep the devil away and changes her outer kimona three times during the ceremony and great feasts follow the wedding.

Sprig Cherry-blossom festival calls for bright lacquer boxes filled with rice-balls covered with sesame or benne seeds and seasoned with salt, carried under the trees and enjoyed like a picnic.

There are summer wild-flower and fall harvest festivals like our Thanksgiving.

Fall moon-viewing in August is accompanied with fruits in season and taro roots with cooked soy-beans.

At Chrysanthemum viewing festivals, rice and soy flour cookies are enjoyed. I attended an Imperial Chrysanthemum party held in the Palace gardens, where many beautiful foods were served on dressy buffet tables. The piece de resistance was small hard rice cakes impressed with the Imperial crest, an 18 petal Chrysanthemum. These were highly prized and taken home by Japanese guests to be placed in the family shrine.

All household and business bills must be paid by New Year's eve and families stay home when small merchants, street cleaners and extra help come to collect their fees. On this day soups and fish with boiled radish are eaten with sweetened bean paste cakes and buckwheat cookies.

From every aspect, the receipts of Japan are worth the effort. The results are culinary feasts and artistic achievements.

Each receipt contained in this volume has the Japanese and American translations on facing pages. Some of our favorite American receipts have been included, with the hope that they may prove enjoyable for our American readers, as well as for those who read them in Japanese and trytthem for the first time.

Marjorie W. Young

近代的家庭

西洋料理法

No. 1   PRUNES STUFFED WITH CREAM CHEESE

Steam till tender, and cool large meaty prunes. Remove pits through slits in side. Mash to a paste some cream cheese, or melt cheese to which add a little cream. Add a little thick, sweet cream and finely chopped nut meats, salt and paprika to taste. Fill the prunes generously full with the cheese mixture and chill before serving.

No. 2   ORANGE SECTIONS WITH COCOANUT

Peel oranges carefully and divide into sections and remove all white skin. Dip the orange sections into fruit juice and roll in toasted cocoanut.

No. 3   PINEAPPLES BOUCHEES

Cut into segments, canned pineapple slices and dip into finely chopped nut meats.

No. 4   BANANA SEGMENTS

Peel ripe bananas and scrape and slice in half inch pieces. Marinate in slightly sweetened lemon juice and drain. Arrange on serving dish and top with a rosette of whipped cream.

No. 5   FIG TASTIES

Marinate whole dried figs in orange juice, then dip in grated lemon rind and garnish with halved blanched almonds.

No. 6   CHEESE PUFFS

Soak in ice water two or three minutes, small round soda crackers. Arrange on buttered baking sheet, and sprinkle with grated cheese. Brown in hot oven till well puffed.

No. 1　　　　プルンズのチーズ詰

作り方—大型のプルンズ（乾西洋梅）を軟くなる迄蒸して一寸ナイフで切目を入れて種子を取出します。別にチーズを少量のクリームで煉り、細く切つた胡桃を加へたものを鹽とパプリカで味をつけて前のプルンズの種子を取つた中に詰め充分冷します。

No. 2　　　　オレンヂとココナツツ

作り方—ネーブル・オレンヂの皮を取り、中の薄皮を取つて實を一つづゝ別々にして、オレンヂ汁に一寸漬けてココナツツを一寸位に切つた中にころがしてオレンヂの外側にココナツツをまぶします。

No 3　　　　バイナツプルと胡桃

作り方—罐詰のバイナツプルの一切れを八ツ位に切つて細く切つた胡桃の中にころがしてまぶします。

No. 4　　　　バ ナ ナ の 前 菜

作り方—バナナの皮を取つて三分の厚さに切り、少量の砂糖を加へたレモン汁に和へ色が變らぬ様にして、上に袋からおし出して花形を作つた泡立てクリームを飾ります。

No. 5　　　　乾 無 花 果

作り方—乾無花果を其の儘オレンヂ汁に和へ、後、レモンの皮を卸したものにまぶします。此の儘又はアーモンドを一個程上に指でおさへてのせ飾りとします。

No. 6　　　　チ ー ズ・バ フ

作り方—小さい丸形のソーダ・クラツカー（ソーダ・ビスケツト）を二三分間氷を入れた冷水に漬け、油を塗つた天パンに並べ、上に卸したチーズを振掛け強火の天火で充分ふくれる迄燒きます。

No. 7 STRAWBERRY JUICE COCKTAIL

2 Cups strawberries	¼ Cup grapefruit juice
2 Tablespoons sugar	1½ Tablespoons lemon
1/3 Cup orange juice	juice

Wash and hull the strawberries, cut them in halves, sprinkle with sugar and let stand half an hour in order to have as much juice as possible. To the sugar and berries add orange juice, grapefruit juice, lemon juice and a few grains of salt. Mix thoroughly and squeeze through cheesecloth and chill in the refrigerator When thoroughly chilled pour into four double cocktail glasses.

No. 8 OYSTER AND RIPE OLIVE COCKTAILS

2 Dozen small oysters	1 Tablespoon Worcestershire
¼ Cup minced ripe olives	sauce
1 Tablespoon horseradish	1 Tablespoon lemon juice
½ Teaspoon tabasco sauce	2 Tablespoon tomato catsup
1 Tablespoon vinegar	½ Teaspoon salt

Arrange the small oysters in cocktail glasses and sprinkle with the minced olives. Make a sauce by mixing together throughly the horseradish, tabasco sauce, vinegar, Worcestershire sauce, lemon juice, tomato catsup and salt. Pour the sauce over the chilled cocktail and serve ice cold.

No. 9 TOMATO JUICE COCKTAIL

1 Can tomato soup	1 Piece celery bruised
1 Cup water	1 Tablespoon Worcestershire
1 Small onion sliced	sauce
1 Tablespoon vinegar	1 Teaspoon soy sauce
2 Teaspoons lemon juice	1 Teaspoon chili sauce
3 Drops tabasco sauce	1 Teaspoon prepared horseradish
2 Bay leaves	

Combine the soup and the water and add the remaining ingredients. Allow to stand at least 15 minutes, then strain and serve very cold. In bruising the celery, twist it slightly to bruise some of the outside fibers. Serves eight.

No. 7　　　　苺コクテール

材料　苺　　　　　　カツプ二杯　　　グレープ・フル
　　　砂　糖　　　　大匙二杯　　　　ーツの汁　　　カツプ四分ノ一
　　　オレンヂ汁　　　　　　　　　　レモン汁　　　大匙一杯半
　　　（又は蜜柑汁）　カツプ三分ノ一　鹽　　　　　極　少　量

作り方――苺はへたを取り、洗つて半分に切り、砂糖を加へて三十分程置きます。
　これに他の材料を全部加へ、（グレープ・フルーツの汁の代りに葡萄酒を使つ
　てもよい）よく混ぜて、さらし布の袋に入れて、汁を全部しぼり、冷藏庫に
　入れて充分冷し、コクテール・グラスに入れ、食前の前菜とします。

No. 8　　　牡蠣とオリーヴ・コクテール

材料　牡　蠣（小）　二十四個　　　　牡蠣コクテール・ソース
　　　ライブオリーヴ
　　　（黒オリーヴ）　カツプ四分ノ一

作り方――牡蠣は一人前六個をガラスに入れ、上に微塵切りにしたオリーヴを振掛
　け、冷したソースを上から掛けて前菜として召上るもの、次のコクテール・
　ソースは牡蠣蟹等のコクテールによいものです。

コクテール・ソース

材料　卸した山葵　　　　大匙一杯　　　レモン汁　　　　大匙一杯
　　　トバスカ・ソース　小匙半杯　　　トマト・ケチヤツプ　大匙二杯
　　　西洋酢　　　　　　大匙一杯　　　鹽　　　　　　　小匙半杯

作り方――材料を全部よく混合せ冷くして用ひるのです。

No. 9　　　トマト・ジユース・コクテール

材料　トマト・スープ罐詰　一　罐　　　ベーリーフ（香料）　二　枚
　　　水　　　　　　　　トマト・スー　セロリの葉　　　一　枝
　　　　　　　　　　　　プと同分量　　ウイスタシヤー・
　　　玉葱輪切り　　　　一切れ　　　　ソース　　　　　大匙一杯
　　　西洋酢　　　　　　大匙一杯　　　チリー・ソース　小匙一杯
　　　レモン汁　　　　　小匙二杯　　　醬　油　　　　　小匙一杯
　　　トバスコ・ソース　三　滴　　　　卸したわさび　　小匙一杯

作り方――トマトのスープを同分量の水で割り、他の材料を全部加へ、十五分位そ
　の儘に置き、裏濾しして、充分に冷し、前菜として、晩餐の一番初めに供し
　ます。

No. 10   PINEAPPLE AND CRAB COCKTAIL

1/3 Cup chopped or ground pineapple

1/3 Cup crab

6 Tablespoons mayonnaise

2 Teaspoons grated horse-radish

2 Teaspoons Worcestershire sauce

Take crab from can and remove all small bones and mix with the chopped pineapple. Combine the mayonnaise, horseradish and sauce. Arrange the crab and pineapple in cocktail glasses and pour the mayonnaise mixture over the top. Serve very cold.

No. 10　　　　　蟹とパイナツプルのコクテール

材料	微塵切りパイ		卸したわさび	小匙二杯
	ナツプル	カツプ三分ノ一	ウイスタシヤー・	
	蟹罐詰	カツプ三分ノ一	ソース	小匙二杯
	マヨネーズ	大匙六杯		

作り方—蟹をほぐして小骨を抜いたものにパイナツプルを混合せ、別にマヨネーズとソースとわさびを併せたものを上に掛け、四個のコクテール・グラスに盛ります。

No. 11   TOMATO SOUP WITH MACARONI

2 Tins tomato soup	3 Teaspoons sugar
1 Cup soup stock	½ Teaspoon celery salt
2 Tablespoon butter	½ Teaspoon salt
1 Cup cooked macaroni cut in two inch lengths	3 Teaspoons mushroom catsup

Put the tomato soup in a double boiler. Slowly add the soup stock, the seasoning, macaroni and butter. When well heated, pour into bowls. On top of each bowlful put one tablespoon puffed rice which has been heated in a saucepan with butter.

No. 12   CORN-TOMATO CHOWDER

1 Tablespoon grated onion	2 Cups water
2 Cups green corn cut from the cob	1 Tablespoon sugar
3 Tablespoons fat	1 Teaspoon salt
2 Tablespoon flour	Few grains pepper and paprika
4 Cups peeled tomatoes cut in small pieces	¼ Teaspoon soda
	1 Cup hot milk

Chop fine or grate the onion and corn and saute in the fat, add flour and cook for three minutes, stirring constantly. Add tomatoes, water, sugar, salt pepper and paprika, cover and cook slowly 30 minutes. Just before serving stir in the soda and milk which has been heated to boiling.

No. 13   CLAM AND TOMATO SOUP

2 Cups shelled clams	2 Slices onion
1 Cup cold water	4 Tablespoons flour
1½ Hot cups milk	¾ Cup canned tomato soup
4 Tablespoons butter	1 Tablespoon salt

Remove the tough parts of the clam and add to the cold water and simmer for 20 minutes, then put through sieve. Brown the onion for five minutes in the butter and remove the onion Add the flour to the butter and add the water in which the clams were cooked, stirring constantly. Allow this mixture to boil up several times, then add the tomato soup, salt and pepper and boil up once more. Just before serving add the hot milk.

No. 11　　　　トマト・マカロニ・スープ

材料	トマト・スープ	二　　　罐	砂　糖	小匙三杯
	スープ・ストツク	カツプ一杯	セロリ・ソルト	小匙半杯
	バター	大匙二杯	鹽	小匙半杯
	マカロニ（茹でゝ一寸の長さに切つたもの	カツプ一杯	松茸ケチヤツプ	小匙三杯

作り方―トマト・スープとスープ・ストツクを二重鍋の上の部に入れ、靜に、マカロニ、バター、鹽、セロリ・ソルト、ケチヤツプ及び砂糖等を加へて熱します。之をスープ皿に盛り、上にパフ・ライス（ふくらましたライス）を一人前に附き大匙一杯位づゝバターでいためたものを振掛け直に召上るのです。

No. 12　　　　玉蜀黍とトマトのチヤウダー

材料	玉葱卸したもの	大匙一杯	冷　水	カツプ二杯
	玉蜀黍罐詰又は生のもの	カツプ二杯	砂　糖	大匙一杯
	バター	大匙三杯	鹽	小匙一杯
	メリケン粉	大匙二杯	胡椒、パプリカ	少　量
	トマト（皮を取り賽の目切り）	カツプ四杯	ソーダ	小匙四分ノ一
			熱したミルク	カツプ一杯

作り方―玉蜀黍は罐詰ならばその儘、生のものならばかぶから切つて用ひます。先づバターで玉蜀黍と玉葱をいため、メリケン粉を加へて、三分間絶えず混ぜながら煮て、トマトと水を加へ、鹽、胡椒、パプリカで味を附け、蓋をして弱火で三十分間煮る。召上る一寸前に熱したミルクとソーダを加へます。

No. 13　　　　蛤とトマトのスープ

材料	むきみ	カツプ二杯	メリケン粉	大匙四杯
	冷　水	カツプ一杯	トマト・スープ（罐詰でよい）	カツプ四分ノ三
	牛　乳	カツプ一杯半	鹽	大匙一杯
	バター	大匙四杯		
	葱の輪切り	二切れ		

作り方―むきみの固い部分を取り冷水に加へて煮立て、弱火で二十分煮て裏漉にします。バターで玉葱を五分間燒き、玉葱を取り去り、メリケン粉を入れ、蛤を茹でた水で次第に延し沸騰したらばトマトと鹽と胡椒を入れて再び煮立て、召上る前に別に煮立てた牛乳に加へます。

No. 14   **TOMATO AND RICE SOUP**

2 Cups boiled rice	1 Teaspoon salt
3 Tablespoons chopped celery leaves	¼ Teaspoon paprika
	3 Cups tomatoes
3 Tablespoons chopped onions	2 Tablespoons fat, melted

Mix all ingredients except butter. Cover and cook slowly for 20 minutes. Add butter and serve hot.

No. 15   **RICE AND ASPARAGUS SOUP**

1 Quart well seasoned soup stock	½ Cup rice
	2 to 4 Tablespoons grated cheese
1 Cup water	1 Small bunch asparagus

Wash the asparagus, cut off the tough parts, and use them for cream soup. Put the tips and the tender portions into the broth and water, boil till half done, about 20 minutes, then add the rice well washed, and cook until it is tender. Serve very hot and pass the cheese with it. This soup should be very thick.

No. 16   **ONION AU GRATIN**

1 Large onion, sliced	4 Tablespoons grated Parmesan cheese
4 Tablespoons olive oil	
	4 Squares dry bread
4 Cups soup stock	1 Teaspoon salt

Slice the onion in a quarter of an inch thickness and cook in the olive oil for about 10 minutes being careful not to brown it. Divide the onion into four au gratin dishes and add the boiling hot soup stock to which salt has been added. Brown the dry bread in the oven float on the top of the soup, and sprinkle each with one tablespoon of chesse. Cover and bake for 15 minutes in a hot oven. Serve in au gratin dishes.

No. 14　　　トマト・ライス・スープ

材料	御　　飯	カツプ二杯	パプリカ	小匙四分ノ一
	セロリ葉微塵切り	大匙三杯	トマト	カツプ三杯
	玉葱微塵切り	大匙三杯	溶したバター又は	
	鹽	小匙一杯	代用品	大匙二杯

作り方―バター以外の材料全部を一緒にして、蓋をして二十分間煮て、バターを
加へ、スープ皿に盛ります。大層濃いスープです。

No. 15　　　アスパラガスとライス・スープ

材料	スープ・ストツク	カツプ四杯	生アスパラガス	二十本位
	水	カツプ一杯	卸したチーズ	大匙二乃至四杯
	白　米	カツプ半杯		

作り方―アスパラガスの先の方の軟い所を切り取り、固い所は別の料理用に取つ
て置きます。スープ・ストツクに充分味を附け、水を加へ、アスパラガスを
五分位に切つたものを入れて火に掛け、二十分間程茹でゝ半煮えにし、洗つ
た白米を加へ、白米が軟くなる迄茹で續けます。スープ皿に盛り、卸したチ
ーズを別に添え召し上る時適當に各自がチーズをスープの上に振掛けるの
です。濃いスープです。

No. 16　　　玉葱グラタン・スープ

材料	玉葱輪切り	大　一　個	パン（一寸角）	四　切　れ
	オリーブ油	大匙四杯	鹽	小匙一杯
	スープ・ストツク	カツプ四杯		
	卸したパーミシア			
	ン・チーズ	大匙四杯		

作り方―玉葱を厚さ二分の輪切りにして、オリーブ油（又はサラダ油、バター等）
で十分位透明になる迄燒き、茶椀蒸の器四個に等分して盛り、此の上に鹽で
味を附け、沸騰したスープを掛け、此の上にパンを天火の中でよく乾したも
のを浮ばせてパンの上にチーズを振掛け蓋をして、天火の中で十五分燒いて
温めます。冬に美味しいスープです。器に入れた儘蓋を取らずに供します。

No. 17   **OYSTER STEW**

1 Pint oysters   Salt, pepper, paprika
4 Tablespoons butter   4 Cups rich milk

Put cleaned oysters, strained osyter liquor, butter, and seasoning into a saucepan and simmer gently until oysters curl at the edges. Add the milk and bring quickly to the simmering point. Serve very hot.

No. 18   **JERUSALEM ARTICHOKE SOUP**

1 Pound Jerusalem   1½ Cups milk
  artichokes   1 Leaf of mace
½ Lemon   1 Teaspoon salt
2 Tablespoons butter   ⅛ Teaspoon pepper
1 Slice onion   ½ Cup whipping cream
1 Cup cold water   1 Tablespoon chopped nuts

Wash artichokes well, peel and cut in thin slices. Add to the water the artichokes and lemon juice and allow to stand for 15 minutes. Melt butter, Add onion and artichokes which have been drained from the water, and cook for five minutes without browning. Add one cup water, mace and cook until artichokes are soft. Put through the potato ricer. Add milk, salt and pepper to the sieved artichokes and juice, heat and serve in soup dishes, topped with whipped cream to which the chopped nuts have been added.

No. 19   **BEETS A LA RUSSE**

1¼ Cups cooked beets   ¼ Cup water
1 Tablespoon butter   ½ Teaspoon salt
1 Tablespoon flour   ¼ Cup sour cream
3 Tablespoons vinegar

Put beets through food chopper. Melt butter, add flour and when well blended add vinegar (less if cream is very sour), water and salt. Stir and cook until sauce boils. Add beets and cook 10 to 15 minutes. Add sour cream, mix well and serve.

No. 17　　　　牡蠣スチユー・スープ

材料　牡　　蠣　　　　　カツプ二杯　　　　鹽、胡椒、パプリカ　　　適宜
　　　バター　　　　　　大匙四杯　　　　　ミルク　　　　　　　カツプ四杯

作り方―牡蠣とその汁、バター、鹽、胡椒及びパプリカを鍋に入れ、弱火で靜か
　　に牡蠣の緣が縮む迄數分間煮て後、ミルクを加へ、火力を强くして、早く熱
　　して煮立ち初めたらば直にスープ皿に盛つて溫い內に供します。

No. 18　　　　八　ツ　頭　の　ス　ー　プ

材料　八ツ頭　　　　　一　封　度　　　ミルク　　　　　カツプ一杯半
　　　レモン汁　　　　　半　個　分　　　鹽　　　　　　　小匙一杯
　　　バター　　　　　　大　匙　二　杯　　胡　　椒　　　小匙八分ノ一
　　　玉葱輪切り　　　　一　切　れ　　　泡立てクリーム　　カツプ半杯
　　　冷　　水　　　　　カツプ一杯　　　胡挑微塵切リ　　　大匙一杯
　　　メース（香料）　　一　　枚

作り方―八ツ頭はよく洗ひ皮を取つて薄く切り、レモン汁と共に冷水に入れ十五
　　分間置きます。バターを溶し、玉葱と八ツ頭を入れ、五分間色を附けずに燒
　　きカツプ一杯の冷水とメースを加へ、八ツ頭が軟くなる迄煮て、裏漉にしま
　　す。ミルクに鹽、胡椒と共に裏漉にしたものを加へ、熱してスープとして召
　　上るのです。別にスープ皿に盛つてから上に泡立てたクリームに胡桃を混ぜ
　　たものを浮ばせると尙よいのですが特にそうする必要もありません。

No. 19　　　　ビーツ・クリーム・スープ

材料　茹でたビーツ（赤蕪）カツプ一杯四分ノ一
　　　バター　　　　　　大匙一杯　　　メリケン粉　　　小匙一　杯
　　　西洋酢　　　　　　大匙三杯　　　水　　　　　　　カツプ四分ノ一
　　　鹽　　　　　　　　小匙半杯　　　腐つたミルク　　カツプ四分ノ一

作り方―茹でたビーツを微塵切りにするか又は挽肉器で挽いて置きます。別にバ
　　ターを熱して溶し、メリケン粉を加へ、混ぜて後酢を加へ、水と鹽を入れて
　　混ぜながら一度沸騰させ、ビーツを加へて十分乃至十五分間煮て火より下し、
　　ミルクを入れてスープ皿に盛ります。ロシヤ式スープです。

No. 20   **LITTLE PIGS IN BLANKETS**

24 large oysters	Salt and pepper
24 very thin short slices fat	Parsley
bacon	

Season the oysters with salt and pepper. Wrap one oyster in each slice of bacon and fasten with a toothpick . Heat a saucepan and put in the little pigs, cook just long enough to crisp the bacon, about five minutes. Cut slices of toast into quarters and place one oyster in slice of bacon on each small slice of toast. Serve immediately, garnished with parsley.

No. 21   **SAVORY OYSTERS**

2 Cups oysters	½ Tablespoon finely chopped
3 Tablespoons fat	onion
2 Tablespoons minced pim-	1½ Cups milk and oyster liquid
ento or green pepper	mixed

Look over and scald the oysters in their own liquor. Drain the liquor from the oysters and add enough milk to make one and a half cups of liquid. Cook the fat, green peppers and onion together for five minutes. Add the oyster liquid gradually stirring well, and cook till thick. Season with salt, pepper, paprika, dash of celery salt, and mace. Arrange the oysters in a baking dish or on an oven proof platter, pour over the sauce. Border with mashed potatoes, sprinkle with grated cheese. Bake till potatoes and cheese are brown. Serve in baking dish.

No. 22   **OYSTER FRITTERS**

2 Cups oysters	1½ Teaspoons baking powder
2 Well beaten eggs	½ Teaspoon salt
1/3 Cup milk	¼ Teaspoon paprika
1½ Cups flour	

Drain the oyster liquid and chop fine. Add the flour, baking powder and paprika sifted together and milk to the beaten eggs and add the chopped oysters. Drop by spoonfuls into heated deep fat and fry until golden brown. Serve with tomato catsup.

No. 20　　　　牡蠣ベーコン巻き

材料　牡蠣大きいもの　　二十四個　　ベーコン極く薄く切つたもの　十二枚
　　　鹽、胡椒、パセリ

作り方—牡蠣に鹽と胡椒を振掛け、ベーコンを横半分に切つたもので巻き、楊子
　　で止めます。鍋を熱し、牡蠣を入れ、強火でベーコンが焼ける迄五分間位返
　　しながら手早く燒き、小型の四角に切つたトーストの上に一個づゝのせ、パ
　　セリを飾ります。これはランチ用の料理ですが、前菜として用ひても結構
　　です。

No. 21　　　牡蠣ホワイト・ソース

材料　牡蠣　　　　　　　　カツプ二杯　　　　バター　　　大匙三杯
　　　ピミエント又はグリーン・ベツパー微塵切り　大匙二杯
　　　玉葱微塵切り　　大匙半杯
　　　牡蠣の汁とミルクを併せたもの　　　　　　カツプ一杯半

作り方—バターを熱して溶し、ピミエントと玉葱を五分間燒き、牡蠣の汁にミ
　　ルクを加へてカツプ一杯半にしたものを少しづゝ加へ、どろどろになる迄煮
　　ます。これに鹽、胡椒、好みにより、パプリカ、セロリ・ソルト、メース等の
　　香料で味をつけます。牡蠣は瀬戸引きの天パンに入れ、上にミルク等を煮た
　　ものを掛け、周圍につぶした馬鈴薯を盛り、卸したチーズを全體に掛け、強
　　火の天火でチーズに色が附く迄燒きます。これは天パンのまゝ食膳に出し
　　ます。

No. 22　　　牡蠣フリツター

材料　牡蠣　　　　　　　　カツプ二杯　　玉子泡立てたもの　　二　　　個
　　　ミルク　　　カツプ三分ノ一　　メリケン粉　　　カツプ一杯半
　　　ベーキング・パウダー　小匙一杯半　　鹽　　　　　　小匙半杯
　　　パプリカ　　　　小匙四分ノ一

作り方—牡蠣は汁を取り細く切ります。別に玉子を泡立てたものにミルクとメ
　　リケン粉、ベーキング・パウダー、鹽及びパプリカを篩つたものを加へ、前
　　の牡蠣を混ぜ、熱した油の中で一度返して狐色に揚げ、トマト・ケチヤツプ
　　をかけて召上るのです。

No. 23 **DEVILLED OYSTERS**

2 Dozen selected oysters	½ Teaspoon salt
2 Tablespoons minced onion	⅛ Teaspoon paprika
2 Tablespoon butter	1 Teaspoon Worcestershire sauce
1½ Tablespoons cornstarch	1 Teaspoon minced parsley
1/6 Teaspoon dry mustard	1 Egg yolk
½ Cup milk	Buttered bread crumbs
¼ Cup oyster liquor	

Wash, drain and coarsely chop the oysters. Cook the onion in the butter until it begins to turn yellow, add the cornstarch and the mustard, mix smoothly. Then put in milk and oyster liquor and bring to the boiling point, stirring constantly. Now add to the sauce the oysters, salt and the paprika, Worcestershire sauce and the parsley. Simmer two minutes, then add the yolk of one egg and turn into buttered scallop or oyster shells or in to a shallow baking dish. Sprinkle buttered crumbs over the top and bake for 10 minutes in a hot oven at 375 degrees F.

No. 24 **LOBSTER MEXICANE**

2 Lobsters	1 Seeded green pepper
1 Small can tomatoes	3 Tablespoons butter
¾ Teaspoon salt	1 Cup cooked mushrooms if desired
1 Tablespoon sugar	sired
¼ Teaspoon powdered clove	3 Tablespoons butter
1 Bay leaf	Dash of tabasco sauce
1 Large onion	

Boil lobster and cut in pieces about as big as walnuts. Simmer the tomatoes about 15 minutes, and season with salt, sugar, powdered clove, and bay leaf. While the tomatoes are cooking, saute one large peeled onion and one seeded green pepper, which have been sliced fine, in the three tablespoons of butter. Cook until tender, but do not let them brown. Put the onion and pepper in the tomatoes. Then if desired add one cup of cooked mushrooms which have been previously sliced in thin pieces and sauted until tender in two tablespoons fat. Put these in the tomato and add three tablespoons butter and tabasco sauce, than add pieces of lobster meat. Simmer until the lobster is heated and serve in a casserole or covered dish. Serve with brown rice.

No. 23　　デプルド・オイスター

材料	牡蠣	二十四個位	微塵切り玉葱	大匙 二 杯
	バター	大匙二杯	コーンスターチ	大匙一杯半
	西洋芥子粉	小匙六分ノ一	ミルク	カツプ半杯
	牡蠣の汁	カツプ四分ノ一位	鹽	小匙 半 杯
	パプリカ（又は胡椒）	小匙八分ノ一	ウイスタシヤー・ソース	小匙 一 杯
	微塵切りパセリ	小 匙 一 杯	玉子の黄味	一　　個
	生パン粉			

作り方──牡蠣は洗つて水を切り、細く切ります。フライパンにバターを入れて玉葱をいため、之に芥子とコーンスターチを混合せて加へ、ミルクと牡蠣汁（二十四個ノ牡蠣について居るだけの汁）で延し、絶えず攪拌しながら沸騰させます。之に牡蠣、鹽、パプリカ、ソース及びパセリを入れ、弱火で二分間煮て黄味を混ぜて加へ、火より下します。別に牡蠣の貝又は天パンに油を塗つた中に牡蠣等を盛り、上にパン粉を振り、バターを點々と置いて強火の天火で十分間燒きます。

No. 24　　メキシコ風鰕と玄米御飯

材料	伊勢鰕	二　　匹	トマト罐詰	一　　罐
	鹽	小匙四分ノ三	砂糖	大匙 一 杯
	クローブ粉（香料）	小匙四分ノ一	ベーリーフ（香料）	一　　枚
	玉葱薄輪切り	一　　個	グリン・ペッパー輪切り	一　　個
	バター又は代用品	大匙 三 杯	バターでいためた松茸（無くとも可）	カツプ一杯
	バター	大匙 三 杯	トバスカ・ソース	數　　滴
	玄米の御飯			

作り方──鰕は茹でゝ身を大きい賽ノ目切りにして置きます。トマトは十五分程弱火で煮詰め、鹽、砂糖、クローブ、ベーリーフ等で味を附けます。別にグリーン・ペッパーと玉葱をバター又は代用品でよくいため、煮詰めたトマトに加

BROWN RICE

Wash one cup of brown rice in cold water, than add it slowy to at least three cups of vigorously boiling water, to which one teaspoon of salt has been added. Boil for 15 minutes. Then drain the rice, put it in a steamer, and continue to cook it 45 minutes.

No. 25   **CREAMED SCALLOPS**

1 Pint scallops, fresh or   2 Cups thin white sauce
  canned

Wash and drain the scallops, add them to the sauce and cook about 15 minutes in a double boiler.

No. 26   **CRAB FLAKES AND TOMATO JELLY**

½ Can tomatoes   1 Tin crab or tuna

1 Teaspoon salt   2 Drops Worcestershire sauce

½ Teaspoon sugar   2 Tablespoons lemon juice

2 Sheets gelatin   1 Tablespoon chopped pickle

Force the tomatoes through a sieve and add the salt, sugar and Worcestershire sauce. Heat this mixture to the boiling point. Meanwhile, soak the gelatine in water to cover for about 10 minutes then drain and squeeze out all water. Add this gelatine to the hot tomato mixture and remove from fire. Cool. When it begins to stiffen add the flaked crab, lemon juice and chopped pickles. Pour in individual molds. Chill. Remove from mold on to plate and serve with mayonnaise. Lay strips of pimento on top if desired.

へ、好みによりバターでいためた松茸を加へ、最後にバターとトバスカ・ソースを入れ、鰻を加へ一度火を通して、玄米御飯を添へて食します。玄米は普通にたいたもので差支へありませんが、洋式の方法は、玄米カツプ一杯を洗ひ、カツプ三杯の沸騰して居る湯に加へ、鹽小匙一杯を入れ十五分煮て後、湯をきり、御飯蒸しで四十五分間蒸すのです。

No. 25　　　貝 柱 の ス カ ロ ツ プ

材料　　貝柱（罐詰でよい）　カツプ二杯　　薄いホワイト・ソース　カツプ二杯

作り方—生の貝柱の場合はよく洗つて水をきり、ホワイト・ソースに加へます。罐詰の場合は貝柱　汁をきり、此の汁とミルクを半々にして作つたホワイト・ソースと和へます。ホワイト・ソースと和へた貝柱を二重鍋の上で十五分煮て召上るのです。簡單で美味しいランチ用の料理です。

No. 26　　　蟹 ト マ ト ・ ジ エ リ ー

材料　　トマト罐詰　　　半　罐　　　鹽　　　　　　　　小匙一杯
　　　　砂糖　　　　　　小匙半杯　　ゼラチン紙　　　　二　　枚
　　　　蟹罐詰（鮪油漬）　小一罐　　ウイスタシヤー・ソース　二　　滴
　　　　レモン汁　　　　大匙二杯　　微塵切り胡瓜漬物　　大匙一杯

作り方—トマトを裏漉こしして、鹽、砂糖、ソースを加へ、沸騰させ、水に漬けて軟くした後、よくしぼつたゼラチン紙をトマト汁に入れて火より下し、混ぜながら溶して冷します。少し固まりはじめたならば、ほぐして小骨を拔いた蟹とレモン汁と漬物を入れ、水でぬらしたゼリー型に流して固め、マヨネーズを添えて食します。ピミエントの繊切りを上に飾つてもよい。

No. 27   **CRAB SOUFFLE**

2 Tablespons fat	½ Cup soft bread crumbs
2 Tablespoons flour	2 Cups flaked canned crab meat
¾ Teaspoon salt	3 Egg yolks
⅛ Teaspoon pepper	2 Teaspoons minced parsley
1 Cup evaporated milk diluted with 1 cup water	3 Egg whites

Make a white sauce using the fat, flour, salt, pepper, and milk diluted with water. Add to this the flaked canned crab meat, bread crumbs and beaten egg yolks. Lastly fold in the well beaten egg whites and minced parsley, and bake in a slow oven as you would a souffle. That is set the pan containing the souffle mixture in a separate pan containing hot water and bake in a slow oven for about 25 minutes.

No. 28   **CRAB MEAT AND TUNA AU GRATIN**

1 Large can crab meat	1 Teaspoon salt
1 Small can tuna	¼ Teaspoon pepper
4 Tablespoons butter	1½ Cups milk
3 Tablespoons flour	¼ Cup Parmesan cheese

Melt two tablespoons of butter in a saucepan, add the flour, salt and pepper, and cook until bubbling, stir in gradually the milk, stirring constantly, cook until smooth and thickened. Cover the bottom of a buttered baking dish with a thin layer of white sauce thus made. Add a layer of crab meat, cover with white sauce, then a layer of tuna, and continue alternating layers until dish is filled. Cover with cheese, dot with butter using the remaining two tablespoons and bake at 500 degrees F. 12 minutes or until cheese has browned nicely.

No. 27　　　　蟹 の ス フ レ ー

材料	バター又は代用品	大匙二杯	メリケン粉	大匙二杯
	鹽	小匙四分ノ三	胡椒	小匙八分ノ一
	ミルク	カツプ二杯	生パン粉	カツプ半杯
	蟹罐詰	カツプ二杯	玉子の黄味	三　　個
	微塵切りパセリ	大匙二杯	玉子の白味	三　　個

作り方――バターを熱して溶し、メリケン粉を加へて混ぜ、ミルクで延して、鹽、胡椒で味を附け、煮立つ迄混ぜてパン粉を加へ、二分間煮て火より下し、直ちに蟹のほぐしたものとよく泡立てた玉子の黄味とパセリを加へ、次に充分泡立てた白味を靜に加へ、油を塗つた瀨戸引天パンに入れ、中火の天火の中で湯煎にして二十五分間程燒きます。蟹の代りに鮭の罐詰を使つてもよい。

No. 28　　　　蟹 と 鮪 の グ ラ タ ン

材料	蟹罐詰	大 一 罐	鮪油漬罐詰	小 一 罐
	バター	大匙四杯	メリケン粉	大匙三杯
	鹽	小匙一杯	胡椒	小匙四分ノ一
	ミルク	カツプ一杯半		

卸したパーミサン・チーズ　　カツプ四分ノ一

作り方――バター大匙二杯を熱して溶し、メリケン粉を加へて煮て、ミルクで混ぜながら延してどろどろのホワイト・ソースを作り、鹽、胡椒で味を附けます。別に瀨戸引き天パンに油を塗り、ホワイト・ソースを薄く底に一段入れ、その上に蟹をほぐして一段入れ、ホワイト・ソースを敷き、次にほぐした鮪を入れ、再びホワイト・ソースを敷き、これを繰返して、材料全部を加へ、上に殘りの大匙二杯のバターを點々と置き、チーズを振掛け（チーズの代りにパン粉でもよい）強火の天火に入れ十二分程上が狐色になる迄燒くのです。

No. 29 BAKED POTATOES WITH CREAMED TUNA

3 Large potatoes	Salt, pepper and paprika
2 Tablespoons melted fat	1 Can tuna fish
1 Tablespoon butter	1 Cup medium white sauce
2 Tablespoons hot milk	

Halve the potatoes lengthwise and brush all over with the melted fat. Bake in a hot oven and scoop out and mash the pulp well adding butter, hot milk and seasoning with salt, pepper and paprika. Whip the mixture until very light. Meanwhile flake and heat the tuna in the heated medium white sauce. Half fill the potato skins with hot creamed tuna, and top with fluffy potatoes. Brown them in a medium oven until delicately colored.

No. 30 SALMON RING WITH GREEN PEAS AND RICE

2 Tablespoons butter	1 Tablespoon parsley
¼ Cup bread crumbs	2 Eggs
1 Cup milk	½ Teaspoon salt
1½ Cups salmon	Pepper and paprika

Melt the butter, then add and heat the milk and the bread crumbs. Remove from the flame and add the beaten eggs, then the salmon and the seasoning. Put into well greased individual ring molds and bake for 40 minutes to one hour in a moderate oven. These rings should be baked in a pan of water. Remove and fill the center with the following pea sauce.

1 Cup cooked rice	1 Tablespoon flour
½ Cup peas	½ Cup milk
2 Tablespoons butter	

Make a white sauce with the butter, flour and milk and season to taste. Stir in the rice and peas and pour over ring, garnish with pasley.

No. 29　　　鮪クリームとポテト

材料　馬鈴薯　　　　　　　大三個　　　油　　　　　　　　大匙二杯

　　　バター　　　　　　　大匙一杯　　熱したミルク　　　大匙二杯

　　　鹽、胡椒、パプリカ　少量づゝ　　鮪油漬又は鮭罐詰　半封度一罐

　　　中位のホワイト・ソース　カツプ一杯

作り方―馬鈴薯を縦半分に切り、表面を油で塗り、強火の天火で他のものを燒く
　　時に軟くなるまで燒き、中をえぐり取り、これにバターと熱したミルクを加
　　へてよくつぶし、鹽、胡椒及びパプリカで味を附けます。別に鮪又は鮭をほ
　　ぐし、ホワイト・ソースと和へて、これを馬鈴薯の皮の中に半分位迄入れ、上
　　に馬鈴薯をつぶしたものを盛り、強火の天火の中で狐色に燒きます。

No. 30　　　サーモン・リング（鮭の輪に御飯を添えたもの）

サーモン・リング

材料　バター　　　　　　大匙二杯　　生パン粉　　　　カツプ四分ノ一

　　　ミルク　　　　　　カツプ一杯　　鮭罐詰　　　　　カツプ一杯半

　　　パセリ　　　　　　大匙一杯　　玉子　　　　　　　二　　　個

　　　鹽　　　　　　　　小匙半杯　　パプリカ又は胡椒　小匙八分ノ一

作り方―バターを溶し、ミルクとパン粉を加へて熱し、火より下して、玉子を泡
　　立てたもの、鮭をほぐしたもの、及び香料を加へ一人附けの輪形のゼリー型
　　に油を塗つた中に入れ、四十分乃至一時間中火の天火で湯煎にして燒き、取
　　り出して、中央に次のソースを盛ります。

ソース

材料　御飯　　　　　　　カツプ一杯　　グリーン・ピース　カツプ半杯

　　　バター　　　　　　大匙二杯　　メリケン粉　　　　大匙一杯

　　　ミルク　　　　　　カツプ半杯

作り方―バターを溶し、メリケン粉を混ぜながら加へ、ミルクで延してホワイト・
　　ソースを作り、鹽、胡椒で味を附け、この中に御飯とグリーン・ピースを混ぜ
　　合せます。パセリを青味に添へると宜しい。

No. 31   SALMON AND MACARONI MOLD

3 Cups cooked macaroni   2 Tablespoons lemon juice
1 Tin salmon   ½ Cup white sauce
½ Teaspoon salt   1 Tablespoon chopped parsley
A few grains paprika

Cook the macaroni or spaghetti until tender and cut in inch long pieces, then measure. Grease a loaf cake pan and arrange cooked macaroni on the bottom and on the sides. Mash salmon and add salt, paprika, lemon juice and white sauce and pile in the middle of the macaroni. Cover the salmon with another layer of macaroni, cover this with a greased sheet of oil paper and steam for 30 minutes. Serve with thin white sauce.

No. 32   SALMONETTES

1 Cup canned salmon   ⅛ Teaspoon pepper
1 Cup soft bread crumbs   ½ Teaspoon salt
1 Tablespoon minced onion   1 Egg, beaten
1 Tablespoon chopped parsley   1 Tablespoon melted fat
1 Teaspoon lemon juice   Fat for deep frying

Bone fish, Stir in bread crumbs. Add egg, all seasonings and fat. Mix. Shape into croquettes. Roll in fine dry bread crumbs (additional). Deep-fry in hot fat, fat is the right heat when it browns cube of bread in 40 seconds (390 degrees F.). Fry until golden brown. Serve with chili sauce or white sauce or tomato catsup.

No. 33   ESCALLOPED CODFISH

2/3 Pound dried codfish   4 Tablespoons flour
2 Cups diced potatoes   2 Cups milk
6 Cups water   1 Teaspoon finely chopped onion
½ Teaspoon salt   ¼ Teaspoon celery salt or salt
3 Tablespoons fat   ¼ Teaspoon paprika or pepper

Flake codfish and add water and soak 30 minutes. Add potatoes and boil gently in covered pan 20 minutes. Drain. Melt fat and add flour and seasonings and milk and cook until creamy sauce forms. Add cooked mixture. Pour into buttered baking dish and bake 20 minutes in moderate oven.

No. 31　　　　鮭とカマロニのローフ

材料	茹でたマカロニ		鮭罐詰	一　　罐
	又はスパゲテイ	カツプ三杯	鹽	小匙半杯
	パプリカ(赤胡椒)	少　　量	レモン汁	大匙二杯
	ホワイト・ソース	カツプ半杯	パセリの微塵切り	大匙一杯

作り方――マカロニ又はスパゲテイが柔くなる迄茹で、一寸位の長さに切つてカツプに三杯使ふのです。別にお菓子の天パンに油を塗り、茹でたマカロニを下と側面に盛り、此の中に鮭をほぐして鹽、パプリカ、レモン汁、パセリ及びホワイト・ソースを加へたものを入れて、殘りのマカロニを上に盛り、上に油を塗つた紙を敷いて、三十分間蒸します。天パンより取出し、薄いホワイト・ソースを掛けて召上るのです。

No. 32　　　　鮭のコロツケ

材料	鮭罐詰	カツプ一杯	生パン粉	カツプ一杯
	微塵切り玉葱	大匙一杯	微塵切りパセリ	大匙一杯
	レモン汁	小匙一杯	胡椒	小匙八分ノ一
	鹽	小匙半杯	玉子の泡立てたもの	一個分
	溶した油	大匙一杯		

作り方――鮭をほぐして、パン粉を加へ、玉子を攪混ぜて入れ、他の材料を全部加へて、コロツケ形に丸め、別のパン粉をまぶして、揚物油で狐色に揚げます。トマト・ケチヤツプ、チリー・ソース又はホワイト・ソースを添えるとよい。

No. 33　　　　鹽鱈スカロツプ

材料	鹽鱈	三分ノ二封度	賽ノ目切り馬鈴薯	カツプ二杯
	冷水	カツプ六杯	鹽	小匙半杯
	バター又は代用品	大匙三杯	メリケン粉	大匙四杯
	ミルク	カツプ二杯	玉葱微塵切り	小匙一杯
	セロリ・ソルト(香料)又は鹽	小匙四分ノ一	パプリカ又は胡椒	小匙四分ノ一

作り方――鹽鱈をほぐして、水を掛け三十分間置き、薯を加へ蓋をして二十分間静かにゆでゝ水をきります。別にバターを熱し、メリケン粉を加へ、ミルクで延してホワイト・ソースを作り、セロリ・ソルト、パプリカ(無い場合は鹽、胡椒)で味をつけ、之に前の薯と鱈を加へて全部を油を塗つた天パンに入れ、中火の天火中で二十分間焼きます。

No. 34   **ROLLED FILLETS OF FISH**

Place a strip of pimento down the centre of each fish fillet, and folde over into a roll. Wrap two strips of bacon around each piece and fasten with a tooth-pick. Bake in a hot oven until the bacon is done.

No. 35   **BAKED FISH RINGS**

6 Thin slices of fish filet	1 1/3 Cup soft bread crumbs
2 Slices of bacon	1/3 Cup hot milk
⅛ Teaspoon pepper	½ Cup chopped mushrooms or
1 Teaspoon salt	½ Cup chopped walnuts

Grease small muffin tins and arrange the fish filets around the inside in a ring. Chop bacon fine and saute in a hot frying pan, then add salt, pepper, bread crumbs, and milk and mix well to make a stuffing. Add this to the center of the fish rings, cover each muffin tin with a piece of oiled paper then arrange the muffin tins in a large greased tin and bake in a moderate oven for 20 minutes. Remove the pieces of oiled paper and dot surface with pieces of butter and brown in the oven. If desired the chopped mushrooms or chopped nuts may be added to the stuffing.

No. 36   **BAKED WHOLE FISH**

To bake whole the fish should measure more than 10 inches. After removing entrails of the fish wash thoroughly and if desired remove the bones. Stuff with stuffing and sew up the side, and place a skewer through the fish to keep it in shape while baking. Put a piece of cloth in the bottom of a baking pan and arrange the fish on this. Lay several slices of bacon across the top of the fish and bake in a moderate oven, allowing 15 minutes per pound. Baste often with a sauce of one fourth cup butter and one cup hot water. When baked remove cloth, string and skewer and arrange on a platter. Serve with butter sauce, or tartar sauce, and garnish with parsley. Stuffing can be ordinary fish stuffing or spinach stuffing for a change.

No. 34　　　　フイツシユのベーコン巻

作り方―白身の魚の薄い切身を四枚用意して、一枚毎に上にピミエントを細長く切つたものを一本宛のせ、浅苔巻の様に魚を巻き、その外にベーコンの薄切りを二枚巻附けて楊子で止め、天パンに並べてベーコンが焼ける迄中火の天火で焼きます。

No. 35　　　　ベークド・フイツシユ・リング

材料	白身の魚、薄く細長		ベーコン	二 切 れ
	く切つたもの	六 切 れ	胡椒	小匙八分ノ一
	鹽	小匙一杯	生パン粉	カツプ一杯三分ノ一
	熱したミルク	カツプ三分ノ一	松茸微塵切り	カツプ半杯
			又は胡桃微塵切り	カツプ杯半

作り方―小型のマフエン用の天パンに油を塗り、魚を周圍に巻く様にして入れます。別にフライパンを熱し、細く切つたベーコンを入れて狐色に焼き、鹽、胡椒、パン粉、ミルクを加へ充分に混ぜて熱し、これを前の魚の中に詰め、上に油を塗つた紙を敷き、小型の天パンを更に油を塗つた四角な天パンに並べ、中火の天火で二十分間焼き、紙を取り上にバターを點々とのせ、色が附く迄焼き續けます。好みによりパン粉等と一緒に松茸又は胡桃を加へても結構です。

No. 36　　　　魚 の 丸 燒 き

作り方―魚は一尺位の長さのものでしたらば何でもよろしいのですが、腹わたを取り、よく洗ひ、場合によつては骨を拔き、腹に何かスタツフイング（詰物）を入れ、切り目を絲で縫合せ、串を差し、形を直して焼きます。焼くには天パンに布の細く切つたのを置いて、其の上に魚をのせ、魚の上にベーコンの薄切りを二、三枚のせ、中火の天火で魚の目方によつて時間を定めて焼きます。焼く時間は魚一封度に對して十五分間ですから、二封度の魚ならば三十分間焼くとよろしいのです。焼きながら時々上からバターカツプ四分ノ一をカツプ一杯の湯に溶して作つたソースを掛けます。焼き上りましたらば絲と布と串を取り皿にのせ、レモン又はパセリで飾ります。タ―タ―・ソ―ス（マヨネーズにピツクルスをきざんで入れたもの）を掛けるとよい。詰物は魚の詰物又は菠薐草の詰物がよい。

No. 37 — FISH STUFFING

2 Cups soft bread crumbs
½ Cup melted butter
½ Teaspoon salt
⅛ Teaspoon pepper

1 Teaspoon chopped onion
1 Teaspoon chopped parsley
1 Tablespoon chopped pickles
½ Cup hot water

Add the melted butter to the bread crumbs, and season with salt and pepper, then add onion, parsley and pickles. Add enough hot water to make it the right thickness to stuff the fish. Use as fish stuffing.

No. 38 — SPINACH STUFFING

1 Cup soft bread crumbs
2 Tablespoons butter
¼ Pound chopped spinach
1 Tablespoons green pepper chopped

1 Tablespoons celery chopped
1 Tablespoon onion chopped
1 Tablespoon carrots chopped
½ Teaspoon salt
⅛ Teaspoon pepper

Heat one tablespoon butter and saute all vegetables, and push over to one side in the frying pan. Melt the remaining one tablespoon of butter and add the bread crumbs. Combine the crumbs and the vegetables and season with salt and pepper ,and use as fish stuffing.

No. 39 — SHRIMP SAUCE

Make a rich white sauce, using part cream and part milk. To one cup sauce add one half cup cooked or canned shrimps, cut in halves, and one fourth teaspoon paprika. Good with any bland fish like halibut, flounder, or pompano.

No. 40 — SAUCE NORMANDE

Melt three tablespoons fat, three tablespoons flour, ½ teaspoon salt and a few grains pepper. Mix well. Add one cup hot fish stock gradually, and cook until mixture thickens, stirring constantly to keep smooth. Add one half cup cream and two beaten egg yolks, and cook two minutes. Add one tablespoon lemon juice and one tablespoon Worcestershire. Good with broiled salmon or baked fillet of sole (flounder).

No. 37　　　　　　　魚 の 詰 物

材料　生パン粉　　　　カツプ二杯　　溶したバター　　　カツプ半杯
　　　鹽　　　　　　　小匙半杯　　　胡椒　　　　　　　小匙八分ノ一
　　　玉葱微塵切り　　小匙一杯　　　パセリ微塵切り　　小匙一杯
　　　ピツクルス（漬物）　　　　　　熱湯　　　　　　　カツプ半杯位
　　　微塵切り　　　大匙一杯

作り方―パン粉に溶したバターを加へ、鹽、胡椒で味を附け、玉葱、パセリ、ピツ
　　クルス等を加へ、熱湯を少しづゝ入れて詰めるによい固さにします。魚の丸
　　燒きの場合にこれを魚の腹の中に詰めるのです。

No. 38　　　　菠薐草の魚の詰物

材料　生パン粉　　　　カツプ一杯　　バター　　　　　　大匙二杯
　　　菠薐草細く
　　　　切つたもの　　四分ノ一封度　　グリーン・ペツパー
　　　　　　　　　　　　　　　　　　　微塵切り　　　　大匙一杯
　　　セロリ微塵切り　大匙一杯　　　玉葱微塵切り　　　大匙一杯
　　　人參微塵切り　　大匙一杯　　　鹽　　　　　　　　小匙半杯
　　　胡椒　　　　　　小匙八分ノ一

作り方―大匙一杯のバターを熱して菠薐草以下の野菜を全部いため、フライパン
　　の端に寄せて置き、次に殘りの大匙一杯のバターを溶して、パン粉と混ぜ、
　　パン粉と野菜を混合せて、鹽、胡椒で味を附けます。これも魚の丸燒きの場
　　合の詰物として用ひるのです。

No. 39　　　　芝鰕ソース

作り方―クリームとミルクを半々に用ひて、ホワイト・ソースを作り、カツプ一杯
　　のソースにカツプ半杯の細く切つた芝鰕を入れ、小匙四分ノ一のパプリカを
　　加へます。此のソースはさつぱりした魚に掛けて美味しいもの。

No. 40　　　　ノーマンデイー・ソース

作り方―大匙三杯のバターを溶し、之にメリケン粉大匙三杯、鹽小匙半杯、パプ
　　リカ少量を加へて混ぜ、熱した魚の煮汁で延して絶えず混ぜながらどろどろ
　　に煮詰め、カツプ半杯のクリームと泡立てた玉子二個を加へ二分間煮ます。
　　火より下してレモン汁大匙一杯と、ウイスタシャー・ソース大匙一杯を加へ
　　ます。これは生鮭の燒いたものによいソースです。

No. 41   OYSTER SAUCE

Fry small oysters in a little fat for three minutes. Add a little cream and heat thoroughly. This is delicious with any broiled or baked white fish.

No. 42   LEMON BUTTER SAUCE

Melt one half cup butter with one clove garlic, and brown slightly. Add juice one lemon and one tablespoons chopped parsley. Heat thoroughly. For baked mackerel, lake trout, scrod (baby codfish), and blue fish.

No. 43   TOMATO SAUCE

Cook one cup canned tomatoes for 20 minutes with one stalk celery, one slice onion, one half teaspoon salt, few grains pepper, and one table-spoon Worcestershire. Rub through a sieve and add few grains cayenne. Add this to one cup white sauce.

No. 44   EGG SAUCE

Chop two hard cooked eggs and add to one cup rich medium thick sauce. Heat thoroughly. If desired, this sauce may be varied by adding chopped parsley, lemon juice or Worcestershire. Very nice with boiled cod.

No. 45   TARTAR SAUCE

Mix one cup mayonnaise with one tablespoon each chopped parsley, chopped pickles, chopped onion, chopped olives and onion juice. Chill well and serve with fried scallops, fillets, or oysters.

No. 46   CUCUMBER SAUCE

Beat one half cup cream until stiff, and season with salt and pepper. Peel one cucumber and discard seeds. Chop fine and drain well. Beat into the cream. Chill. A little horse-radish may be added, if desired. This is delicious served with cold or hot flounder or broiled fresh salmon.

No. 41　　　　牡　蠣　ソ　ー　ス

作り方―小型の牡蠣を少量の熱した油で三分間フライして少量のクリームを加
へ、丸燒きの魚に掛けます。

No. 42　　　レモン・バター・ソース

作り方―カツプ半杯のバターを熱して溶し、大蒜を一枚入れて狐色にし、取り出
　　してレモン汁一個分とパセリの微塵切りを大匙三杯加へ、熱して、丸燒又は
　　網の上で燒いた魚に掛けます。

No. 43　　　　トマト・ソース

作り方―トマト罐詰カツプ一杯にセロリー本、玉葱一切れ、鹽、胡椒及びウイス
　　タシャー・ソース大匙一杯を加へ二十分間煮ます。裏漉にしてケアネ・ペパー
　　を少量入れ、これをカツプ一杯のホワイト・ソースに加へます。これは特に
　　鱈の料理によいソースです。

No. 44　　　　玉子のソース

作り方―二個の茹で玉子を細く切り、熱したホワイト・ソースに加へ、好みにより
　　微塵切りのパセリ、レモン汁又はウイスタシャー・ソース等を加へます。こ
　　れも鱈の料理によいソースです。

No. 45　　　　ターター・ソース

作り方―カツプ一杯のマヨネーズに微塵切りのパセリ、微塵切りのピツクル、微
　　塵切りの玉葱、微塵切りのオリーブ及び玉葱汁を大匙一杯づゝ入れ、充分冷
　　して、フライの牡蠣又は魚に掛けて用ひます。

No. 46　　　　胡瓜のソース

作り方―生クリームをカツプ半杯泡立て、鹽、胡椒で味を附けます。別に胡瓜大
　　一本の皮をむき、種子を取り、卸します。汁をよくしぼり、前のクリームに
　　折込み、わさびの卸したものを小匙半杯加へ、冷して溫い又は冷した生鮭に
　　用ひます。

No. 47   **COSMOPOLITAN SAUCE**

1 Tablespoon butter
1 Tablespoon flour
3 Tablespoons oyster juice
1½ Tablespoons chili sauce
¼ Teaspoon Worcestershire
    sauce

1 Teaspoon lemon juice or vinegar
⅛ Teaspoon salt or celery salt
¼ Teaspoon onion juice
1 Tablespoons chopped pimento
Few drops Tabasco sauce
3 Tablespoons mayonnaise dressing

Melt the butter and when it is slightly brown add the sifted flour and stir. To this add the oyster liquid and when it boils add all other ingredients with the exception of the mayonnaise, allow to boil up. Then place over hot water and add mayonnaise and heat before serving.

No. 48   **PAPRIKA PEPPER SAUCE**

3 Tablespoons salad oil
3 Tablespoons flour
Teaspoon salt
1½ Teaspoons paprika
1 Cup milk

½ Cup rich chicken soup
1 Tablespoon chopped green pepper
1 Tablespoon chopped pimento
Few drops onion juice
1 Teaspoon lemon juice

Heat the oil and add the salt, paprika and flour which have been sifted together, and cook. Next add the milk with the soup stirring all the time and allow to come to a boil and cook until thick. Add lemon juice, onion juice and chopped green pepper and pimento. Serve on baked fish, roast chicken, boiled potatoes or boiled cauliflower.

No. 47　　　コスモポリタン・ソース

材料　バター　　　　　　大匙一杯　　　メリケン粉　　　　大匙一杯

牡蠣の汁　　　　　大匙三杯　　　チリー・ソース　　大匙一杯半

黑ソース　　　　　小匙四分ノ一

西洋酢
（又はレモン汁）　小匙一杯　　　鹽（又は
　　　　　　　　　　　　　　セロリ・ソルト）小匙八分ノ一

玉葱汁　　　　　　小匙四分ノ一

ピミエントの
　微塵切り　　　　大匙一杯　　　タバスコ・ソース　　數　　滴

マヨネーズ・
　ドレツシング　　大匙三杯

作り方―バターを熱して溶し、狐色になつたならばメリケン粉を篩つて加へ、混
　ぜ、牡蠣の汁で延し、煮立つたらばマヨネーズ以外の材料を入れ、再び沸騰
　させ、湯煎にしてマヨネーズを加へ湯の上で熱してソースとします。魚のフ
　ライ又は牡蠣のフライに用ひます。

No. 48　　　パプリカ・ペツパー・ソース

此のソースは茹でた薯、花きやべつ、燒いた魚又は鶏によい。

材料　サラダ油　　　　　大匙三杯　　　メリケン粉　　　　大匙三杯

鹽　　　　　　　　小匙一杯　　　パプリカ（赤胡椒）　小匙一杯半

ミルク　　　　　　カツプ一杯　　　濃い鶏スープ　　　カツプ半杯

グリーン・ペツパー　　　　　　　　ピミエント
　微塵切り　　　　大匙一杯　　　　微塵切り　　　　大匙一杯

玉葱汁　　　　　　數　　滴　　　　レモン汁　　　　　小匙一杯

作り方―サラダ油を熱し、鹽、パプリカと共に篩つたメリケン粉を加へ、よく混
　ぜながら煮て後、ミルクとスープを併せたもので延し、沸騰する迄煮詰め、
　レモン汁、玉葱汁、グリーン・ペツパー及びピミエントを加へます。このソ
　ースは丸燒きの魚又は鶏、薯、花きやべつ等に掛けます。

No. 49   **HAMBURGER STEAK**

1 Pound chopped beef	½ Cup milk
1 Teaspoon salt	Soft stale bread crumbs
¼ Teaspoon pepper	2 Tablespoons butter

Mix beef, salt, pepper and milk. Form into one large steak, cover on both sides with soft stale bread crumbs and broil on rack in broiling oven until half done, or from five to 10 minutes. Turn over and cook on other side. Remove to hot platter, spread with butter and garnish with parsley.

No. 50   **POT ROAST**

4 or 5 pounds piece of rump beef	8 Small carrots
½ Cup water	1 Cup hot water
Salt and pepper	1 Teaspoon Worcestershire sauce
6 Small onions	1 Teaspoon soy sauce
4 Potatoes	2 Tablespoons tomato catsup

Coat beef with flour and place in an iron kettle in which a little fat has been heated and sear the surface. Add the water and cook over slow fire, turning the beef often. Wash, peel and dice potato, carrots and onion and add t o the beef with the salt, pepper, tomato catsup, soy sauce, Worcestershire sauce and boiling water, and cover and cook until the vegeta les are cooked. The gravy will make itself if the meat is well floured.

No. 51   **SWISS STEAK WITH TOMATO**

3 Tablespoons flour	1 Pound lean beef
½ Teaspoon salt	1 Tablespoon melted fat
Few grains pepper	1 Cup hot tomatoes

Sift flour with salt and pepper and pound thoroughly into steak. Sear steak in fat in heavy pan. Add tomatoes. Cover and simmer two hours or until meat is very tender. Add water as needed.

No. 49　　　　　　　　ハンバーガー・ステーキ

材料　挽牛肉　　　　　　　一封度　　　　　鹽　　　　　　　小匙一杯
　　　胡椒　　　　　　　　小匙四分ノ一　　ミルク　　　　　カツプ半杯
　　　古いパン粉　　　　　カツプ半杯位　　バター　　　　　大匙二杯

作り方——肉に鹽、胡椒及びミルクを加へ、一塊に丸めて、パン粉によくまぶし
　　ます。熱したフライパン又はグリル・オブンに入れ、五分乃至十分間半分程
　　焼ける迄焼き、返して他の面を焼き、熱した皿に取り上にバターを塗りま
　　す。パセリを飾ります。

No. 5o　　　　　　　　ポツト・ロースト

材料　牛肉(ランプ、脚の肉でも　　　水　　　　　　　カツプ半杯
　　　よい)一塊　　　　四封度　　　鹽、胡椒　　　　適宜
　　　小さい玉葱　　　　六個　　　　馬鈴薯　　　　　四個
　　　人參小さいもの　　八個　　　　熱湯　　　　　　カツプ一杯
　　　ウイスタシヤー・　　　　　　　醬油　　　　　　小匙一杯
　　　ソース　　　　　　小匙一杯　　トマト・ケチヤツプ　大匙二杯

作り方——牛肉は此の料理には固い安い肉でよいのです。表面全體をよくメリケ
　　ン粉にまぶし、鐵の鍋に油を少量熱し、此の中で肉の表面を強火でよくいた
　　め、水を加へ蓋をよくして、時々返しながら弱火で肉が軟くなる迄煮ます。
　　後、人參馬鈴薯及び玉葱を洗つて皮をむき適當の大きさに切つて入れ、鹽胡
　　椒を加へ、トマト・ケチヤツプ、醬油、ウイスタシヤー・ソース及び熱湯を加
　　へ再び蓋をして野菜と肉が充分軟くなる迄煮續けます。初め肉につけたメリ
　　ケン粉が煮汁を濃くしますから、煮汁が其の儘肉のソースになります。安い
　　肉の切れを應用した天火無しの肉の料理として美味しいものです。

No. 51　　　　　　　　スヰス・ステーキ

材料　メリケン粉　　　　大匙三杯　　　鹽　　　　　　　小匙半杯
　　　胡椒　　　　　　　小匙八分ノ一　牛肉一枚に切つた
　　　肉脂を溶したもの　大匙一杯　　　　もの　　　　　一封度
　　　トマト煮たもの又は
　　　　罐詰　　　　　　カツプ一杯

作り方——メリケン粉、鹽、胡椒を篩ひ、牛肉の中にたゝきこみ、肉を熱したフ
　　ライパンの中に肉の脂を入れ、肉の兩面を狐色に焼きます。上にトマトを掛
　　け、蓋をして二時間弱火で肉が軟くなる迄焼きます。水分が少くなつたらば
　　水を少し加へながら焼くのです。

No. 52   VEAL FIESTAS

1½ Pounds veal steak	3 Large onions, sliced
⅛ Teaspoon pepper	½ Cup chili sauce
2 Tablespoons flour	1½ Cups hot water
4 Tablespoons fat	½ Cups cooked macaroni
1 Teaspoon salt	½ Cup grated cheese

Buy veal from lower hind shank. Have it cut into six thin slices —or pound them thin. Season, then dredge in flour. Heat skillet, add fat. Fry veal until brown on both sides. Cover with onions. Add chili sauce and hot water. Cover skillet. Transfer to moderately hot oven (375 degrees F.) or cook slowly over burner about 30 minutes. Remove cover. Sprinkle in grated cheese. Bake until cheese melts. Remove Veal Fiestas to platter. Put cooked macaroni in skillet. Stir in gravy until heated. Serve as border.

No. 53   STUFFED MEAT LOAF

1½ Pounds ground beef	1 Cup soft bread crumbs
1 Egg well beaten	½ Teaspoon salt
½ Cup milk	⅛ Teaspoon pepper
1 Teaspoon salt	½ Teaspoon sage
⅛ Teaspoon pepper	1 Tablespoon grated onion
1 Tablespoon Worcestershire sauce	4 Tablespoons melted fat

Mix together the beef, beaten egg, milk, salt pepper and Worcestershire sauce. Line the bottom and sides of a loaf pan with this mixture. Make a stuffing of the remaining ingredients. Fill the center of the pan with the latter mixture . Cover the top with more of the meat and cook in a hot oven of 400 degrees F. for 45 minutes. Serve six.

No. 54   BEEF AND RICE BALLS

1 Pound hamburger or ground beef	¼ Teaspoon salt
1 Cup rice	¼ Teaspoon chili powder
1 Onion, cut fine	1 Tin tomato soup

Mix the above and roll into small balls. Then make sauce of one can tomato soup mixed with same amount of water, seasoned with salt, pepper. Pour this mixture over all. Bake about one hour, or until rice is finished.

No. 52　　　　　犢 と マ カ ロ ニ

材料	犢ステーキに切つ		鹽	小匙一杯
	たもの	一封度半	胡椒	小匙八分ノ一
	メリケン粉	大匙二杯	油	大匙四杯
	玉葱輪切り	三個	チリー・ソース（又はトマト・	
	熱湯	カツプ一杯半	ケチヤツプ）	カツプ半杯
	茹たマカロニ	カツプ一杯半	おろしたチーズ	カツプ半杯

作り方──犢は一封度半を六切れのビーフステーキの様に切つたものを使ひ、よ
　　くたたいて、鹽、胡椒を振掛け、フライパンを熱して油を加へた中で手早く
　　兩面を燒き、玉葱を上にかぶせ、チリー・ソースと熱湯を加へ、蓋をして天
　　火又は弱火の上で三十分燒き、蓋を取つて溶したチーズを振掛け、チーズが
　　溶ける迄燒き又は煮續け、犢を皿に取り、マカロニを犢の煮汁に入れ、よく
　　混ぜて皿に犢の周圍に盛ります。

No. 53　　　　スタツフト・ミート・ローフ

材料	挽牛肉	一封度半	玉子の泡立てたもの	一個
	ミルク	カツプ半杯	鹽	小匙一杯
	胡椒	小匙八分ノ一	ウイスタシヤー・	
	生パン粉	カツプ一杯	ソース	大匙一杯
	鹽	小匙半杯	胡椒	小匙八分ノ一
	セーヂ	小匙半分	卸した玉葱	小匙一杯
	溶したバター又は 　代用品	大匙四杯		

作り方──初めの六種の材料を混ぜて四角なパン燒天パンの底と側面に此の肉等
　　を盛ります。別にパン粉以下の材料を併せてこれを天パンの中の肉の中央に
　　詰め上に殘りの肉をのせ強火の天火で四十五分間燒き、皿に取り出し、三分
　　の厚さの切れにして、供します。肉の中にパンが詰つた料理です。

No. 54　　　　　肉のライス・ボール

材料	挽牛肉	一封度	白米	カツプ一杯
	玉葱薄い輪切り	一個	鹽	小匙四分ノ一
	チリー又はカレー粉	小匙四分ノ一	トマト・スープ	一罐

作り方──材料全部を混ぜ小型の團子に丸め、天パンに入れます。之にトマト・
　　スープ一罐と同分量の水を鹽胡椒で味附けして混合せたものをかけ、中火の
　　天火で一時間燒きます。

No. 55   **ROULANDEN**

12 Pieces round steak, cut thin	12 Slices bacon
12 Slices onions	1 Teaspoon curry powder
	Salt and pepper and cayenne

Cut the steak in pieces of four or five inches square. Place on each piece one or two slices of onion and one or two slices of bacon on the onion. Sprinkle with salt and pepper and roll up tightly, inserting several toothpicks, or if you wish you can tie them with a string. Slowly brown the rolls on both sides, place in a kettle or cooker then barely cover with boiling water and cook slowly for three hours, or until nice and tender add curry powder. Celery, cut up and cooked in the gravy improves the flavor. Mushrooms may be added if desired. Thicken the gravy and serve hot.

No. 56   **VEAL AND PORK LOAF**

1½ Pounds veal finely chopped	¼ Teaspoon pepper
¾ Pound chopped lean pork	½ Cup chopped raisins
1½ Teaspoons salt	2 Slices stale bread, crumbed
¼ Teaspoon pepper	2 Tablespoons melted fat
	1 Egg

Mix the finely chopped veal and pork and raisins and season with salt and pepper. Soak the bread which has been crumbed in hot water, drain and press them dry and add the melted fat. Combine all the ingredients and moisten with one well beaten egg and form into a roll, bake in a slow oven of about 350 degrees F., for one and a quarter hours.

No. 55　　　　　肉　の　カ　ー　レ　煮

材料　牛肉（二分の厚さに　　　　　　　　玉葱薄輪切り　　　大十二枚
　　　　切つたもの　　　四封度　　　　ベーコン薄切り　　十二枚
　　　　カレー粉　　　　小匙一杯　　　　鹽、胡椒

作り方——肉は五寸四角位の大きさが宜しい。此の上に玉葱とベーコンを一切れ
づつのせ、鹽、胡椒を振掛け、海苔巻の様に肉を巻き、糸で結ぶか楊子で止
めるかして置きます。フライパンを熱して肉を入れ、表面を燒いて後、鍋に
入れ、かぶる位に熱湯を加へ、蓋をして弱火で三時間程煮て肉を軟くし、汁
にカレー粉を加へ、メリケン粉で汁をどろどろにして召上るのです。有れば
セロリの枝、松茸、竹の子等を最後の三十分間に肉と一緒に煮ると味がつき
ます。

No. 56　　　　　　犢と豚のローフ

材料　犢挽肉　　　　　一封度半　　　豚肉　　　　　四分ノ三封度
　　　　鹽　　　　　　　小匙一杯半　　胡椒　　　　　小匙四分ノ一
　　　　細く切つた乾葡萄　カツプ半杯　　古いパン　　　二枚
　　　　溶した油　　　　大匙二杯　　　玉子　　　　　一個

作り方——犢の肉と豚肉を混合せ、鹽胡椒で味を附け、乾葡萄を併せます。パン
はちぎつて水に數分間漬けて後、水をよくしぼつて溶した油と混ぜ前の肉の
中に入れ最後に少し混ぜた玉子を加へて一塊に手で丸め、天パンに入れて弱
火の天火で一時間十五分程燒きます。

No. 57   PORK ROAST WITH CARROT DRESSING

1 Beaten egg

2 Cups shredded carrots

1 Green pepper, chopped

1 Medium sized onion, chopped

1 Cup cracker crumbs

½ Cup chopped raisins

Salt and pepper to taste. Mix above ingredients well with the egg.

3 Pounds pork roast

Divide a pork roast into two layers. Flour well. On first layer place the carrot dressing. Then cover with the second piece of pork. Bake for 30 minutes at 550 degrees F., then at 450 degrees F. at the rate of 25 minutes per pound.

No. 58   ROAST PORK BRITANNY STYLE

4 to 5 Pounds of lean pork

4 Medium potatoes

6 Small white onions

3 Peeled and quartered apples

3 Turnips

Rub the pork with fat or oil, and sprinkle with salt and pepper. Place in covered roasting pan in hot oven. 30 minutes later add the pared and halved potatoes, onions, apples and pared and quartered turnips. Cover and bake till well done. Serve meat with vegetables as border. Make gravy from liquid in pan, seasoning to taste. If preferred, lamb may be used in place of pork.

No. 59   ARABIAN CHOPS

6 Pork chops

6 Slices tomato

6 Slices green pepper

6 Tablespoons rice

1 Cup hot water

Salt and pepper

Sear the pork chops in heated frying pan, and place in a casserole, place a slice of tomato, green pepper, and a tablespoon of rice boiled, pour one cup of hot water over all, and bake. Chops fixed in this way fit very nicely with almost every vegetable and make a nice dish for luncheon or for dinner.

No. 57　　　　人參を詰めたポーク・ロース

材料	玉子充分泡立てた		人參纖切り	カツプ二杯
	もの	一個	微塵切りのグリン・	
	玉葱微塵切り	中一個	ペパー	一個
	生パン粉	カツプ一杯	セーヂ(香料)	小匙四分ノ一
	鹽、胡椒	少量	豚肉ロース一塊に	
			切つたもの	三封度

作り方――人參、グリン・ペパー、玉葱、生パン粉等を混合せ、セーヂ、鹽及び
胡椒で味をつけ、泡立てた玉子を加へて混ぜます。豚肉を横半分に切り、メ
リケン粉と鹽をよくまぶし、二切れの間に前の人參等を詰め、天パンに入れ
極く強火の天火で三十分間燒き、のち、火を少し弱めて一封度の豚肉に對し
て二十五分づゝ燒きつゞけます。（三封度の豚肉ならば七十五分）

No. 58　　　　ロース・ポーク・ブリタニー

材料	豚肉丸燒き川のもの	四封度	馬鈴薯	四個
	小さい玉葱	六個	林檎	三個
	蕪	三個		

作り方――豚肉は丸燒川の脂の少い處の肉の一塊に切つたものを使ひ、表面に油
を塗り、胡椒を振掛けます。蓋の出來る天パンに入れ強火の天火で三十分間
燒き、馬鈴薯と蕪と林檎の皮をむいて四ツに切つたもの及び外皮をむいた玉
葱を肉の周圍に入れ、再び蓋をして、肉と野菜がよく爛ける迄燒き、肉と野
菜を一緒に皿に盛り、天パンに殘つた油でグレービー・ソース(油を熱し、メ
リケン粉を加へて煮て、湯で延したソース)を作つて添へます。

No. 59　　　　ポーク・チヤツプ野菜燒

材料	ポーク・チヤツプ	六切れ	トマト三分厚さの	
	グリン・ペパー一分		輪切り	六切れ
	厚さの輪切り	六切れ	御飯	大匙六杯
	熱湯	カツプ一杯	鹽、胡椒	

作り方――ポーク・チヤツプに鹽と胡椒を振掛け、熱したフライパンで兩面を手
早く狐色に燒きます。次に蓋の出來る土鍋の底にチヤツプを並べ、一個づつ
上にトマトとグリン・ペパーの輪切りを重ねてのせ、御飯大匙一杯を盛り、鹽
胡椒を振ります。上から靜かに熱湯を入れ、蓋をしてポークが軟くなる迄燒
き、蓋を取り上に色を附けるのです。
　　此の場合の野菜は此處に書いてあるものに限りません他の物を使つても宜
しいのです。

No. 60   DEVILLED PORK CHOPS AND SPICED PRUNES

6 Pork chops	½ Teaspoon dry mustard
4 Tablespoons chili sauce	½ Teaspoon Worcestershire sauce
2 Tablespoons lemon juice	½ Teaspoon soy sauce
1 Small onion grated	

Have the chops cut quite thick. Trim off most of the fat and cut into the lean part on both sides with a sharp knife. Make a sauce of chili sauce, lemon juice, onion, mustard, Worcestershire sauce and soy sauce. Spread the sauce on both sides of the chops and sprinkle with salt and pepper. Let stand for one hour, turning occasionally. Fry out some pork trimmings in a heavy pan, add the chops, and brown. Cover and let cook until tender. When almost done add the prunes and let cook for a few minutes. Arrange the chops on a platter with the prunes around the pork.

Put large soft prunes in a boiling pan and cover with water, simmer until soft and add some vinegar, cloves, cinnamon bark and one teaspoon sugar and cook over low flame until almost all of the juice is gone.

No. 61   BRAISED TONGUE

1 Fresh tongue	1 Teaspoon soya sauce
4 Tablespoons fat	2 Tablespoons minced onion
4 Tablespoons flour	2 Tablespoons minced celery
1 Pint strained canned tomatoes	1 Teaspoon Worcestershire
	Few grains cayenne
1 Pint stock	Salt and pepper
2 Tablespoons minced carrot	1 Teaspoon soy sauce

Cover the tongue with water and simmer for two hours. Remove the outer tough skin and cut away all loose ends. Make a sauce by melting the butter and sauteing the onion, celery, carrots and flour, add tomato soup and make a sauce as you would make a white sauce. Season with salt and pepper and pour over the tongue which has been placed in a casserole. Cover and bake in a medium oven for about two hours or until the tongue is tender. This is good hot or cold served with the sauce in which the tongue is cooked.

No. 60　　デブルド・ポーク チヤツプとプルンズ

材料　ポーク・チヤツプ		チリー・ソース	大匙四杯
（豚肉骨附き）	六個	レモン汁	大匙二杯
玉葱卸したもの	小一個	西洋芥子粉	小匙半杯
ウイスタシヤー・ソース	小匙半杯	醤油	小匙半杯

作り方――ポーク・チヤツプの脂身を切り取り、　肉の脂の少い所にナイフで切目を附けて、此の脂を挟みます。他の材料全部併せてソースを作り、前のポーク・チヤツプの両面へ塗附け、　鹽胡椒を振掛けソースの中に一時間置き、　時々肉を返して、充分ソースをしみ込ませます。フライパンの中に豚脂の切れ端を入れて、熱して油を出し、此の中で前のソースに漬けて置いた豚肉を軟くなる迄時々返しながら蓋をして焼きます。殆んど焼き上つた時に次のスパイスド・プルンズを入れ数分間豚と共に焼き皿に取ります。

スパイスド・プルンズ

作り方――プルンズを鍋に入れ、ひたひたに水を加へ、弱火で軟く茹でて、西洋酢、クローブ及びニツケの枝等を少しづつ入れ、黒砂糖を小匙一杯程入れて弱火で汁が殆んど無くなる迄煮ます。此の方法で煮たプルンズは肉の附合せとしてよいものです。

No. 61　　　　ブレーズド・タング

材料　タング（牛の舌）	一枚	バター	大匙四杯
メリケン粉	大匙四杯	茹でたトマト又は罐詰トマト	カツプ二杯
スープ・ストツク（舌の茹汁）	カツプ二杯	人参微塵切り	大匙二杯
玉葱微塵切り	大匙二杯	セロリ微塵切り	大匙二杯
ウイスタシヤー・ソース	小匙一杯	鹽、胡椒、ケアネペパー	少量
醤油	小匙一杯		

作り方 ― 牛の舌はかぶる位の水を入れ弱火で二時間程茹でて、皮を取り、不要の部分を切取り、土鍋に入れます。別にバターを熱して溶し、玉葱、セロリ、人参をいため、メリケン粉を加へ、トマト・スープを併せたもので延して、ホワイト・ソースを作るのと同様な方法でソースを作り、鹽、胡椒で味を附け土鍋の中の舌の上に掛け、蓋をして天火の中で舌が充分軟くなる迄二時間程焼きます。皿に舌を盛り上にソースを掛けます。これは溫いまゝでも又は冷くして召し上つても結構です。

No. 62   HAM FONDUE

1 Cup fresh bread crumbs	1 Cup ground ham
1 Cup milk	1 Egg
2 Tablespoons butter	

Pour the milk over the bread crumbs and allow to stand until the milk is entirely absorbed by the crumbs. Add melted butter and ham and the egg which has been slightly beaten. Season with salt and pepper and simmer five minutes or until thick then serve on toast squares.

No. 63   SAVORY HAM LOAF

2 Pounds ground ham	1 Teaspoon prepared mustard
2 Small onions minced	4 Tablespoons minced green
2 Cup soft bread crumbs	pepper
2 Beaten eggs	½ Cup tomato catsup
2 Tablespoons horseradish	

Combine all ingredients and pack into a greased bread pan and bake in a moderte oven of 350 degrees F. for 45 minutes. Serve hot or cold. Serves six to eight.

No. 64   HAM ROLLS

8 Slices boiled ham	2 Tablespoons shortening
1 Cup dry bread crumbs	Salt and pepper
½ Pound mushrooms, diced	1½ Cups thin cream sauce
1 Green pepper, chopped	

Saute the chopped pepper and mushrooms in the shortening, then add the crumbs, a small amount of the sauce, and the salt and pepper to taste. Mix thoroughly, then place equally on the sliced ham. Roll and hold in place with toothpicks. Fry until brown in a little fat, then place in a baking pan, and cover with the remaining sauce . Bake until thoroughly heated in a moderate oven of 375 degrees F. Eight servings.

No. 62　　　　ハムのフオンデユー

材料　生パン粉　　　　カツプ一杯　　　ミルク　　　　　カツプ一杯
　　　バター　　　　　大匙二杯　　　　ハムの挽肉　　　カツプ一杯
　　　玉子　　　　　　一個

作り方——生パン粉にミルクを掛けて、　ミルクが全部パン粉に吸取られたらば、溶したバターとハムを、一寸混ぜた玉子と一緒に加へ、鹽、胡椒で味を附け弱火で五分間煮て、四角に切つたトーストの上に掛けます。

No. 63　　　セーブリ・ハム・ローフ

材料　ハム挽肉　　　　二封度　　　　微塵切り玉葱(小)　二個
　　　生パン粉　　　　カツプ二杯　　　玉子泡立てたもの　二個
　　　卸したわさび　　大匙二杯　　　　西洋芥子　　　　　小匙一杯
　　　グリン・ペパー微塵　　　　　　　トマト・ケチヤツプ　カツプ半杯
　　　切り　　　　　　大匙四杯

作り方——材料全部を併せてよく混ぜ、一塊に丸め、油を塗つた細長い天パンに詰め、中火の天火で四十五分間燒きます。溫いまゝ又は冷して薄く切つて召し上るのです。

No. 64　　　　ハ ム・ロ ー ル

材料　ボイルド・ハム　　　　　　　　パン粉　　　　　カツプ一杯
　　　(厚さ一分のもの)八枚　　　　松茸
　　　グリン・ペパー　　　　　　　　(細く切つたもの)　カツプ半杯
　　　(細く切つたもの)一個　　　　バター　　　　　　大匙二杯
　　　鹽、胡椒　　　　少量　　　　　薄いホワイト・

　　　　　　　　　　　　　　　　　　ソース　カツプ一杯半

作り方——バターを熱して松茸とグリン・ペパーを軟くなる迄いため、　パン粉と少量のホワイト・ソースを加へて鹽、胡椒で味を附け、　輕く固められるかたさにして八等分してハムの上にのせ、ハムを海苔卷の様に卷いて楊子で止めこれを少量の油を熱したフライパンの中でいためます。　後、天パンに並べ、残りのホワイト・ソースを上に掛けて充分火が通る迄燒きます。

No. 65   **HAM LOAF**

2 Cups bread crumbs   1 Cup milk

1 Egg   1 Pound lean pork, ground

¼ Teaspoon pepper   1 Pound smoked ham, **ground**

1 Teaspoon salt

Mix bread crumbs, egg, seasonings and milk together and work into the meat. Knead gently. Mold into a loaf and place in the pan, which has been lined with strips of bacon. Bake 1 hour in a 375 degree F. oven. Strips of bacon may be placed over the top during the baking. Serve surrounded with broiled bananas.

No. 66   **HAM AND RICE**

1 Cup ground ham   2 Green peppers

1 Cup rice   2 Tablespoons butter

1 Large onion

Grind left over baked ham, onion and pepper. Cook and blanch rice. Put butter in frying pan, when hot add other ingredients, salt and pepper to taste. Brown slowly.

No. 67   **HAM AND MACARONI ROLLS**

1½ Cups macaroni   ⅛ Teaspoon pepper

½ Teaspoon salt   2 Cups milk

4 Cups boiling water   1 Cup grated cheese

2 Tablespoons butter   1 Tablespoon horseradish

2 Tablespoons flour   8 Slices of boiled ham

¼ Teaspoon salt

Add half teaspoon salt to boiling water and cook macaroni which has been broken in three inch lengths. Boil until tender and wash out in cold water. Mix butter, flour, salt, pepper, and milk and make a white sauce, to which add cheese and horseradish. Arrange about eight pieces of macaroni on each slice of ham and pour some white sauce over the macaroni, then roll up slice, and fasten with toothpick. Arrange in baking pan and bake in a moderate oven for 35 minutes.

No. 65　　　　スモークド・ハム・ローフ

材料	生パン粉	カツプ二杯	玉子	一個
	胡椒	小匙四分ノ一	鹽	小匙一杯
	ミルク	カツプ一杯	豚肉(なるべく	
	スモークド・ハム	一封度	脂の少い所)挽肉	一封度

作り方——パン粉、鹽、胡椒と、ミルクと玉子を一寸混ぜたものを混合せ、豚肉とハムの中に手で混込みます。別に細長い天パンの底にベーコンを數枚並べその中に前の材料を入れ、手でよくおさへます。上にもベーコンを數枚のせ中火の天火で一時間燒き、天パンより取り出して皿にのせ、溫いまゝ、又は冷してナイフで二分の厚さの切れにして召上るのです。この肉ローフの周圍にバナナの皮をむいてフライしたものを盛り合せるとよい。

No. 66　　　　　　ハ　ム・ラ　イ　ス

材料	ハム挽肉	カツプ一杯	御飯	カツプ一杯
	玉葱微塵切り	一個	グリン・ペパー微塵	
	バター	大匙二杯	切り	二個

作り方——挽肉器でハム、グリン・ペパー、玉葱を併せて挽きます。フライパンにバターを入れ、挽き併せた材料をいため、御飯を加へて充分混合せ弱火でよく燒きます。

No. 67　　　　　マ　カ　ロ　ニ　の　ハ　ム　巻

材料	マカロニ又はウドン	カツプ一杯半	鹽	小匙半杯
	熱湯	カツプ四杯	バター	大匙二杯
	メリケン粉	大匙二杯	鹽	小匙四分ノ一
	胡椒	小匙八分ノ一	牛乳	カツプ二杯
	卸したチーズ	カツプ一杯	わさび	大匙一杯
	ボイルド・ハム	八枚		

作り方——熱湯に鹽小匙半杯を加へマカロニを四ツに折つて入れ、柔くなる迄茹で水で洗ふ。バターを溶しメリケン粉、鹽、胡椒を入れよく混ぜ、牛乳で延して十五分程混ぜながら弱火で煮て、ホワイト・ソースを作り、チーズとわさびを加へます。別にハムはなるべく大きい薄切りを選び平に並べ、一枚の上にマカロニを八本程置き、その上に前のソースを流して、ハムでマカロニを巻きます。これを絲又は楊子で止め天パンに並べ三十分程中火の天火で燒くのです。

No. 68   HAM HAWAIIAN STYLE

2 Cups ground boiled ham
1/3 Cup soft bread crumbs
2 Eggs
⅛ Teaspoon salt
1 Teaspoon mustard
5 Tablespoons fat

6 Slices pineapple
3 Boiled sweet potatoes
¼ Teaspoon clove
¼ Cup brown sugar
1 Cup pineapple juice

Mix ham, egg, bread crumbs, mustard and salt and roll into six patties. Heat the fat in the frying pan and brown the pineapple slices on both sides. Also brown ham patties in the same fat and place on top of pineapple slices in a greased baking pan. Cut boiled sweetpotatoes in half lengthwise and coat with sugar mixed with the clove, and saturate in the same fat in the frying pan. When the sugar is melted put the potatoes in the baking pan also, pour pineapple juice over all and bake for 10 minutes and arrange all on large platter.

No. 69   CORNED BEEF PUFFS

2 Eggs
1 Tin corned beef
1/3 Cup Tomato catsup
¼ Cup water

2 Tablespoons pickles chopped or
a little lemon juice
1 Tablespoon chopped onion

Break corned beef into small pieces with a fork and mix thoroughly with beaten egg yolks. Add one quarter teaspoon salt and fold into stifly beaten egg whites. Drop by large spoonfuls onto greased baking sheet and bake in a moderate oven for 20 minutes. Make a sauce by combining the catsup, water and pickles or lemon juice and onion. Bring this sauce to a boil and use as a sauce for corned beef puffs.

No. 70   SCALLOPED CORNED BEEF

1 Can corned beef cut into
cubes
1 Cup medium white sauce
Butter

1 Stalk celery
2 Slices onion
Bread crumbs

Cook chopped celery and onions in the sauce. Put the corned beef in a shallow baking dish and add the sauce. Sprinkle with bread crumbs moistened with melted butter. Brown in a hot oven.

No. 68　　　　　　　ハムと甘藷のパイナツプル燒

材料　挽肉のハム　　　　カツプ二杯　　　　パン粉　　　　カツプ三分ノ一
　　　玉子　　　　　　　二個　　　　　　　鹽　　　　　　小匙八分ノ一
　　　西洋芥子　　　　　小匙一杯　　　　　油　　　　　　　大匙五杯
　　　パイナツプル　　　六切れ　　　　　甘藷茹でたもの　　三本
　　　クローブ粉　　　　小匙四分ノ一　　黒砂糖
　　　パイナツプル汁　　カツプ一杯　　　（花見砂糖）　　　カツプ四分ノ一

作り方——ハム、玉子、パン粉、芥子及び鹽をよく混合せ、六個の平な團子に丸めます。フライパンで熱した油の中でパイナツプルの兩面をよく燒いて天パンに取出し、同じ油でハムの團子を狐色に燒き、パイナツプルの上にのせます。甘藷は皮を取り縱半分に切り、砂糖とクローブを混ぜたものでよくまぶしてフライパンで同じ油で燒き、砂糖が溶けて甘藷の周圍に附く樣にして天パンにパイナツプルと並べて入れ、上からパイナツプル汁を掛け、中火の天火で十分間程燒き、全部を皿に盛合せます。

No. 69　　　　　　　コンビーフ・パフ

材料　玉子　　　　　　　二個　　　　　罐詰のコンビーフ
　　　トマト・ケチヤツプ　カツプ三分ノ一　　をほぐしたもの　　一罐
　　　水　　　　　　　　カツプ四分ノ一　ピツクルス微塵切り　大匙二杯
　　　玉葱微塵切り　　　大匙一杯　　　　（又はレモン汁少量）

作り方——コンビーフをよくほぐして、充分泡立てた玉子の黃味に加へ、鹽小匙四分ノ一を入れ、固く泡立てた白味をこれに折込み、油を塗つた天パンに大匙一杯づつ落して、中火の天火で二十分程燒きます。別にトマト・ケチヤツプに水を加へ、ピツクルス又はレモン汁及び玉葱を加へ、火に掛けて沸騰させ前の燒いたコンビーフのパフの上に掛け、直に召上るのです。手輕な美味しいコンビーフの即席料理です。

No. 70　　　　　　　コンビーフ・スカロツプ

材料　コンビーフ罐詰　　一罐　　　　　ホワイト・ソース　　カツプ一杯
　　　セロリ　　　　　　一本　　　　　玉葱輪切り　　　　　二切れ
　　　パン粉　　　　　　　　　　　　　バター

作り方——セロリと玉葱を細く切り、中位の固さのホワイト・ソースの中に入れ二重鍋の湯の上で十五分程煮ます。コンビーフは賽の目に切り、油を塗つた瀬戸引き天パンに入れ、上にホワイト・ソース等を掛け、パン粉を少量のバターでいためたものを上に振掛けて強火の天火で色を附けます。

No. 71   **BAKED CORNED BEEF HASH**

2 Cups corned beef, finely-   Salt
   chopped   Pepper
2 Cups cooked potatoes,   Hot milk or water
   finely-chopped   1 Egg per person

Mix corned beef and potatoes and season to taste with salt and pepper. Moisten with a little hot milk or water. Spread evenly in greased baking dish. Sprinkle a few buttered crumbs over the top and bake in a moderate oven (350 degrees F.) until heated through. Remove from oven, make slight depressions in hash, and drop an egg into each one. Return to oven for a few moments for egg to set.

No. 72   **CORNED BEEF CHARTREUSE**

1 Tin corned beef   ¼ Teaspoon pepper
2 Teaspoons onion juice   ¼ Cup bread crumbs
1 Tablespoon chopped parsley   1 Egg
1 Teaspoon salt   4 Cups cooked rice

Add the onion juice, parsley, salt, pepper and bread crumbs to the corned beef and add the beaten egg. Add a little water or soup to this so as to moisten it. Grease a deep baking dish thoroughly and place three cups of rice in it, building it up on the sides. Place the corned beef in the center surrounded by rice, cover the top of the corned beef with more rice. Cover closely and steam for 45 minutes. Mashed potatoes may be used in place of the rice, while ground beef may be added in stead of the corned beef, or fish, crab, etc.

No. 73   **BARBECUE SAUCE**

1 Small onion   3 Tablespoons Worcestershire
2 Tablespoons butter   sauce
3 Tablespoons vinegar   ½ Tablespoon dry mustard
2 Tablespoons brown sugar   1 Cup water or stock from roast
Juice ½ lemon   ½ Cup diced celery
1 Small bottle tomato catsup   Salt and pepper to taste

Slice the onion and fry slightly in the butter, add the other ingredients and cook for one hour. Add more water if necessary. This is a delicious gravy with roast lamb or veal, or in fact with any roast meat except fowl.

No. 71　　　　　　コンビーフのハツシユと玉子

材料　コンビーフ　　　　　　　　茹でて細く切つた
　　（ほぐしたもの）　カツプ一杯　　馬鈴薯　　　　カツプ二杯
玉子　　　　　　一人前に附一個　　鹽、胡椒、熱したミルク

作り方──馬鈴薯とコンビーフを混ぜ、鹽、胡椒で味を附け、ミルクを少し加へ
　　て油を塗つた天パンに平に入れ、上にバターでいためたパン粉を少量振掛け
　　中火の天火で充分火が通る迄燒き、天火より取出し、上に玉子の數だけ淺く
　　丸く穴をあけ、玉子を一個づつ落して、再び天火に入れ、數分間玉子を燒い
　　て取出します。

No. 7　　　　　　コンビーフ・シヤートルーズ

材料　コンビーフの　　　　　　　玉葱汁　　　　　小匙二杯
　　　ほぐしたもの　　一罐　　　パセリ微塵切り　大匙一杯
　　　鹽　　　　　　小匙一杯　　胡椒　　　　　　小匙四分ノ一
　　　パン粉　　　　カツプ四分ノ一　玉子　　　　　一個
　　　御飯　　　　　カツプ四杯

作り方──コンビーフに玉葱汁、パセリ、鹽、胡椒及びパン粉を加へ、玉子を少
　　し混ぜて入れ、これにスープ又は水を少量加へて一塊にします。瀬戸引き天
　　パンに充分バターを塗りその中に御飯をカツプ三杯入れて、底と側に盛り、
　　中に前のコンビーフを盛り、上に殘りの御飯をのせて肉をすつかりかくす樣
　　にして蓋を密閉して、四十五分間蒸すのです。此の料理は御飯の代りにつぶ
　　した馬鈴薯を用ひても、又はコンビーフの代りに牛肉の挽肉をよくいためた
　　もの或は茹でゝほぐした魚か罐詰の鮭等を使つてもよいのです。

No. 73　　　　　　肉類用の美味しいソース

材料　玉葱(小)微塵切り　一個　　　バター　　　　大匙二杯
　　　西洋酢　　　　大匙三杯　　黑砂糖(花見砂糖)　大匙二杯
　　　レモン汁　　　半個分　　　トマト・ケチヤツプ　小一瓶
　　　ウイスタシヤー・　　　　　西洋芥子粉　　　大匙半杯
　　　　ソース　　　大匙三杯　　水又は肉の燒汁と水　カツプ一杯
　　　セロリ賽ノ目切り　カツプ半杯　鹽、胡椒　　　少量

作り方──玉葱をバターでいため、他の材料を加へ、一時間弱火で煮て、ソース
　　とします。餘り煮詰つたらば水を少し加へると宜しい。これは牛肉、豚肉、
　　犢肉等によいソースです。

No. 74   CHICKEN AND MACARONI

3 Pound chicken	1 Small onion
2 Teaspoons salt	2 Tablespoons butter
1 Bay leaf	1 Pint of tomatoes
1 Large onion	1 Pint chicken broth
2 Outside stalks of celery	3 Tablespoons chopped mushrooms
1 Package macaroni	½ Teaspoon Worcestershire sauce
4 Quarts of rapidly boiling water	3 Tablespoons flour
1 Tablespoon salt	1 Cup grated cheese

Simmer the chicken in water to cover, to which two teaspoons salt, bay leaf, onion and celery have been added, until tender. When tender take the meat off the bones and leave in good sized pieces. Strain the broth. Parboil for seven minutes the macaroni in the rapidly boiling water, to which one tablespoon of salt has been added. Drain in a colander, saute the chopped onion in the butter, when onion is soft add the tomato which has been strained, chicken broth and chopped mushrooms, salt to taste and sauce and cook as slowly as possible at a low temperature for one half hour to to blend the flavoring. Thicken with flour, moistened with cold water. Lastly add the chicken. Put a layer of macaroni in the bottom of a baking dish, cover with the sauce and sprinkle with the cheese. Continue until the dish is filled. Sprinkle the top generously with the cheese, dot with a little butter and bake at 325 degrees F. for one hour.

No. 75   CHICKEN ROLL

Prepare a nice short biscuit dough, roll it into a rectangular sheet and spread over it two cupfuls of finely chopped boiled chicken moistened with a nicely seasoned white sauce which may be made in part from the liquid left from boiling the chicken. Roll the dough up securely like a jelly roll, brush with milk and bake in a hot oven. Serve with a white sauce to which a few canned mushrooms or a teaspoonful of chopped parsely has been added.

No. 74　　　　チキンとマカロニ

材料					
鶏三封度位のもの	一羽		鹽	小匙二杯
ベーリーフ（香料）	一枚		玉葱	一個
セロリの葉	二枚		マカロニ又はウドン	一包
湯	カツプ十六杯		鹽	大匙一杯
玉葱微塵切り	小一個		バター	大匙二杯
トマト茹でたもの	カツプ二杯		鶏の煮汁	カツプ二杯
松茸細く切つたもの	大匙三杯		ウイスタシヤー・	
メリケン粉	大匙三杯		ソース	大匙半杯
チーズ卸したもの	カツプ一杯			

作り方――此の場合の鶏は少しかたくてもよいのです。普通に十二切れに切り、
かぶる程の湯を入れ、鹽、ベーリーフ、玉葱及びセロリの葉を入れて、数時
間弱火で煮て軟くします。煮えたならば肉を骨より取り、スープは漉して置
きます。マカロニは、沸騰して居る鹽を加へた湯の中に静に入れ、軟くなる
迄八分間茹で、湯をきり水で洗つて置きます。別に微塵切りの玉葱をバター
で軟くいため、トマト、鶏を煮たスープ、松茸、ウイスタシヤー・ソース等
を加へ、出來るだけ弱火で三十分間煮て味を附け、メリケン粉を少量の水と
混ぜたものを加へて、此のスープのソースを濃くし、最後に鶏を入れます。
天パンは二寸五分位の深さのものを選び、底にマカロニを一段入れ、鶏のソ
ースを掛け、卸したチーズを振掛けます。此の三種の材料を交互に天パンに
入れ、一番上にチーズをたつぷり掛け、バターを點々と置いて中火の天火で
一時間燒きます。

No. 75　　　　チキン・ロール

作り方――これは丸燒き又は茹でた燒肉の残物を應用した料理です。鶏は細く切
つて鹽、胡椒でよく味を附けたホワイト・ソースに和へます。別にベーキン
グ・パウダーとビスケツトの材料を混合せ、メリケン粉を振つた板の上で四
角に三分の厚さに延して、その上に鶏を掛け、海苔巻の様に巻き、上にミル
クを塗つて強火の天火で燒きます。この上にホワイト・ソースに薄く切つた
松茸を入れ、パセリの微塵切を加へたものを掛けて召上るのです。

No. 76 **ROAST CHICKEN WITH SPANISH SAUCE**

1 Fat young hen	Salt and pepper
1/3 Cup butter	

Prepare chicken by cleaning and cutting into pieces. Brush with melted butter and season with salt and pepper. Place pieces in a roaster, adding one cup hot water. Have oven heated to 440 degrees or hot oven. Bake for 20 minutes, than reduce heat to moderate. When about half done add another cup of water, when done there should be one and a half cups of rich broth. Drain off the broth and prepare the following sauce

No. 77 **SPANISH SAUCE**

4 Tablespoons butter	¼ Teaspoon soda
2 Spanish onions, minced	1 Cup canned mushrooms or
2 Green peppers	bamboo sprouts
1 Cup strained canned	1½ Cups broth from baked chicken
tomatoes	1 Cup evaporated milk
2 Tablespoons flour	1 Diced pimento

Melt butter in a saucepan, saute minced onion to a golden brown, add the minced green pepper and cook for five minutes. Stir in flour, blending well, add cream and broth gradually, stirring until the mixture thickens. Cook for 10 minutes. Add soda to tomatoes, then add to the sauce with mushrooms or bamboo sprouts, pimento and salt and pepper to season well. Bring to the boiling point, pour over the tender roast chicken and serve piping hot garnished with parsley.

No. 78 **CHICKEN ALMOND STEW**

1½ Pounds chicken meat,	1½ Cup thinly sliced celery
cut into small pieces	½ Cup thinly sliced mushrooms
3 Tablespoons olive oil or	½ Cup finely sliced almonds
butter	1 Tablespoon soy sauce
1 Teaspoon onion juice	½ Tablespoon flour
A little garlic	1 Cup cold water

Have the pieces of chicken cut in thin slices, and brown in hot olive oil. Add the onion juice and garlic if desired and cook five minutes, then add the celery, almonds and mushrooms, next the soy sauce and boil up once. Then add the flour and cook for 10 minutes longer. Add water and cook slowly for 30 minutes. This is good served with boiled rice.

No. 76　　　　鶏の蒸燒スパニツシユ・ソース

材料　鶏（四百匁位のもの）一羽　　　　　バター　　　　　カツプ三分ノ一
　　　鹽、胡椒

作り方──鶏はフライの時と同じ樣に十二切れに切り離してバターを溶したもの
　　を塗り、鹽、胡椒を振り掛け、深い天パンに入れ、上に湯カツプ一杯を掛け
　　強火の天火で二十分間燒き、のち、火を弱くして中火で燒きつゞけるのです
　　が、三十分程燒いて、更に湯をカツプ一杯加へ燒きつゞけます。燒けたらば
　　汁を別に取ります。此の時汁（スープ）がカツプ一杯半程有ればよいので
　　す。

No. 77　　　　スパニツシユ・ソース

材料　バター　　　　　大匙四杯　　　微塵切りの玉葱　　　二個
　　　グリン・ペパー　　二個　　　　トマト罐詰（又は柔
　　　メリケン粉　　　　大匙二杯　　　く煮たもの）　　　一罐
　　　ソーダ　　　　　　小匙四分ノ一　松茸又は竹の子　　　小一罐
　　　鶏を燒いた汁（ス　　　　　　　クリーム　　　　　　カツプ一杯
　　　　ープ）　　　　カツプ一杯半　ピミエント賽ノ目
　　　　　　　　　　　　　　　　　切り　　　　　　　　一枚

作り方──バターを熱し、玉葱をいため、グリン・ペパーを細く切つたものを入
　　れ、五分間いため、メリケン粉を加へて混ぜ、クリームとスープで延し、混
　　ぜながら十分間煮ます。別にトマトにソーダを加へたものを前の材料に加へ
　　松茸、ピミエント（竹の子等もよい）等を入れ鹽、胡椒にて味を附け一度沸
　　騰させて前の燒いた鶏に掛け、直に召上るのです。

No. 78　　　　チキン・アーモンド・スチユー

材料　鶏肉薄切り　　　　一封度半　　　オリーブ油又はバ
　　　玉葱汁　　　　　　小匙一杯　　　ター　　　　　　　大匙三杯
　　　大蒜　　　　　　　極少量　　　　セロリ薄切り　　　カツプ一杯半
　　　松茸薄切り　　　　カツプ半杯　　アーモンド薄切り　カツプ半杯
　　　醬油　　　　　　　大匙一杯　　　メリケン粉　　　　大匙半杯
　　　冷水　　　　　　　カツプ一杯

作り方──鶏肉を熱した油で狐色にいため、玉葱汁と大蒜を加へ、五分間いため
　　てセロリ、アーモンド及び松茸を加へ、醬油を入れ、混ぜて一度沸騰させ、
　　メリケン粉を入れて、十分間煮て後、冷水を加へて靜に三十分間煮ます。こ
　　れには御飯を附合せます。

No. 79   CHICKEN PORTOLA

1 Spring chicken
3 Tablespoons shredded
    coconut
½ Can corn
4 Tablespoons olive oil
1 Onion, sliced fine
1 Tablespoon chopped lean bacon
1 Green pepper, chopped
Little garlic
½ Can tomatoes
½ Teaspoon sugar

Cut the spring chicken into four pieces. Mix the shredded coconut with the corn. Next put the oil into an iron pan, and brown onion and chopped lean bacon. Add finley chopped green pepper, a sliver of garlic if desired and the tomatoes and blend all these flavors with the sugar. Cook together until it thickens, then strain and mix with the coconut and corn. Add the chicken, place in a small baking crock, cover tightly and seal with a paste of flour and water. Stand crock in a pan of water in a hot oven for an hour. When you open it the aroma of coconut and chicken will be very delicious.

No. 80   CHICKEN MUSHROOM

1 Spring chicken
1 Green pepper chopped fine
1 Sliver of garlic
Sherry
Tomato paste
French button mushrooms
½ Tablespoon butter

Into a hot iron pan coated with olive oil put two spring chickens cut in pieces. Season with salt and pepper and keep turning until the bird is browned on all sides. Add chopped green pepper, garlic and a little sage if desired. Add one wineglass of sherry. Then put in the tomato paste, and mushrooms and a dash of sugar. When all has simmered 10 minutes, add the butter and take out the chicken on to a hot plate.

No. 81   JELLIED CHICKEN

Prepare a lemon-flavored gelatin using your own recipe, cool almost to the point of congealing. Then add one and a half cupfuls of cold cooked sliced chicken, half a cupful of diced celery, half a cupful of canned pineapple drained and diced, a quarter of a cupful of shredded olives, and half a cupful of chopped nut meats. Turn into a wet mold and set aside for twelve to twenty-four hours, turn out, and serve with mayonnaise dressing and garnish with parsley.

No. 79　　チキン・ポートラ

材料　若鶏　　　　　　　　一羽　　　　ココナツツ　　　　大匙三杯
　　　コーン(玉蜀黍)罐詰　カツプ半杯　オリーブ油　　　　大匙四杯
　　　玉葱薄輪切り　　　　一個　　　　ベーコン細く切つ
　　　グリン・ペパー微塵　　　　　　　　たもの　　　　　大匙一杯
　　　　切り　　　　　　　一個　　　　大蒜　　　　　　　極少量
　　　トマト罐詰　　　　　半罐　　　　砂糖　　　　　　　小匙半杯

作り方——鶏は先づ縦半分に切り、次に横半分に切つて、四ツにして置きます。
　フライパンにオリーブ油を入れ、玉葱を入れてベーコンと共によくいため、
　これにグリン・ペパー、トマト、大蒜及び砂糖を加へ、全部をよく混ぜ、少
　しどろどろになる迄煮續けて裏漉にします。別に玉蜀黍とココナツツを混ぜ
　て置いたものに此のトマト等を加へます。小さい蓋のある土鍋に鶏と裏漉に
　した材料を入れ、蓋をして緣を水とメリケン粉をねつたのりで密閉して、强
　火の天火の中で水を入れた犬パンに土鍋を入れて、一時間燒きます。これは
　召上る時テーブルで初めて蓋を取るのです。此の樣にしますと香と味が少し
　も逃げず美味しく燒けます。

No. 80　　キチン・ア・ラ・レイン・ドオール

材料　雛鶏　　　　　　　　二羽　　　　グリン・ペパー微塵
　　　大蒜　　　　　　　　極少量　　　　切り　　　　　　一個
　　　シエリー酒　　　　　大匙三杯　　トマトペースト
　　　シヤムピニオン(西　　　　　　　　(罐詰)　　　　　一罐
　　　　洋松茸)　　　　　一瓶　　　　砂糖　　　　　　　小匙半杯
　　　バター　　　　　　　大匙半杯

作り方——フライパンの底にオリーブ油を入れ、熱した四ツに切つた鶏を入れ、
　鹽、胡椒を加へて返しながら鶏がよく狐色に燒ける迄燒きます。これにグリ
　ン・ペパー、大蒜、好みによりセーヂ等を入れ、シエリー酒、松茸及びトマ
　ト・ペースト、砂糖等を加へ、十分間煮てバターを加へ、一度沸騰して鶏を
　皿に取出します。上にソースとして煮汁を掛けます。

No. 81　　チキン・ジエリー

作り方——丸燒き又は茹でた鶏の殘り物應用の料理です。先づ普通のレモンのジ
　エリーを作り、冷してどろどろに固まつたらば鶏肉を薄く切つて之をカツプ
　一杯半とセロリの賽の目切りカツプ半杯、パイナツプル微塵切りカツプ半杯、
　オリーブの薄い輪切りカツプ四分ノ一（無くてもよい）、及び胡椒を細く切
　つたものカツプ半杯を加へ、水でぬらしたジエリー型に流して十二時間乃至
　二十四時間置き、冷して皿に盛りマヨネーズを掛け、パセリを飾ります。

No. 82   ROAST GOOSE WITH POTATO STUFFING

Select a goose that is about four months old, an old goose is better braized than roasted. Singe the goose, wash it carefully in hot water, and wipe it dry before drawing it. Flatten the breast bone by striking it with the rolling pan. Partly fill the goose with potato stuffing, stitch up the openings and truss it. If it is not fat, lay thin slices of bacon upon the breast, but if the goose has considerable fat, omit the pork. Bake in a hot oven of 400 degrees to 480 degrees F. for 45 minutes, remove it from the oven, pour out all the fat, sprinkle the bird all over with salt and pepper, dredge with flour, and return it to the oven. When the flour is a good brown, pour one cup of hot water into the pan and baste the goose often, dredging it each time with a slight sifting of flour to absorb the fat. Allow 18 minutes to the pound for a young goose and 25 for one that is old. Remove the goose from the pan, add a cup of hot water to the gravy and thicken it, if necessary with browned flour. Garnish the goose with parsley and serve with giblet gravy.

No. 83   POTATO STUFFING

2 Cups hot mashed potatoes
1 Cup bread crumbs
½ Teaspoon pepper
½ Tablespoon salt

1 Teaspoon sage
4 Tablespoons melted butter or other fat
2 Tablespoons onion juice

Mix the ingredients in the order given.

No. 84   RICE AND SAUSAGE STUFFING

½ Cupful evaporated milk
1 Cupful bread crumbs, moistened in beef broth
1 Medium onion, minced
1 Small clove garlic, minced
1 Tablespoonful shortening

4 Cupfuls cold boiled rice
½ Pound sausage meat
Salt, pepper, cayenne
1 Tablespoonful minced parsley
Sage and poutry seasoning to Taste

Mix the moistened and squeezed-dry bread crumbs with the evaporated milk. Brown the onion and garlic in the shortening. Mix with the bread crumbs. Add all the other ingredients.

No. 82　　　　　鷲　鳥　丸　燒

作り方——鷲鳥は四ケ月位の物がよく目方が八封度位有ればよろしい。羽毛を取り、火であぶつて生毛を燒き、充分水で洗つて後、臟物を取り出し、胸の骨の突出して居るのを棒でたたいて平にして、腹の中に馬鈴薯の詰物を入れ、切り目を針と糸で縫ひ、強火の天火で四十五分間燒き、天火より取出し、天パンの油を全部取り、鷲鳥に鹽、胡椒、メリケン粉をよくまぶして再び天火に入れて燒きます。鷲鳥にまぶしたメリケン粉が狐色に燒けたらば湯をカツプ一杯上から振掛けます。時々鷲鳥の表面に油が出ますから此の時は少量のメリケン粉を振掛け、後、天パンの中の湯を匙ですくつて鳥の上から掛けます。此の樣にして鷲鳥一封度に對して二十分間と見て、八封度のものならば二時間四十分燒くのです。（初めからの時間です。）燒き上つたならば大皿に取り、天パンの中の汁に湯をカツプ一杯加へ、火の上に掛けて混ぜながら、グレービー・ソースを取ります。ソースが餘り薄い場合はメリケン粉を少し加へます。

正月やクリスマス等に七面鳥の代りに用ふる鷲鳥の料理です。

No. 83　　　　　　馬　鈴　薯　詰　物

材料	溫いつぶした馬鈴薯	カツプ二杯	パン粉	カツプ一杯
	胡椒	小匙半杯	鹽	小匙半杯
	セーヂ粉	小匙一杯	溶したバター	大匙四杯
	玉葱汁	大匙二杯		

作り方——材料を並べた順に混合せ、鷄、鷲鳥、魚等に詰めます。

No. 84　　　　ライスとソーセーヂの詰物

材料	クリーム	カツプ半杯	生パン粉に肉のスープを加へたもの	カツプ一杯
	微塵切り玉葱	小一個		
	微塵切り大蒜	一切れ	バター又は代用品	大匙一杯
	御飯	カツプ四杯	ソーセーヂ肉	半封度
	鹽、胡椒、ケアネペ		微塵切りパセリ	大匙一杯
	パー（赤胡椒）	適宜		
	セーヂ（香料）ボルトリー・シーズニング（香料）			

作り方——生パン粉を一塊に固め得る程度にスープを加へ、クリームと混ぜ、これにバターでいためた玉葱と大蒜を加へ、他の材料を入れて鷄又は七面鳥の詰物とします。

No. 85 **CROUSTADES**

Croustades make excellent containers for creamed mixtures, such as chicken. Make them by removing the crusts from a loaf of bread, cutting the bread in half lengthwise and place oval cutter on the half loaf as near the end as possible. With a sharp vegetable knife trim off the corners of the loaf and follow around the cutter. When four ovals are cut, make a cut all the way around them a quarter of an inch from the edge, and extending to within a quarter of an inch of the bottom. Take out the section of bread in the middle, leaving a boxlike container. Thoroughly brush with butter both inside and out of these bread boxes and put into the oven to dry out and toast a golden grown.

No. 86 **EGG DUMPLINGS**

3 Cups flour
3 Teaspoons baking powder
½ Teaspoon salt

¾ Cup milk
1 Well beaten egg

Sift the flour, baking powder and salt together and add the milk which has been mixed with the well beaten egg. Work quickly and mix well, then drop from end of a tablespoon into hot chicken stew. Cover closely and cook for 12 minutes.

No. 85　　　クラステード

作り方——クラステードは食パンを用ひて作つたものですが、クリーム・ソース
　　等で和へた魚、鳥、野菜等を詰めるのによいものです。食パンの外側の堅い
　　部分を全部切り取り、縦半分に切ります。これを直径三寸位の四　又は丸形
　　にくり抜き、へりの厚さが三、四分程の蓋の無い箱形を作ります。此のパン
　　の箱の内側と外側及び底に溶したバターを充分塗り、天火の中に入れ、すつ
　　かり乾いて狐色になる迄焼きます。此の中にホワイト・ソースで和へた野菜
　　肉等を盛ります。次のクリームド・エツグにも此のクラステードが用ひてあ
　　ります。

No. 86　　　玉子のダンプリング

材料　メリケン粉	カツプ三杯	ベーキング・パウ	
鹽	小匙半杯	ダー	小匙三杯
ミルク	カツプ四分ノ三	泡立てた玉子	一個

作り方——メリケン粉とベーキング・パウダーと鹽を篩ひ、ミルクを入れて混ぜ
　　よく泡立てた玉子を加へ、手早く充分混ぜ、大匙一杯づつを沸騰した肉又は
　　鳥のシチューの中に落し、蓋をして十二分間煮て直ちにシチューと一緒に皿
　　に盛つて召上るのです。

No. 87   **VOLCANO POTATOES**

2 Cups mashed potatoes	½ Teaspoons salt
8 Tablespoons grated cheese	¼ Teaspoons paprika

Shape potato in irregular cones, three inches high on baking dish or small platter. Make a deep indentation in the top of each and fill with seasonings. Sprinkle with cheese and bake 10 minutes in a hot oven of 450 degrees F.

No. 88   **SPANISH HASH**

4 Medium, peeled, cooked potatoes	⅛ Teaspoon paprika
½ Small onion	3 Tablespoons butter
1 Seeded green pepper	3 Eggs
1 Pimento	6 Tablespoons milk
½ Teaspoon salt	1 Tablespoon melted butter
	⅛ Teaspoon salt

Chop the potatoes rather coarsely and add the onion, green pepper, pimento, salt and paprika. Turn into a hot frying pan in which the butter has been melted, and cook gently until the mixture is well heated. Then pour in eggs which have been beaten with the milk, melted butter and salt and stir until the egg coats the potatoes and has a scrambled appearance. Serves six.

No. 89   **POTATO PANCAKES**

1 Egg	2 Cups grated raw potatoes
2 Tablespoons flour	Onion juice
¼ Teaspoon salt	Milk
Few grains pepper	

Beat egg and add flour, salt, pepper, potatoes and a few drops onion juice. Add enough milk to make a stiff batter. Heat fat in frying pan —have about half an inch deep. Drop a tablespoon of the batter in the fat and fry on both sides until golden brown.

No. 87　　　　火　山　ポ　テ　ト

材料　馬鈴薯を茹でゝ　　　　　　　　　　卸したチーズ　　　大匙八杯
　　　つぶしたもの　　　カツプ二杯　　鹽　　　　　　　　小匙半分
　　　胡椒又はパプリカ　小匙四分ノ一

作り方——つぶした馬鈴薯を大匙二杯位手に取り、丸く尖つた富士山の様な形に
　　固め上に穴を明けます。チーズと鹽と胡椒を混ぜたものを穴の中に大匙一杯
　　程入れ、上にも少量振掛けて強火の天火で十分間燒きます。

No. 88　　　スパニツシユ・ハツシユ

材料　茹でた馬鈴薯　　　四個　　　　玉葱(小)　　　　　　半分
　　　グリン・ペパー　　一個　　　　ピミエント　　　　　一個
　　　鹽　　　　　　　　小匙半杯　　パプリカ　　　　　　小匙八分ノ一
　　　バター又は代用品　大匙三杯　　玉子　　　　　　　　三個
　　　ミルク　　　　　　大匙六杯　　バター溶したもの　　大匙一杯
　　　鹽　　　　　　　　小匙四分ノ一

作り方——茹でた薯は賽の目に切り、微塵切りの玉葱、グリン・ペパー、ピミエ
　　ントと混ぜ、鹽及びパプリカを加へ、熱したバターの中で充分に火が通る迄
　　燒き、上に泡立てた玉子にミルクと溶したバター及び鹽等を混合せたものを
　　流し、輕く混ぜながら、玉子が軟く固まる迄フライパンで燒き續けます。残
　　り物のハム、肉等を加へても宜しい。

No. 89　　　ポ　テ　ト　・　ケ　ー　キ

材料　玉子　　　　　　　一個　　　　メリケン粉　　　　　大匙二杯
　　　鹽　　　　　　　　小匙四分ノ一　胡椒　　　　　　　少量
　　　卸した生馬鈴薯　　カツプ二杯　玉葱汁　　　　　　　數滴
　　　ミルク

作り方——玉子を泡立て、メリケン粉、鹽、胡椒を篩つて加へ、馬鈴薯と玉葱汁
　　を入れ、ミルクを適當に加へて、かたいマヨネーズ位のかたさにして、フラ
　　イパンに油を熱した中に大匙一杯づつ落して、兩面を狐色に燒きます。

No. 90   **SURPRISE CROQUETTES**

2 Cups mashed potatoes	2 Eggs
4 Tablespoons cream	Left over meat, vegetable or
1 Teaspoon onion juice	cheese

Add the hot milk and onion juice to mashed potatoes and season with salt and pepper and mix over fire until smoothly mixed. Slightly cool and add to egg yolks. Mix left over meat, vegetables or cheese with white sauce and put in the center of croquetts made using the potato mixture. Dip each croquette first in egg white beaten with a little water, then in bread crumbs. Fry in hot deep fat until golden brown.

No. 91   **MASHED SWEET POTATOES**

4 Cups mashed boiled sweet potatoes	¼ Cup brown sugar
¾ Cup milk	2 Tablespoons sherry
4 Tablespoons butter	3 Tablespoons molasses
⅜ Teaspoon salt	1 Tablespoon butter

Boil or steam sweet potatoes in their jackets, then peel and mash and while hot moisten with milk, which is enriched with butter and season with salt, a little pepper and brown sugar. Add cooking sherry to flavor them delicately and turn into a buttered baking dish about two inches deep. Over the top spread a dressing made by boiling together for three or four minutes the molasses and one tablespoon of butter. Place the potatoes in a hot oven of 425 degrees F. for 25 minutes to brown delicately. A little cinnamon or chopped peanuts can be added to varey flavor.

No. 92   **CARAMEL SWEET POTATOES**

Steam sweetpotatoes and remove skin and cut in one third lengthwise. Arrange in greased baking pan, sprinkle with brown sugar and salt, dot with butter and bake in a hot oven until the sugar is melted and coats the potatoes.

No. 90　　　　サプライズ・コロツケ

材料　つぶした薯　　　　　カツプ二杯　　　クリーム　　　　　大匙四杯
　　　玉葱汁　　　　　　　小匙一杯　　　　玉子　　　　　　　二個
　　　殘り物の肉、野菜、チーズ等

作り方――溫いつぶした薯に熱した牛乳と玉葱汁を加へ、鹽、胡椒で味を附け火
　の上でなめらかになる迄混ぜます。これを少し冷して泡立てた黄味二個を加
　へます。別に殘り物の肉等をクリーム・ソースの濃物と和へ、これを中心に
　して、馬鈴薯をコロツケ形に丸め白味を一寸混ぜた中に入れ、パン粉をまぶ
　し、熱した油に入れて揚げます。

No. 91　　　特別マツシユ・スキート・ポテト

材料　甘藷(大)茹でて　　　　　　　　　　ミルク　　　　　カツプ四分ノ三
　　　　つぶしたもの　　カツプ四杯　　　バター　　　　　　大匙四杯
　　　鹽　　　　　　　　小匙四分ノ三　黒砂糖(花見砂糠)　カツプ四分ノ一
　　　シエリー酒　　　　大匙二杯
　　　モラセズ(黒蜜)　　大匙三杯　　　バター　　　　　　大匙一杯

作り方――甘藷は軟く蒸して皮を取り、つぶして溫い間に熱したミルクを加へ、
　バターを入れ、砂糖、鹽、胡椒、シエリー酒を加へてよく混合せます。これ
　を二寸位の深さの瀬戸引き天パンに油を塗つた中に入れます。黒蜜とバター
　大匙一杯を四分間程煮詰めて、甘藷の上に流し、天パンを強火の天火に入れ
　二十五分程燒きます。美味しい甘藷料理です。シナモン又は微塵切りの落花
　生を入れると味がよくなります。

No. 92　　　キヤラメル・スキート・ポテト

作り方――甘藷を蒸して皮を取り、縦に三分ノ一位に切り、油を塗つた天パンに
　並べ、上に黒砂糖、バター、鹽をのせて強火の天火で砂糖が溶ける迄燒きま
　す。

No. 93 **SWEET POTATO BALLS**

Shape mashed sweet potato in balls, using if desired a piece of pineapple a marshmallow or a cooked prune in the center. Roll each ball in flaked cereal, crushing the cereal first if preferred or bread crumbs. Cover the potato with it completely, and cook thirty minutes in a moderate oven. These balls may be cooked in the pan with roast meat during the last half hour of cooking, basting once or twice with the fat.

No. 94 **SWEET POTATOES IN ORANGE CUPS**

3 Large sweet potatoes
4 Tablespoons butter
4 Tablespoons evaporated
   milk
4 Tablespoons brown sugar
4 Slices of canned pineapple
   chopped

Select large sweet potatoes and boil until tender. Peel and mash, adding butter, milk, brown sugar and the chopped pineapple. Season to taste with salt and beat until light and fluffy. Fill the above into orange cups. The Japanese oranges are good for this purpose if the tops are cut off in half inch slices and the pulp scooped out. Fill with the potato mixture and sprinkle with sugar and dot with butter. Brown in hot oven.

No. 95 **HAWAIIAN SWEET POTATOES**

4 Sweet potatoes
Butter
1 Small tin pineapple chopped

Slice steamed or boiled sweet potatoes in a quarter of an inch thicknesses and arrange one layer in well buttered baking pan. Sprinkle the top with chopped pineapple then arrange another layer of sweet potatoes and pour melted butter over the top. Bake.

No. 96 **FRIED STUFFED ONIONS**

4 Large flat onions
½ Cup soft bread crumbs
¼ Cup nut meats
¼ Teaspoon pepper
½ Teaspoon poultry seasoning
Few grains salt
Egg and crumbs
Deep hot fat

Remove tops and skins from onions and cook until tender. Take out centers, chop fine, add bread crumbs, nut meats and seasonings and use this mixture to stuff onions solidly. Coat with crumbs, egg and crumbs and fry in deep fat heated to 375 degrees F.

No. 93　　　　　ス井ート・ポテト・ボール

作り方——茹でた又は蒸した甘藷を裏漉にして、鹽で味を附け、眞中にパイナツプル、マシマロ又はプルンズの小片を入れて、團子形に丸め、コンフレークス又はパン粉を少しくづした中にころがしてまぶし、中火の天火で三十分間燒きます。これはロース・ビーフ等を作る場合に肉と同じ天パンで燒くとよい。

No. 94　　　　　蜜　柑　と　甘　藷

材料　甘藷	大三本	バター	大匙四杯
クリーム	大匙四杯	黑砂糖（花見砂糖）	大匙四杯
パイナツプル微塵切り	四切れ		

作り方——柔く蒸した甘藷をよくつぶし、バター、クリーム及び砂糖を入れて輕くなる迄泡立てる様にして手早く混ぜ、パイナツプルを加へ、鹽で味を附けます。別に蜜柑は上を二分位の厚さに切り取り、匙で中の實をえぐり取り、皮だけを丸く殘して、此の中に前の甘藷等を入れ上にバターと砂糖を少し掛け、天火の中で狐色に燒きます。

No. 95　　　　　ハワイ風甘藷

材料　甘藷	四個	パイナツプル細くきざんだもの	小一罐
バター			

作り方——蒸した（又は茹でた）甘藷を三分位の厚さの輪切りにし、バターを充分に塗つた淺い天パンに並べ、上にパイナツプルを振掛け又甘藷を並べ、此の上から溶したバターを流して天火で燒きます。

No. 96　　　　　玉葱詰フライ

材料　玉葱	四個	生パン粉	カツプ半分
胡桃	カツプ四分ノ一	胡椒	小匙四分ノ一
ボルトリー・シーズニング（香料）	小匙半分	鹽、パン粉、揚物用油等	

作り方——玉葱の上の方を三分位の厚さに切り取り外の皮をむき、熱湯に鹽を入れたものの中で軟くなる迄煮ます。此の玉葱の芯の方を形をくづさぬ様になるべく澤山取り細く切つて、パン粉、胡椒、香料と混ぜ、前の玉葱の中にしつかり詰込みます。玉葱をパン粉にまぶし、玉子の中に一寸漬け、再びパン粉にまぶして揚物油の中で揚げます。

No. 97　　　**TOMATO ON TOAST**

Heat canned tomatoes and season with a little salt, pepper and sugar. Saute as many slices of bacon as persons to serve and toast as many pieces of bread as persons to serve. On a plate arrange slices toast, pour over them some bacon fat, then place tomatoes. On the tomatoes place one soft boiled egg and a slice of bacon. This is a simple but good luncheon dish.

No. 98　　　**CHEESE SOUFFLE ON TOAST**

4 Slices bacon	4 Rounds of taost
2 Large tomatoes	Cheese souffle

Peel tomatoes and cut in half crosswise, cut the toast in rounds the size of the tomatoes. Cut each slice of bacon in half crosswise. Arrange bread, bacon and tomatoes on the rack of the grill or the oven and bake until the bacon is well done. But slices of toast on plate, pour some of the bacon fat over it, then arrange slice of tomato then pile on this cheese souffle made as follows, and bake in a hot oven 10 minutes. Serve with two short slices of bacon on the top.

Cheese Souffle	½ Teaspoon salt
2 Tablespoons	⅛ Teaspoon pepper
Butter or other shortening	½ Cup grated cheese
2 Tablespoons flour	2 Eggs
½ Cup milk	

Make a white sauce by melting the butter, adding the flour and stirring constantly while adding the milk. Cook until it boils, then add cheese, salt and pepper and continue stirring until the cheese melts. Remove from fire and add well beaten egg yolks. Just before serving fold in the well beaten whites of eggs and pile on tomatoes and bake as mentioned.

No. 99　　　**STUFFED FRIED EGGPLANT**

Split half slices of large fried eggplant, making a pocket. Insert a slice of raw tomato and a strip of broiled bacon in each half slice. Put on broiler, sprinkle with grated cheese, brown quickly and serve at once.

No. 97　　　　トマトとトースト

作り方——トマトの罐詰を熱し、少量の鹽、胡椒、砂糖で味をつけ、別にベーコンの薄切りを人數だけフライパンで燒き、同じ數だけトースト（燒パン）を作つて置きます。皿にトーストをのせ、ベーコンの油をかけ、トマトを盛り、此の上に半熟の玉子の皮を靜かに取つたものを一個のせ、ベーコンを添えます。手輕な晝食向きの御料理です。

No. 98　　　チーズ・スフレー・トマト・トースト

材料	ベーコン	四切れ	大きいトマト	二個
	二三日經た古いパン丸く切つたもの	四枚	ヂーズ・スフレー（作り方後述）	

作り方——トマトの皮をむき横半分に切り、ベーコンは二つに切り、パンはトマトの大きさに丸く切ります。此の三つをフライパン又は強火の天火の中（グリル・オブンがあればその中で）で燒きます。天火の中に入れても差支へ無い皿にトーストをのせ、ベーコンの油を掛け、トマトをのせ、上に次の方法で作つたチーズ・スフレーを盛り、強火の天火の中で十分間燒き、前のベーコンを二切れづつ上にのせます。是は直に召上るのです。

チーズ・スフレー

材料	バター又は代用品	大匙二杯	メリケン粉	大匙二杯
	ミルク	カツプ半杯	鹽	小匙半杯
	赤胡椒	小匙八分ノ一	卸したチーズ	カツプ半杯
	玉子	二個		

作り方——バターを溶し、メリケン粉を加へ、ミルクで延してホワイト・ソースを作り、チーズ、鹽胡椒を加へ、チーズが溶ける迄煮ます。火より下して、よく混ぜた黄味を加へ、召し上る一寸前迄置き、此の時に泡立てた白味を折込み、前の方法で燒くのです。

No. 99　　　　茄子とトマトのフライ

作り方——茄子は大きいものを選び、三分位の輪切りにしてフライします。これに半分位迄切り目を入れ、トマトの薄輪切り一切れと短く切つたベーコンの薄切りをはさみ、天火のグリルの天パンに並べ、上に卸したチーズを振掛けて、強火で上から早く燒き上げます。

No. 100   **SPANISH STYLE EGGPLANT**

1 Large eggplant	3 Small onions
or 8 small ones	1 Can tomatoes

Peel, dice and drop the eggplant into cold water, then slice the onions. Put generous amount of bacon grease or any cooking fat you may have into a deep iron fry pan. Drop the diced egg plant into the hot fat. Cover with the sliced onions, salt and pepper to taste, then pour the tomatoes over all, cover closely, turn the flame quite low and place on back part of range and simmer for one hour, stirring occasionally to keep it from sticking. If it should be watery when done, just leave lid off and cook more rapidly for a few minutes. It should be quite thick.

No. 101   **BAKED STUFFED EGGPLANT**

1 Eggplant about five inches in diameter	½ Tablespoon poultry seasoning
	2 Tablespoons melted butter
1 Cup wholewheat bread crumbs	1 Medium onion chopped
	Salt and pepper
3 Tablespoons tomato ketchup	

Cut eggplant in half lengthwise and bake until tender. The pulp should then be removed from the shell and mixed thoroughly with all the ingredients. Fill the shell with the mixture and brown well in oven.

No. 102   **VEGETABLE BALLS**

2 Cups cooked left over vegetables	1 Egg yolk
	½ Teaspoon salt
2 Tablespoons butter	2 Tablespoons cheese
2 Tablespoons grated onion	1 Egg white
1 Cup soft bread crumbs	

Combine the vegetables, egg yolk, butter, salt, pepper, cheese and one half cup of bread curmbs and allow to stand for 10 minutes. When it becomes soft and light, mold into round using your hands. Add a little water to the whites of the eggs and mix. Dip vegetable balls in some bread crumbs, then in the egg whites and again in crumbs. Then fry in deep fat until golden brown.

No. 1oo　　スペイン風茄子

材料　茄子　　　　　　　大一個又は小
　　　　　　　　　　　八個　　　玉葱　　　　　小三個
　　トマト罐詰　　　　一罐

作り方──茄子の皮をむき賽ノ目に切り水の中に漬けて置きます。玉葱は薄輪切りにします。深いフライパンの底に油をたつぷり入れて熱し、茄子を入れ、上に玉葱をのせ、トマトを掛け、鹽、胡椒で味を附け、固く蓋をして弱火の上で一時間燒き、時々焦げぬ樣攪拌ぜます。煮詰つてどろどろになればよいのですから水が多過ぎる場合は蓋を取つて少し煮立てゝ水分を取ります。

No. 1o1　　　茄　子　詰　物

材料　茄子直徑五寸位の　　　　　黑パン粉　　　　カツプ一杯
　　　もの　　　　　一個　　　トマト・ケチヤツプ　大匙三杯
　　ボルトリ・シーズニ　　　　溶したバター　　　大匙二杯
　　　ング　　　　大匙半杯　　玉葱微塵切り　　中一個
　　鹽、胡椒

作り方──茄子は縱半分に切り、他のものを燒く時一緒に天火に入れて軟くなる迄燒いて置きます。茄子の實をえぐり取りよくつぶして他の材料全部と混ぜ、再び茄子の皮の中に盛り、天火の中で上に色を附けます。

No. 1o2　　　野　菜　ボ　ー　ル

材料　煮た野菜細く切つ　　　　　バター又は代用品　大匙二杯
　　　たもの　　　カツプ二杯　卸した玉葱　　　大匙二杯
　　パン粉　　　　カツプ一杯　玉子の黃味　　　一個
　　鹽　　　　　　小匙半杯　卸したチーズ　　大匙二杯
　　玉子の白味　　一個

作り方──野菜、黃味、バター、鹽、胡椒及びチーズをカツプ半杯のパン粉と併せて十分間置き、軟くふくらんだらば團子に丸め、白味に水を加へて混ぜた中に入れ、パン粉をまぶし、熱した揚げ油に入れて輕く揚げます。

No. 103   **MOCK MUSHROOM SAUCE**

Add to brown sauce one half cup radishes cut in thin slices and pan-fried for 15 minutes in two tablespoons fat.

No. 104   SCALLOPED CAULIFLOWER AND MUSHROOMS

2 Small cauliflowers	1¼ Cup milk
½ Pound dried Japanese shiitake	¼ Cup water in which shiitake are cooked
½ Onion chopped	½ Teaspoon salt
5 Tablespoons butter	¼ Cup bread crumbs
3 Tablespoons flour	

Break cauliflower into small pieces and boil until soft. Wash shiitake (kind of Japanese mushroom), remove stems and soak both stems and tops in water. Cut tops of shiitake in small pieces and saute for two or three minutes in two tablespoons of butter. Put the stems in water and cook for 30 minutes. Saute the onions in the remaining three table-spoons of butter, add flour to this, stir and add milk and water in which shiitake were cooked, stirring all the time. Cook until it boils and becomes thick. Season with salt and pepper and add sauted shiitake. Arrange boiled cauliflower in greased baking dish and cover with the sauce. Sprinkle with bread crumbs and dot with two tablespoons of butter. Bake in a moderate oven for 25 minutes.

No. 105   TURNIP DICE EN CASSEROLE

2 Cups turnip dice	2 Tablespoons shortening
1 Teaspoon salt	4 Tablespoons water or stock
1 Teaspoon sugar	

Put turnip dice in baking dish. Add remaining ingredients, cover and bake in a moderate oven until soft, 20 minutes to one hour. Other vege-tables may be substituted.

No. 1o3　　　　手　輕　な　松　茸　ソ　ー　ス

作り方――普通のグレービー・ソースの中にラデツシユ（赤蕪）カツプ半杯を極
　く薄く切つて大匙二杯のバターでいためたものを加へますと、一寸松茸の様
　な味がして美味しいものです。ビーフステーキ等に掛けるによいソースです。

No. 1o4　　　　花きやべつと椎茸のスカロツプ

材料	花きやべつ	二個	椎茸乾した物	五十匁
	玉葱微塵切り	半個	バター	大匙五杯
	メリケン粉	大匙三杯	牛乳	カツプ一杯四分ノ一
	椎茸の煮汁	カツプ四分ノ一		
	鹽	小匙半分	パン粉	カツプ四分ノ一

作り方――花きやべつを細くちぎつて柔く茹で、乾椎茸は水に漬けて傘の方を細
　く切つてバター大匙二杯で二三分いため、他の部は水を加へて三十分程煮て
　煮汁をカツプ四分ノ一作ります。別に残りの大匙三杯のバターに玉葱を入れ
　ていためメリケン粉を加へ牛乳及び椎茸の煮汁でそろそろ延します。次に鹽
　胡椒で味を附けてきざんだ椎茸を加へ前に油を塗つた天パンに並べた花きや
　べつの上に流し上にパン粉を大匙二杯のバターと混ぜた物を振掛け中火の天
　火で二十五分程燒きます。

No. 1o5　　　　蕪　の　バ　タ　ー　蒸　燒

材料	蕪賽ノ目切り	カツプ二杯	鹽	小匙一杯
	砂糖	小匙一杯	バター	大匙二杯
	水又は			
	スープストツク	大匙四杯		

作り方――蕪を蓋の出來る天パン又は土鍋に入れ、他の材料を上から掛け、中火
　の天火で軟くなる迄二十分乃至一時間燒きます。野菜は他の物を使つても差
　支へありません。

No. 106   CREAMED DAIKON

6 Cups boiled daikon	1½ Cups milk
1½ Teaspoons salt	½ Teaspoon pepper
2 Tablespoons butter	Few grains cayenne pepper
2 Tablespoons flour	

Wash daikon and dice, then cook until soft in salted water. Make a white sauce with remaining ingredients and mix with the daikon which has been cooked and drained.

No. 107   BRAISED CELERY IN GREEN PEPPER RINGS

1 Bunch celery	1 Sprig parsley
1½ Cups stock	1 Green pepper
1 Onion	

Wash and scrape celery and cut in three inch pieces. Place in a casserole on sliced onion and parsley, cover with beef stock and bake one hour. Remove celery and serve in rings of green pepper.

No. 108   CELERY ROOT

Three or Four celery roots are steamed, peeled, and cut in small pieces. Two teaspoonfuls of finely grated onion are mixed with this, and they are served with a thin cream sauce seasoned with curry powder or melted butter with chopped parsley.

No. 109   BOILED JERUSALEM ARTICHOKES

Wash Jersalem artichokes thoroughly and scrub with a brush, then remove skin and cut in half inch squares. Soak in water immediately. Boil enough water to cover one pound of artichokes and add one tablespoon of vinegar and salt. Add artichokes and cook until tender, which should take about 25 minutes.

No. 1o6　　　　大根のクリーム・ソース

材料　大根の茹でたもの　　カツプ六杯　　　鹽　　　　　　　小匙一杯半
　　　バター　　　　　　　大匙二杯　　　　メリケン粉　　　大匙二杯
　　　牛乳　　　　　　　　カツプ一杯半　　胡椒　　　　　　小匙半杯
　　　赤胡椒　　　　　　　少量

作り方――大根をよく洗つて賽の目に切り鹽湯で柔く茹で、水をきつて次のソー
　　スを掛けます。ソースはバターを溶し、メリケン粉、鹽胡椒及び赤胡椒をい
　　れてグラグラ煮立つ迄攪拌しながら煮て、牛乳を少量づつ入れ、攪拌しなが
　　ら弱火でどろどろになる迄煮てつくります。

No. 1o7　　　　　セ　ロ　リ　蒸　燒

材料　セロリ　　　　　　　大一本　　　　　スープ・ストツク　カツプ一杯半
　　　玉葱　　　　　　　　一個　　　　　　パセリ　　　　　　一枝
　　　グリン・ペパー　　　一個

作り方――セロリをよく洗ひ、ナイフで皮をそぎ取り二寸位の長さに切ります。
　　土鍋に玉葱の輪切りと細く切つたパセリを入れ、上にセロリをのせ、スープ
　　を掛け、蓋をして一時間天火の中で燒き、セロリを取出し、三、四本をグリ
　　ン・ペパーの輪切りの中に通して皿に盛ります。残りのストツクは美味しい
　　スープになります。此の樣にして作つたセロリは肉のロースの附合せとして
　　よいものです。

No. 1o8　　　　セロリの根のクリーム和

作り方――セロリの根を三、四個蒸して軟にし、皮を取り賽の目に切ります。こ
　　れに微塵切りの玉葱小匙二杯を加へ、薄いホワイト・ソースを熱して、カレ
　　ー粉で味を附けたものに和へます。

No. 1o9　　　　八　ツ　頭　の　茹　で　方

作り方――八ツ頭はブラシでこすつてよく洗ひ、皮を取り、五分位の賽ノ目に切
　　り、直に水に漬けて置きます。別に八ツ頭一封度に對してかぶる程の湯を沸
　　騰させ、大匙一杯づつの鹽と酢を加へ、水に漬けて置いた八ツ頭を加へ、軟
　　くなる迄煮るのです。（二十五分から三十分位）

No. 110   BUTTERED JERUSALEM ARTICHOKES

1 Pound boiled Jerusalem
  artichokes
4 Tablespoons butter

½ Teaspoon salt
2 Tablespoons lemon juice
2 Tablespoons parsley

Add the other ingredients to the boiled Jerusalem artichokes and cook together for three minutes and serve hot.

No. 111   JERUSALEM ARTICHOKES AU GRATIN

1 Pound boiled Jerusalem
  artichokes
2 Tablespoons butter
3 Tablespoons flour

1 Cup chicken soup
Salt, and pepper
1/3 Cup cream

Melt butter, add flour, stir well and add soup, stirring constantly, cook until smooth and thick, then season. Add cream, heat and add artichokes.

No. 112   SQUASH   AKED WITH BACON

Cut squash in strips one and a half inches wide and five inches long. Remove skin, sprinkle with salt, cover with tiny squares of bacon and bake, covered closely, until squash is tender, then uncover until bacon is crisp and brown.

No. 113   SQUASH PUDDING WITH BACON

4 Cups steamed or boiled
  squash
¾ Teaspoon salt
¼ Teaspoon pepper
½ Teaspoon sugar

3 Tablespoons fat
1 Well beaten egg
1 Cup milk
Strips of bacon

Mash fine or press through a sieve the steamed or boiled squash and season with salt, pepper and sugar. Add melted fat, well beaten egg and milk and turn into a baking dish and top with strips of bacon. Bake in a moderate over of 375 to 400 degrees F. for about 15 minutes or until nicely browned.

No. 11o　　　八ツ頭のバター・ソース和へ

材料　八ツ頭茹でたもの　　一封度　　　　バター　　　　　大匙四杯
　　　鹽　　　　　　　　　小匙半杯　　　レモン汁　　　　大匙二杯
　　　パセリ微塵切り　　　大匙二杯

作り方——茹でた八ツ頭を他の材料と和へ、三分間煮て食膳に供します。

No. 111　　　八ツ頭オグラタン

材料　八ツ頭茹でたもの　　一封度　　　　バター　　　　　大匙二杯
　　　メリケン粉　　　　　大匙三杯　　　鷄スープ　　　　カツプ一杯
　　　鹽、胡椒　　　　　　少量　　　　　クリーム　　　　カツプ三分ノ一

作り方——バターを溶し、メリケン粉を和へ、スープで延し、鹽、胡椒で味を附
け、混ぜながら一度沸騰させて、クリームを加へて熱し、八ツ頭を入れてよ
く温めます。

No. 112　　　南瓜とベーコン

作り方——南瓜は幅一寸、長さ三寸の細長い形に切り、皮を取り鹽を掛け、ベー
コンを賽ノ目に切つたものを上に振振け天パンに入れ、蓋をよくして、南瓜
が軟くなる迄燒き、蓋を取り、ベーコンがからつと燒き上る迄天火の中で燒
續けます。

No. 113　　　南瓜の天火燒

材料　茹でて裏漉にした　　　　　　　　　鹽　　　　　　　小匙四分ノ三
　　　　南瓜　　　　　　　カツプ四杯　　胡椒　　　　　　小匙四分ノ一
　　　砂糖　　　　　　　　小匙半杯　　　バター　　　　　大匙三杯
　　　玉子　　　　　　　　一個　　　　　ミルク　　　　　カツプ一杯
　　　ベーコン薄切れ　　　四切れ

作り方——南瓜に鹽、胡椒、砂糖で味を附け、溶したバターと泡立てた玉子及び
ミルクを加へ、バターを塗つた天パンに入れ、上にベーコンの薄切れをのせ
て、中火の天火で上のベーコンが燒けて色が附く迄二十五分間程燒きます。

No. 114　　STUFFED GREEN PEPPERS

6 Large green peppers	1 Egg
1 Cup corn cut from cob	3 Tablespoons butter, melted
1 Cup soft bread crumbs	½ Teaspoon salt
1 Tablespoon chopped onion	¼ Teaspoon pepper
1 Tablespoon chopped green pepper	¼ Teaspoon celery salt

Wash peppers, cut off and discard tops, remove seeds and fibrous portions on inside. Mix rest of ingredients. Stuff peppers. Fit side by side in small baking pan. Add one half inch of water. Bake 30 minutes.

No. 115　　CORN CREOLE

2 Cups canned corn	1 Pimento chopped
2 Cups soft bread crumbs	2 Teaspoon onion chopped
2 Tablespoons butter	2 Cup tomato juice
1 Green pepper chopped	Salt and pepper

In a deep baking dish arrange alternate layers of corn and bread crumbs. On each layer of bread crumbs place pieces of butter, chopped green pepper, pimento, salt and pepper. When all ingredients have been put in the baking dish, pour the tomato juice or soup over the top and bake in a moderate oven for 45 minutes.

No. 116　　SPINACH CROQUETTES

2 Cups cold cooked spinach	¼ Cup grated cheese
1 Tablespoon butter	1 Egg yolk, beaten
¼ Tablespoon grated onion	1 Egg white, beaten
1 Tablespoon sifted flour	1 Tablespoon chopped parsley
¼ Cup bread crumbs	⅛ Teaspoon pepper

Drain the spinach and chop very fine. Melt the butter in a frying pan. Add the onion and brown lightly, then add the spinach and stir until well heated. Slowly add the remaining ingredients except the cheese. Mix well, and heat until lukewarm Turn out on a board spread with crumbs. Sprinkle with the parsley. Form into small balls or croquettes and roll in crumbs. Fry in deep hot fat of 365 degrees F. until brown. Remove from the fat, sprinkle with the grated cheese and crumbs, and brown in a hot oven of 400 degrees F.

No. 114　　　グリン・ペパー玉蜀黍詰

材料　グリン・ペパー	六個	玉蜀黍（ゆでゝ實を	
生パン粉	カツプ一杯	取つたもの）	カツプ一杯
微塵切り玉葱	大匙一杯	微塵切りグリン・ペ	
玉子	一個	パー	大匙一杯
溶したバター	大匙三杯	鹽	小匙半杯
胡椒	小匙四分ノ一	セロリ・ソルト	小匙四分ノ一

作り方──グリン・ペパーを洗ひ、枝の方を二分の厚さに切取り、中の種子を取
　り、他の材料を混ぜたものを中に詰め、天パンに並べ、周圍に五分の深さに
　熱湯を入れ、中火の天火で三十分間燒きます。

No. 115　　　コーン・クレオール燒

材料　玉蜀黍罐詰	カツプ二杯	生パン粉	カツプ二杯
バター	大匙二杯	グリン・ペパー纎	
ビミエント纎切り	一個	切り	一個
玉葱微塵切り	小匙二杯	トマト汁	カツプ二杯
鹽、胡椒	少量		

作り方──深い瀬戸引き天パンに玉蜀黍とパン粉を交互に一段づつ入れパン粉の
　各段の上にはバターを小さくちぎつたもの、グリン・ペパー、ビミエント、
　鹽、胡椒等を振り掛けます。一番上の段のパン粉にも同樣に他の材料をの
　せ、全部の上からトマト汁又はトマト・スープを流し中火の天火で四十五分
　間燒きます。

No. 116　　　菠薐草コロツケ

材料　茹でた菠薐草	カツプ二杯	バター	大匙一杯
卸した玉葱	小匙四分ノ一	メリケン粉	小匙一杯半
生パン粉	カツプ四分ノ一	卸したチーズ	カツプ四分ノ一
玉子白味	一個	玉子黃味	一個
微塵切りパセリ	大匙一杯	胡椒	小匙十六分の一

作り方──菠薐草は軟く茹でて細くきざみ、別にフライパンにバターを入れて熱
　し、玉葱を入れ、之に菠薐草を加へていため、徐々にパセリとチーズ以外の
　材料を加へます。此の時玉子は白味と黃味を別々によく泡立てゝ加へるので
　す。微温程度に熱してパン粉を振つた皿又は板の上に延してのせ、上にパセ
　リを振掛け、小さいコロツケ形に丸め、パン粉にまぶして、熱した揚物油に
　入れて狐色に揚げ、取出してパン粉と卸したチーズを振掛け強火の天火で色
　附けてチーズを溶します。

No. 117   MOULDED SPINACH WITH MUSHROOMS

Steam spinach, drain thoroughly, chop fine, and season with butter and salt, press in a buttered ring mould and set in warm water for five minutes. Remove from the mold, place on a serving plate, and fill center with mushrooms.

No. 118   SPINACH AND TOAST

Chop one small onion and saute in three tablespoons of butter for five minutes, add two cups of cooked and mashed spinach, and two hard boiled eggs sliced. Heat while stirring and place on hot slices of toast. Good for luncheon or childrens supper.

No. 119   SAVORY SPINACH

2 Pounds spinach	2 Tablespoons chopped green pepper
½ Cups butter	¼ Teaspoon salt
2 Tablespoons vinegar	2 Tablespoons chopped pimento

Cook spinach until tender. Drain thoroughly, chop fine and serve with a sauce made from the remaining ingredients. Melt the butter in a saucepan. Add the vinegar, chopped green pepper, salt and chopped pimento. Heat until the green pepper is tender. Serves six.

No. 120   GREEN PEAS AND LETTUCE

Two cups of peas and one head of lettuce are put in a saucepan with two tablespoonfuls of butter, one slice of onion, and one cupful of water and cooked over the flame for five minutes, stirring constantly with a fork. The heat is reduced, and the vegetables are allowed to simmer gently until the peas are tender.

No. 117　　　　菠薐草こ松茸

作り方――菠薐草を軟く蒸し、裏漉にするか又はすりつぶしてバター、鹽、胡椒を加へ、バターを塗つた輪形のジェリー型に指先でおさえて詰め、熱湯の中にジェリー型を五分間漬けて置きます。菠薐草をジェリー型より皿の上に取り出し、松茸を薄切りにし、バターでいためてホワイト・ソースで和へたものを菠薐草の輪の中央に盛ります。

No. 118　　　　菠薐草こトースト

作り方――玉葱の小さいもの一個を微塵切りにして大匙三杯のバターの中で五分間いため、茹でて裏漉にした菠薐草カップ二杯を加へ、茹玉子二個細く切つたものを加へます。之を混ぜながら熱してトースト（燒パン）の上に盛ります。畫食用又は子供用によい御料理です。

No. 119　　　　菠薐草セーブリ・ソース

材料			
菠薐草	二封度	バター溶したもの	カップ半杯
酢	大匙二杯	微塵切りグリン・	
鹽	小匙四分ノ一	ペパー	大匙二杯
ピミエント微塵切り	大匙二杯		

作り方――菠薐草は軟く茹でて裏漉にし、他の材料を用ひ次の方法でソースを作り上に掛けます。溶したバターに、酢、グリン・ペパー、鹽、ピミエントを加へ、グリン・ペパーが軟くなる迄數分間煮ます。此の方法で料理した菠薐草は美味しく召上れます。

No. 12o　　　　レタスこグリン・ピース

作り方――生のグリン・ピースをカップに二杯位と玉レタス一個を輪切りにしたものを鍋に入れて、大匙二杯のバター、玉葱一切れ、水カップ一杯を加へ、五分間強火で絶えず混ぜながら茹でゝ後、火力を減じてピースが軟くなる迄煮るのです。

No. 121   BEAN SAUSAGES

½ Cup dried lima beans	2 Teaspoons poultry seasoning
1/3 Cup soft bread crumbs	¼ Teaspoon salt
3 Tablespoons milk	1 Teaspoon vinegar
¼ Teaspoon pepper	1 Egg, beaten

Wash beans, and soak water to cover over night. Pour out the water and add to salted boiling water and cook beans until tender. Pour out water and put the beans through the potato ricer. Add all other ingredients to the mashed beans and roll in to sausage shapes. Put in frying pan in which some fat has been heated and fry on both sides until brown. Serve with tomato catsup.

No. 122   PARSLEY FRITTERS

½ Cup flour	½ Tablespoon melted fat
¼ Teaspoon salt	1 Egg white
1/3 Cup milk	Parsley
1 Egg yolk	

Sift together flour and salt, add gradually milk, egg yolk beaten until thick, melted fat and egg white beaten stiff. Dip sprigs of parsley in the batter and fry in deep hot fat.

No. 123   FRIED ASPARAGUS

Canned asparagus rolled in beaten eggs and bread crumbs and fried in deep fat, makes a good vegetable.

No. 124   ORANGE SAUCE FOR ASPARAGUS

2 Beaten egg yolks	5 Tablespoons orange juice
2 Tablespoons butter	1 Tablespoon lemon juice
¼ Teaspoon salt and paprika	Grated rind of 1 orange
1 Teaspoon sugar	

An unusually delicious dish is asparagus served with orange sauce. Put in a double boiler the beaten egg yolks and butter, salt, paprika and sugar. Cook until the mixture thickens. Then add the orange juice, lemon juice and the grated rind of the orange. Mix well and serve over the asparagus. This is equally good served with boiled or baked beets.

No. 121　　　　　　豆　の　ソ　セ　ー　ヂ

材料　乾白ゐんげん豆　　カツプ半杯　　　生パン粉　　　　カツプ三分ノ一
　　　ミルク　　　　　　大匙三杯　　　　胡椒　　　　　　小匙四分ノ一
　　　ボルトリ・シーズニ　　　　　　　　鹽　　　　　　　小匙四分ノ一
　　　　ング　　　　　　小匙二杯　　　　西洋酢　　　　　小匙一杯
　　　玉子、一寸泡立て
　　　　たもの　　　　　一個

作り方――ゐんげんをよく洗ひ、かぶる位の冷水に一晩漬け水をすて、鹽を加へ
　　た熱湯に入れ、軟くなる迄茹で、湯をすてゝ豆を裏漉にし、パン粉と他の材
　　料全部を加へ、團子に丸め、熱したフライパンに油を少し入れ、兩面を燒き
　　トマト・ケチヤツプ等を掛けて召上るのです。

No. 122　　　　　　パ　セ　リ・フ　リ　ツ　タ　ー

材料　メリケン粉　　　　カツプ半杯　　　鹽　　　　　　　小匙三分ノ一
　　　ミルク　　　　　　カツプ三分ノ一　玉子の黄味　　　一個
　　　溶したバター　　　大匙半杯　　　　玉子の白味　　　一個
　　　パセリ

作り方――メリケン粉と鹽を篩ひ、ミルクと、よく泡立てた黄味を加へ、油と最
　　後に泡立てた白味を靜に入れます。此の中にパセリを一枝づつ一寸漬け、揚
　　物油で輕く揚げ肉、魚の料理に飾り、附合せとします。

No. 123　　　　　　ア　ス　パ　ラ　ガ　ス　の　フ　ラ　イ

作り方――罐詰のアスパラガスの汁をよく切り、アスパラガスを少量のメリケン
　　粉でまぶし、玉子と水を混ぜた中に一寸漬け、パン粉をまぶして、熱した揚
　　物油の中で狐色に手早く揚げます。トマト・ケチヤツプを掛けるのも宜しい。

No. 124　　　　　　オレンヂ・ソース（アスパラガス用）

材料　玉子の黄味　　　　二個　　　　　　バター　　　　　大匙二杯
　　　鹽　　　　　　　　小匙四分ノ一　　パプリカ　　　　少量
　　　砂糖　　　　　　　小匙一杯　　　　オレンヂ汁　　　大匙五杯
　　　レモン汁　　　　　大匙一杯　　　　オレンヂ皮卸した
　　　　　　　　　　　　　　　　　　　　　もの　　　　　一個分

作り方――これはアスパラガスの上に掛けると大層美味しいソースです。二重鍋
　　の上に玉子、鹽、パプリカ、砂糖及びバターを入れ湯の上でどろどろになる
　　迄煮ます。これにレモンとオレンヂ汁を加へ、卸した皮を入れ、溫めてアス
　　パラガスの上に掛けます。此の他ビーツ（赤蕪）の上に掛けても結構です。

No. 125   **BANANAS ROLLED IN BACON**

3 Bananas   6 Slices bacon

Cut bananas in half crosswise, and wrap each piece with a slice of bacon and fasten with toothpick. Bake in a hot oven or saute in a heated frying pan. Serve with meat course.

No. 126   **BAKED BANANAS WITH PINEAPPLE**

Cut bananas in half lengthwise, and cut each slice of pineapple in half crosswise. Arrange bananas and pineapple in baking pan and sprinkle with sugar. Bake in moderate oven for 10 minutes or until the sugar is melted. Serve with meat.

No. 127   **PINEAPPLE AND BACON**

12 Slices bacon   Salt and flour
6 Slices pineapple

Put the bacon in a cold frying pan and place over fire and fry, pouring the excess fat out of the frying pan from time to time. Put the bacon on a hot plate, and fry the pineapple which has been coated with flour and salt, in the bacon fat. This is a good breakfast dish.

No. 128   **MACARONI CROQUETTES**

1 Cup broken macaroni   ¼ Cup grated cheese
1 Cup thick white sauce   1 Egg yolk

Cook the finely broken macaroni in boiling salted water about 15 minutes. Make the thick white sauce, season with salt and pepper, add the grated cheese, beaten yolk of an egg, and mix well, spread on platter cool. Shape into croquettes, roll in crumbs, dip in beaten egg and crumbs again and fry in deep, hot fat. Drain and serve with cheese sauce.

No. 125　　　バナナのベーコン巻

材料　バナナ　　　　　三本　　　　ベーコン　　　　六切れ

作り方——バナナは横半分に切り、ベーコンの薄切れで巻き、揚子で止め、強火の天火で焼くか又は熱したフライパンで焼きます。肉の附合によい料理です。

No. 126　　　バナナとパイナツプルの砂糖焼

作り方——バナナを縦半分に切り、パイナツプルは一切れを半分に切り、浅い天パンに並べ、上に砂糖を振掛けます。中火の天火で十分程焼き砂糖が溶ければよいのです。肉の附合せによい料理です。

No. 127　　　ベーコン・パイナツプル

材料　ベーコン　　　　十二切れ　　　パイナツプル　　　六切れ

　　　鹽、メリケン粉　　少量

作り方——ベーコンを冷えたフライパンに入れ、火にかけて熱し、からつと焼き上げます。（此時油が出ますが、これは別の皿にへ時々流してとる様にします）。此のベーコンを温めた皿に取り温い所に置きます。パイナツプルは鹽とメリケン粉にまぶし、ベーコンの油の入つて居るフライパンで兩面をいため、ベーコンと一緒に盛ります。朝食向きの變つた料理です。

No. 128　　　マカロニ・コロツケ

材料　一寸の長さに折つ　　　　　濃いホワイト・

　　　たマカロニ（又は　　　　　ソース　　　　カツプ一杯

　　　ウドン　　　カツプ一杯　　　卸したチーズ　カツプ四分ノ一

　　　玉子の黄味を泡立

　　　てたもの　　　一個

作り方——マカロニを多量の熱湯に入れ、鹽を加へて軟くなる迄十五分程沸騰させ、水で洗つて後、他の材料全部と合せ、皿の上に延して敷き、充分冷します。これをコロツケ形に手で丸め、パン粉をまぶし、玉子一個を大匙一杯の水と混ぜた中に漬け、再びパン粉をまぶし、熱した揚物油の中で狐色に揚げて、チーズ・ソースを掛けます。チーズ・ソースはホワイト・ソースに卸したチーズを加へて溶したものです。

No. 129   **TOMATO SALAD**

Select one medium sized tomato for each person. Pour boiling water over the tomatoes then dip in cold water and remove skins. Chill thoroughly. Make slits all over the tomatoes and insert thin slices of cucumbers in these slits. Serve with mayonnaise. This makes a simple but unusual tomato salad.

No. 130   **CARDINAL SALAD**

2 Large beets	½ Cup asparagus tips
2 Tablespoons vinegar	Mayonnaise made with vinegar
½ Cup wax beans	from beets
½ Cup peas	

Boil beets until tender, slice, cover with vinegar and let stand until the following day. Drain off the vinegar and use it in making the mayonnaise. Arrange white wax beans, peas, asparagus tips and red mayonnaise in little rose like nest of lettuce leaves, and garnish with red radishes.

No. 131   **APPLE-RING-AND-CARROT SALAD**

Cut large rosy apples into inch slices. Core but do not pare. Place on lettuce nests. Fill the centers with grated raw carrot, top with a green-pepper star and serve with French dressing.

No. 132   **RAISIN AND SALMON SALAD**

1 Cup canned salmon	½ Cup chopped dill pickles
½ Cup chopped raisins	Few drops of tabasco sauce
1 Cup diced celery	

Wash the raisins in hot water and cut each one in half and mix with the canned salmon which has been made into small pieces. Add celery, pickles and mix with mayonnaise to which a few drops of tabasco sauce has been added. This salad is best garnished with slices of tomatoes and hard boiled eggs which have been marinated in French dressing.

No. 129　　　　ト　マ　ト・サ　ラ　ダ

作り方——トマトは一人に一個附け位の大きさの物を選び、**熱湯**を掛け、冷水に漬けて皮を薄くむきます。トマトの表面にナイフで切目を半吋置き位に附けて、その所に薄く切つた胡瓜を挟み、トマトの上からマヨネーズ・トレツシングを掛けます。

No. 13o　　　カ ー デ イ ナ ル・サ ラ ダ

材料	ビーツ（赤蕪）	大二個	酢	大匙二杯
	ライマ・ビーンズ（又		グリン・ピース	カツプ半杯
	はセロリ）	カツプ半杯	アスパラガス	カツプ半杯
	ビーツの酢で作つたマヨネーズ			

作り方——ビーツはよく洗つて皮を取らず莖も五分位ついた儘輕くなる迄茹でて皮をむき、輪切りにして酢を掛け、一晩置きます。次の日ビーツを漬けた酢を用ひて普通にマヨネーズを作ります。大皿にレタスの葉を敷き、冷した野菜（此處に書き並べた以外の物でもよい）を色取りよく盛合せて赤い色のマヨネーズ・ドレツシングを添えます。

No. 131　　　林 檎 と 人 參 の サ ラ ダ

作り方——林檎を厚さ三分位の輪切りにして芯を抜き、皮は取りません。レタスの葉を敷いた一人附けのサラダ皿に林檎を一切れのせ、中央に卸した生の人參を盛り、グリン・ペパーを星形に切つたものをのせ、マヨネーズを掛けます。色の美しい滋養のあるサラダです。

No. 132　　　乾 葡 萄 と 鮭 の サ ラ ダ

材料	鮭罐詰	カツプ一杯	乾葡萄半分に切つ	
	賽の目切りセロリ	カツプ一杯	たもの	カツプ半杯
	ジル・ピツクル（漬物）	カツプ半杯	トバスコ・ソース	數滴

作り方——乾葡萄は熱湯で洗ひ、半分に切り、ほぐした鮭と混合せ、セロリ及びピツクルを加へます。次にトバスコ・ソースとマヨネーズにこれを和へます此のサラダにはフレンチ・ドレツシングで和えたトマトと茹玉子の輪切りを添えると㗵しい。

No. 133　　　CRAB SALAD

1½ Cups canned crab or
　lobster
½ Cup diced celery

1 Teaspoon vinegar
Mayonnaise dressing

Remove small bones from canned crab or use canned lobster and pour the vinegar over it and allow to stand in the refrigerator until thoroughly chilled. Dice the celery and chill with a piece of ice in it. Just before serving drain both the crab and celery and mix with mayonnaise.

No. 134　　　ORANGE AND SHRIMP SALAD

1 Cup walnut meats, broken
　in pieces
6 Oranges peeled and cut in
　sections

1 Can shrimps

2 Tablespoons cooking wine

Mix all in stiff mayonnaise and serve chilled in orange cups or on crisp lettuce, and garnish with orange and then slices of lemon.

No. 135　　JELLIED PINEAPPLE AND CHEESE SALAD

1 Small can crushed pineapple
2 Tablespoons lemon juice
½ Cup sugar

2 Sheets gelatine
½ Cup grated cheese
½ Cup whipping cream

Heat pineapple, add lemon juice and sugar and stir until sugar is dissolved. Meanwhile soak the gelatine in cold water to cover for 10 minutes, remove from the water and squeeze well. Add this gelatine to the hot mixture and remove from the fire and chill. When beginning to set add the grated cheese mixed with whipped cream. Chill until firm. Place in refrigerator and chill. Serve with the following dressing.

No. 136　　　PIQUANT SALAD DRESSING

2 Tablespoons chopped celery
2 Tablespoons chopped
　peppers

2 Teaspoons onion, minced
½ Cup mayonnaise

Mix the chopped vegetables with the mayonnaise and mix well.

No. 133　　　蟹　の　サ　ラ　ダ

材料　蟹又は鰕罐詰　　　カツプ一杯半　　　賽の目切りセロリ　　カツプ半杯
　　　酢　　　　　　　　小匙一杯　　　　　マヨネーズ・ドレツシング

作り方——蟹又は鰕をよくほぐして小骨を拔き、酢を掛けて冷して置きます。セ
　ロリは切つて氷を一塊入れ、充分冷します。召し上る直前にセロリの水を切
　り蟹と混ぜ、マヨネーズで和へます。

No. 134　　　蜜柑こ芝鰕のサラダ

材料　胡桃細く割つたもの　カツプ一杯　　　蜜柑又はオレンヂ　　六個
　　　芝鰕　　　　　　　　一罐　　　　　　料理用葡萄酒　　　　大匙二杯

作り方——蜜柑の皮を取り實を薄く輪切りにして他の材料全部と混ぜ固く作りま
　したマヨネーズ・ドレツシングに和へて、蜜柑の皮の中に詰めるか、皿の上
　のレタスの葉の上にのせます。レモン又はオレンヂの輪切りを飾るのもよ
　い。

No. 135　　　パイナツプルこチーズ・サラダ

材料　パイナツプル微塵　　　　　　　レモン汁　　　　　　大匙二杯
　　　　切り　　　　　　小一罐　　　砂糖　　　　　　　　カツプ半杯
　　　ゼラチン紙　　　　二枚　　　　卸したチーズ　　　　カツプ半杯
　　　生クリーム(泡立用)　カツプ半杯

作り方——パイナツプルの微塵切りを汁と共に熱し、レモン汁、砂糖を加へ、砂
　糖が溶ける迄混ぜ乍ら熱し、水に漬けて軟くして、しぼつたゼラチン紙を加
　へ、火より下して溶し、冷します。どろどろに固まりはじめたならば泡立て
　た生クリームと卸したチーズを折込み、水でぬらしたヂエリー型に流して固
　め、次のドレツシングをかけてサラダとして召上るのです。

No. 136　　　ピカント・サラダ・ドレツシング

材料　セロリ繊切り　　　大匙二杯　　　グリン・ペパー繊切
　　　玉葱微塵切り　　　　小匙二杯　　　　り　　　　　　大匙二杯
　　　マヨネーズ　　　　　カツプ半杯

作り方——微塵切りの野菜をマヨネーズと和へて用ひます。

No. 137   **STRAWBERRY SALAD**

Select large, perfect berries, halve them and sprinkle with powdered
sugar; chill and arrange in lettuce nests, top with fruit dressing.

No. 138   **FRUIT DRESSING**

Fruit Dressing. Beat the yolks of two eggs with a third of a cupful
of pineapple juice and one and a half tablespoonfuls of lemon juice, cook
over hot water till thick, adding half a cupful of sugar gradually and
stirring well. Chill, then fold into one cupful of whipped cream.

No. 139   **JELLIED CUCUMBER SALAD**

4 Cupfuls diced cucumbers	1 Teaspoonful salt
½ Tablespoonful chopped	⅛ Teaspoonful pepper
onion	2 Tablespoonfuls vinegar
3½ Cupfuls boiling water	4 Sheets gelatine

Cook the cucumbers and onion in the boiling water until the cucumbers
are tender. This will take about 20 minutes. Add the salt, pepper, and
vinegar. Remove from the fire and add the gelatine, which has soaked for
5 minutes in the cold water. Stir until the gelatine is dissolved. Press the
mixture through a sieve and pour into individual molds. Chill and serve
with mayonnaise and cold cuts of meat. Serves 6.

No. 140   **PINEAPPLE AND CUCUMBER SALAD**

5 Sheets gelatine	½ Cup sugar
½ Cup boiling water	3 Cups grated pineapple
Juice of 1 lemon	½ Cup finely chopped cucumber
1/3 Cup vinegar	1 Pimento, chopped
1 Teaspoon salt	

Soak the gelatine in cold water for about 10 minutes and squeeze the
water out. Add the gelatine to the boiling water, remove from the fire and
stir until dissolved. Add lemon juice, vinegar, salt and sugar. Chill. When
it has begun to set add pineapple, cucumber and pimiento. Pour into six
wet individual molds. and chill. Serve with following salad dressing

No. 137　　　苺　サ　ラ　ダ

作り方——苺は大きいのを選び、へたを取つて半分に切り、粉砂糖を振掛け、充
　　分冷してレタスの葉の上に盛り、上に次のフルーツ・ドレツシングを掛けま
す。

No. 138　　　フルーツ・ドレツシング

作り方——黄味二個をよく泡立てカツプ三分ノ一のパイナツプル汁と大匙一杯半
　　のレモン汁を加へ、二重鍋の湯の上で混ぜながらカツプ半杯の砂糖を加へ、
　　どろどろになる迄煮て火より下し、冷してからカツプ一杯のクリームを泡立
　　てて折込みます。これは果物のサラダ類によいドレツシングです。

No. 139　　　胡瓜のジエリー・サラダ

材料			
胡瓜の賽ノ目切り	カツプ四杯	微塵切り玉葱	大匙半杯
熱湯	カツプ三杯半	鹽	小匙一杯
胡椒	小匙八分ノ一	酢	大匙二杯
ゼラチン紙	四枚		

作り方——玉葱と胡瓜を熱湯の中で軟くなる迄茹でゝ（約二十分間）鹽、胡椒、
　　酢を加へ、水に漬けて後、しぼつたゼラチン紙を加へ、火より下して溶しま
　　す。之を裏漉にして水でぬらしたジエリー型に流して冷し、マヨネーズを添
　　へます。冷肉の附合せによいサラダです。

No. 14o　　　パイナツプルと胡瓜のジエリー・サラダ

材料			
ゼラチン紙	五枚	熱湯	カツプ一杯
レモン汁	一個分	西洋酢	カツプ三分ノ一
鹽	小匙一杯	砂糖	カツプ半杯
微塵切りパイナツプル	カツプ三杯	細い賽ノ目切り胡瓜	カツプ半杯
		ピミエント微塵切り	一個

作り方——ゼラチン紙は水に漬けて軟にして後、よく水をしぼり熱湯に加へてよ
　　く溶します。これにレモン汁、砂糖、鹽及び酢を加へ、冷して少し固まり初
　　めたならばパイナツプル、胡瓜、ピミエントを混込み、水にぬらした小型の
　　ジエリー型に流して冷します。レタスの葉を敷いた皿に取出し、上にマヨネ
　　ーズ又は次のドレツシングを掛けます。

No. 141   WHITE DRESSING

1 Teaspoon mustard	1 Teaspoon sugar
1 Teaspoon salt	2 Eggs
Few grains cayenne pepper	½ Cup hot vinegar
2 Tablespoons salad oil	1 Cup cream

Beat the eggs well, add salt, pepper, sugar and cream, then pour in the hot vinegar and cook over boiling water in the double boiler stirring constantly. When thick remove from the fire and add the salad oil and beat thoroughly. Chill and use on salad.

No. 142   SHRIMP AND VEGETABLE SALAD TOMATO ASPIC

1½ Cups cooked diced potatoes	Few grains cayenne pepper
½ Cup celery	1 Teaspoon salt
¼ Cup mayonnaise	1 Cup diced celery
1 Tablespoon minced green pepper	1 Teaspoon minced onion
1 Teaspoon salt	3 Cloves
2 Tablespoon vinegar	1 Small leaf mace
1 Tablespoon chopped onion	1 Finely chopped seeded green pepper
4 Cups canned tomatoes	4 Sheets gelatine
½ Cup diced raw carrots	1 Tin canned shrimp
1 Sprig parsley	

Combine the first seven ingredients. Prepare a tomato aspic by cooking for 30 minutes the tomatoes, raw carrots, parsley, peppercorns, salt, diced celery, onion, cloves, mace and green pepper. Strain this mixture and add the gelatine which has been soaked in cold water for 10 minutes and thoroughly drained. Stir until the gelatine dissolves. Cover the bottom of a wet individual mold with a layer of tomato aspic. Next arrange a layer canned or fresh cooked shrimp and then place a tablespoon of the potato salad mixture on top. Pour tomato aspic over all to fill the molds completely. Chill until set, then unmold on individual plates. Garnish with whole shrimp and parsley and serve with mayonnaise dressing.

No. 141　　白 ド レ ッ シ ン グ

材料　西洋芥子粉	小匙一杯	鹽	小匙一杯
ケアネ・ペバー（赤胡		サラダ油	大匙二杯
椒）	少量	砂糖	小匙一杯
玉子	二個	熱した西洋酢	カツプ半杯
クリーム	カツプ一杯		

作り方——玉子をよく泡立て鹽、胡椒、砂糖を加へて混ぜ、クリームを入れ、熱
　　した酢を混ぜながら入れ、二重鍋の湯の上で混ぜながら濃くなる迄煮て火よ
　　り下し、油を加へて全部が混ざる迄攪拌します。これは冷して使ふのです。

No. 142　　芝鰕と野菜のトマト・ジエリー

材料（十人前）　茹でた賽ノ		賽ノ目切りセロリ	カツプ半杯
目切り馬鈴薯	カツプ一杯半	マヨネーズ	カツプ四分ノ一
微塵切りグリン・ペ		鹽	小匙一杯
パー	大匙一杯	西洋酢	大匙二杯
玉葱微塵切り	大匙一杯	トマト罐詰カツプ四杯（又は生ト	
賽ノ目切り人参	カツプ半杯	マト軟く煮たも	
パセリ微塵切り	一枝	の	カツプ四杯
鹽	小匙一杯	ケアネ・ペバー（赤胡	
セロリ賽ノ目切り	カツプ一杯	椒）	少量
玉葱微塵切り	小匙一杯	クローブ（香料）	三個
メース（香料）	一枚	グリン・ペバー微塵	
ゼラチン紙	四枚	切り	小一個
芝鰕	カツプ一杯位		

作り方——初めのし種の材料を混合せて、薯のサラダを作り冷して置きます。別
　　にトマト以下ケアネ・ペバー迄の材料を一緒にして、三十分間弱火で煮て裏
　　漉にします。再びトマトの汁等を火に掛けて沸騰させ、冷水に十分程漬けて
　　軟くしたゼラチン紙を充分しぼり、トマト等の中に入れて火より下し、全部
　　溶ける迄混ぜて冷します。トマト等がどろどろに固まり初めたらば水で濡ら
　　した小型のジエリー型の底に三分ノ一の所迄入れ、その上に芝鰕を少し入れ
　　薯のサラダを加へ、上に再びトマトのジエリーを入れて固めます。これは御
　　客様向きの料理でマヨネーズを掛けて召し上るのです。トマト・ジエリーの
　　中に薯のサラダと芝鰕が入つた美しいジエリーです。（材料は左より右へ讀
　　む事）

No. 143   GINGERALE SALAD

¾ Cup diced pineapple
¾ Cup natsumikan or grape-
    fruit
1/3 Cup shredded almonds

1 Cup gingerale
2 Tablespoons gelatine
½ Cup lukewarm water
Salt and paprika

Allow the gelatine to stand in the warm water for five minutes, then place over hot water and dissolve. Add one fourth cup of gingerale and the fruit and mix, then add the remaining gingerale and the dissolved gelatin and pour into jelly molds. Chill and harden then unmold, and serve on lettuce leaves with mayonnaise.

No. 144   VEGETABLE SALAD DRESSING

1 Teaspoon salt
1 Teaspoon mustard
1 Teaspoon celery seed
1 Teaspoon chopped onion
4 Tablespoons chopped pickles

2 Tablespoons horseradish
½ Teaspoon paprika
4 Tablespoons sugar
2 Tablespoons vinegar
2/3 Cup salad oil

Mix dry ingredients and add rest of ingredients. With rotary beater, beat two minutes. Chill. Beat well and serve. This dressing will keep for a long time if stored in a cold place.

No. 145   COMBINATION DRESSING

1 Cup mayonnaise
½ Cup French dressing

Juice of 1 lemon
1 Tablespoon finely minced onion

Stir the ingredients together in a bowl. Serve with salad greens. This dressing is perfect for lettuce salad; it is also delicious with pears.

No. 143　　　　ジンヂヤエールのサラダ

材料　パイナツプルの賽
　　　の目　　　　　カツプ四分ノ三　　夏蜜柑又はグレー
　　アーモンド纖切り　　　　　　　　プ・フルーツ　カツプ四分ノ三
　　（なくてもよい）　カツプ三分ノ一　ジンヂヤーエール　カツプ一杯
　　微溫湯　　　　　カツプ半杯　　　ゼラチン粉　　　大匙二杯
　　　　　　　　　　　　　　　　　鹽、パプリカ　　少量宛

作り方――ゼラチン粉を湯に五分間位漬けて置いて後熱湯の上にのせてゼラチン
　を溶します。これにカツプ四分ノ一のジンヂヤーエールを加へ、パイナツプ
　ル、グレープ・フルーツ、アーモンド及び殘りのジンヂヤーエールを入れゼ
　ラチン粉の溶したものを合せジエリー型に流し込みます。冷して固め、型よ
　り取り出しレタスの葉の上にのせ、マヨネーズを掛けて召上るのです。

No. 144　　　　野菜サラダ用ドレツシング

材料　鹽　　　　　　　小匙一杯　　　西洋芥子　　　　小匙一杯
　　セロリ・シード　　小匙一杯　　　微塵切り玉葱　　小匙一杯
　　ピツクルス（西洋漬　　　　　　　卸したわさび　　大匙二杯
　　　物）微塵切り　　大匙四杯　　　パプリカ　　　　小匙半杯
　　砂糖　　　　　　　大匙四杯　　　西洋酢　　　　　大匙二杯
　　サラダ油　　　　　カツプ三分ノ二

作り方――初めに鹽と芥子とセロリ・シードを混ぜ、之に他の材料を加へ、玉子
　攪拌器で二分間攪混ぜて用ひます。蓋の出來る瓶に入れ冷藏庫の中に貯藏し
　て置けば二週間位保ちます。キヤベツ、レタス又は他の野菜サラダによいド
　レツシングです。

No. 145　　　　コンビネーシヨン・ドレツシング

材料　マヨネーズ・ドレツ　　　　　　フレンチ・ドレツシ
　　　シング　　　　カツプ一杯　　　ング　　　　　　カツプ半杯
　　レモン汁　　　　一個分　　　　　玉葱微塵切り　　大匙一杯

作り方――材料を全部混合せて、レタスの葉のドレツシング又は果物のドレツシ
　ングに用ひます。

No. 146   **FOUNDATION OMELET**

    1 Tablespoon hot water   Salt and Pepper
    1 Egg

Use one egg for each person served. Separate yolks and whites. Season the yolks with salt and with either pepper or nutmeg, according to taste, add water and beat well. Beat the whites until stiff and fold in the yolks. Pour gently into a well greased pan and cook slowly until the underside is a delicate brown, then place the pan in the oven, keeping the temperature between 325 and 350 degrees F. When the omelet responds to the touch it is done Make two cuts part of the way down into the omelet at right angles to the handle of the pan, dividing it about in thirds. Then tip the pan, slide a patula under the omelet and fold it over as you slip it out of the pan onto a warmed plate.

No. 147   **FRUIT OMELET**

Before folding the cooked omelet made according to the foundation recipe spread its surface with either jam, preserves, cooked figs, or peach, pear or plum jelly; or fresh fruits, well sugared, may be used. Also reserve sufficient fruit for garnishing the top. A plain omelet surrounded with fruit or preserves also makes an attractive serving.

No. 148   **CHOPPED-HAM OMELET**

Before folding the omelet made following the foundation omelet recipe, spread with a generous quantity of butter, add chopped cooked ham, and sprinkle lightly with chopped parsley.

No. 149   **CREAMED-CHICKEN OMELET**

Make a white sauce as follows: Melt one and a half tablespoonfuls of butter in a saucepan, add two tablespoonfuls of flour and salt and pepper seasonings, and blend well. Add a cupful of liquid—half evaporated milk and half water—and stir constantly until thickened to sauce consistency. To the sauce add one cupful of diced, cooked chicken and cook two or three minutes, until meat is well heated. Serve between folded omelet.

No. 146　　　標　準　オ　ム　レ　ツ

材料　湯　　　　　　　　　大匙四杯　　　玉子　　　　　　　　四個
　　　鹽、胡椒　　　　　　適宜

作り方——玉子は一人前に附き二個づつの割合で用ひ、黄味と白味を別々にして
　黄味に鹽、胡椒其の他好みによりナツメグ等で味を附け、湯を加へてよく泡
　立てます。白味は輕く泡立て此の中に黄味等を折込み、油を熱したフライパ
　ンの中に入れ、下が狐色になる迄燒き、これをフライパンに入れた儘中火の
　天火の中に入れ、上に指でふれてみてオムレツの表面が一寸かたまる樣にな
　る迄燒いて取出し、中央に切目を横に入れて半分に折り、温めた皿に取出し
　ます。

No. 147　　　　フ　ル　ー　ツ・オ　ム　レ　ツ

作り方——オムレツが燒けたらば、半分に折る前に上にジヤム、甘く軟く煮た果
　物或は罐詰の果實等を少し盛り、半分に折り皿に附けて周圍に果物を少し添
　へて飾るのです。

No. 148　　　　ハ　ム・オ　ム　レ　ツ

作り方——標準オムレツを作り、半分に折疊む前に表面にバターを塗り、細く切
　つたハムを振掛け、パセリを微塵切りにして掛けます。之を等分に折り皿に
　盛るのです。

No. 149　　　　鶏ホワイト・ソース・オムレツ

作り方——バター大匙一杯半を溶し、メリケン粉大匙二杯を加へて混ぜ、鹽、胡
　椒でよく味を附け、カツプ一杯のミルクで延してホワイト・ソースを作り、
　これにカツプ一杯の鶏肉の燒いたものの残りを賽の目に切つて加へ、二三分
　間煮て火を通し、標準オムレツの折目の間に流します。

No. 150   NUT OMELET

Any chopped nuts may be used, preferably black-walnut meats. Stir nuts into egg mixture (See foundation omelet for ingredients). Before serving, garnish omelet top with a light sprinkling of nuts and powdered sugar.

No. 151   CHIPPED-BACON OMELET

Fry bacon strips and break into small pieces. Either stir the pieces into the egg mixture or sprinkle over the surface of the cooked omelet before folding. See foundation omelet recipe for ingredients for omelet.

No. 152   CHEESE OMELET

Sprinkle grated cheese over the surface of the foundation omelet before folding, or the cheese may be stirred into the egg mixture before cooking.

No. 153   ASPARAGUS OMELET

Drain canned asparagus tips—reserve the liquid for creamed asparagus soup—and heat thoroughly in either a steamer, a covered colander placed over hot water, or a double boiler. Place asparagus between foundation omelet folds and add a generous quantity of melted butter and a light sprinkling of nutmeg.

No. 154   COD FISH OMELET

2 Cups hot mashed potatoes	2 Tablespoons butter
1 Cup softened salted codfish	⅛ Teaspoon pepper
2 Eggs	

Take salted codfish and pick into small pieces, pour boiling water over the fish and allow to stand for a few minutes and drain well. Combine the fish with the hot mashed potatoes, beaten egg yolk and pepper and fold in well beaten white of eggs. Heat butter in a frying pan and pour the potato mixture in when hot. Cook until the under side is well brown, and fold in two and serve, garnished with a little parsley.

No. 15o　　　胡 桃 の オ ム レ ツ

作り方——胡桃の細く切つたものを標準オムレツの材料に靜に加へ、普通に燒い
　　て皿に盛り、上に胡桃の微塵切りと粉砂糖を振掛けます。

No. 151　　　ベ ー コ ン ・ オ ム レ ツ

作り方——ベーコンの薄切りをよくからからにフライして細くくづします。これ
　　を標準オムレツの材料の中に靜に加へるか出來上つたオムレツの上に振掛け
　　るのです。

No. 152　　　チ ー ズ ・ オ ム レ ツ

作り方——標準オムレツの材料の中に好みの分量の卸したチーズを混込んで燒き
　　上げます。他の方法はオムレツを折疊む前に表面に卸したチーズを振掛ける
　　のです。

No. 153　　　ア ス パ ラ ガ ス ・ オ ム レ ツ

作り方——アスパラガスを罐より取出し、汁をきつて蒸してよく溫め、標準オム
　　レツを折疊む時、間にアスパラガスを入れ、溶したバターを掛け、ナツメグ
　　を少し振ります。

No. 154　　　鹽 鱈 オ ム レ ツ

材料	溫いつぶした薯	カツプ二杯	鹽鱈を水に漬けほぐ	
	玉子	二個	した物	カツプ一杯
	溶したバター	大匙二杯	胡椒	小匙八分ノ一

作り方——ほぐした鹽鱈に一度手早く熱湯を掛けて水をきり、馬鈴薯と泡立てた
　　玉子の黃味と胡椒に混合せ、よく泡立てた白味を折込み、バターを溶して熱し
　　たフライパンに入れ、よく色が附く迄燒き二ツ折にして皿に取りパセリ等で
　　飾るのです。

No. 155   POTATO OMELET

2 Cups mashed potatoes	Salt and pepper
¼ Cup hot milk	2 Eggs well beaten
2 Tablespoons melted butter	1 Tablespoons chopped parsley

Mix the potatoes, milk, butter, salt and pepper and add the well beaten eggs. Heat shortening in frying pan and add the mixture and cook until the under side is brown. Then springle the surface with chopped parsley and fold in two and serve on a hot plate.

No. 156   CORN AND BACON SCRAMBLED EGGS

8 slices bacon	1½ Cups canned corn
½ Seeded green pepper or pimento chooped fine	2 Eggs
	½ Teaspoon salt
1 Small onion chopped fine	⅛ Teaspoon paprika

Crisp bacon. When light golden brown remove to hot platter. In four tablespoons bacon fat cook the pepper and onion until tender but not brown. Stir in corn. Beat two eggs lightly, season with salt, paprika. Add to corn mixture and cook gently until scrambled. Mold on hot platter and garnish with bacon.

No. 157   EGGS MOLLETT IN TOMATO SAUCE

Prepare as many hardcooked eggs as there are persons to be served. For the sauce heat one can of tomato soup without water and add teaspoonful of chopped parsley, also a teaspoonful of tarragon vinegar. Arrange the eggs on squares of toast and pour the hot sauce over them.

No. 158   BAKED EGGS WITH BACON RING

6 Eggs	¼ Teaspoon salt
6 Slices bacon	½ Teaspoon pepper
1 Teaspoon butter	

Put the bacon in a frying pan and cook until almost done. Wrap the bacon slices around the sides of a muffin tin and drop an egg in the center of each bacon ring. Sprinkle the egg with salt and pepper and dot with little pieces of butter. Bake in a medium oven until the egg is set and serve on a hot plate, taking the bacon ring and egg out of the muffin tin on to the plate.

No. 155　　　ポテト・オムレツ

材料	つぶした薯	カツプ二杯	熱したミルク	カツプ四分ノ一
	溶したバター	大匙二杯	鹽、胡椒	少量
	玉子泡立てたもの	二個	パセリ微塵切り	大匙一杯

作り方――薯、ミルク、バター、鹽、胡椒を混ぜ合せ、泡立てた玉子を加へます
　　別にフライパンを熱し、前の薯等を入れ、下が狐色になる迄燒き、上にパセ
　　リを振掛け、半分に折疊んで、溫めた皿に取出して召上るのです。

No. 156　　玉蜀黍・ベーコン・スクランブル

材料	ベーコン	八切れ	グリン・ペパー又はピミエント微	
	玉葱微塵切り	小一個	塵切り	半個
	玉蜀黍の罐詰	カツプ一杯半	玉子	二個
	鹽	小匙半杯	パプリカ	小匙八分ノ一

作り方――ベーコンをフライパンでよく燒き、溫めた皿に取つて置きます。ベー
　　コンの油大匙四杯の中で玉葱とグリン・ペパーを軟くいため、玉蜀黍を入れ
　　玉子を輕く泡立て丶之に鹽とパプリカを加へたものを加へ、混ぜながら玉子
　　が軟く燒ける迄煮てベーコンに添へて皿に盛ります。

No. 157　　　玉子・トマト・ソース

作り方――人數だけ茹玉子を用意して縱六つ位に切ります。トマト・スープの罐
　　詰をその儘熱して微塵切りのパセリをスープ一罐に附小匙一杯加へ、酢小匙
　　一杯を入れ、充分熱してトーストの上にのせた玉子に掛けます。

No. 158　　　ベーコン・リング

材料	玉子	六個	ベーコン薄切り	六切れ
	バター	小匙一杯	鹽	小匙四分ノ一
	胡椒	小匙八分ノ一		

作り方――ベーコンを熱したフライパンで半燒き位にいため、マフエンの天パン
　　（小さい丸形）の周圍に卷く樣にして入れ、其の中に玉子を一個づ丶落しま
　　す。一個づつ上にバター、鹽及び胡椒を掛けて、中火の天火で玉子が軟く燒
　　ける迄七、八分間燒くのです。天パンより皿の上に取り出します。

No. 159   **BAKED ASPARAGUS WITH EGGS**

25 stalks of asparagus, canned or cooked
6 Eggs
½ Cup grated cheese
¼ Teaspoon paprika

Grease a casserole and arrange the asparagus stalks on the bottom. Drop eggs on top and sprinkle with cheese and paprika. Bake in a medium oven for about 15 minutes. Cooked mashed spinach may be substituted for the asparagus in this recipe.

No. 160   **WOODSTOCK**

1½ Cups medium thick cream sauce
½ Pound fresh mushrooms
1 Green pepper
5 Hard-cooked eggs, diced
2 Pimentoes, diced
½ Pound cheese
Salt and pepper

To make the medium thick cream sauce use a proportion of one cupful of milk, two tablespoonfuls of flour, and one tablespoonful of fat.

Wash and slice the mushrooms. Dice the green pepper. Add these to the cream sauce, and set over boiling water for 20 minutes. Add the cheese, cut in pieces, and the diced pimentoes and eggs. Blend carefully, adding the salt and pepper to taste, and heat until the cheese is melted. Serve very hot in patty shells or on mounds of hot, boiled rice. Eight servings.

No. 161   **CREAMED EGGS AND ASPARAGUS**

Croustades
12 Stalks asparagus
3 Tablespoons butter
3 Tablespoons flour
½ Teaspoon salt
1½ Cups milk
4 Sliced hard boiled eggs

Make a white sauce by melting the butter and stirring in the flour, then gradually add the milk and cook while stirring until thick, season with salt and pepper. Mix the white sauce and the quartered eggs and put in croustades. Top with three stalks of asparagus which have been cut in the same lengths as the croustades and sprinkle with grated cheese if desired, and bake in a hot oven until the cheese is browned.

No. 159　　アスパラガスと玉子のチーズ燒

材料　アスパラガス　　　二十五本位　　　玉子　　　　　　　六個
　　　卸したチーズ　　　カツプ半杯　　　パプリカ　　　　小匙四分ノ一

作り方——油を塗つた瀬戸引天パンにアスパラガスを並べ、その上に玉子を落し
　　上にチーズとパプリカを振掛け、中火の天火で十五分間燒きます。アスパラ
　　ガス　　りに裏漉にして味を附けた菠薐草を用ひても結構です。

No. 16o　　　ウッド・ストツク

材料　中位の濃さのホワ　　　　　　　松茸　　　　　　カツプ半杯
　　　　イト・ソース　　カツプ一杯半　グリン・ペパー微塵
　　　茹玉子細く切つたも　　　　　　　切り　　　　　　一個
　　　　　の　　　　　　五個　　　　ピミエント微塵切り　二個
　　　チーズ卸したもの　半封度　　　　鹽、胡椒

作り方——中位の濃さのホワイト・ソースはメリケン粉二杯バター大匙一杯ミル
　　クカツプ一杯と鹽、胡椒で作ります。松茸を薄く切つて量り、グリン・ペパ
　　ーを輪切りにしてホワイト・ソースに加へ、二重鍋の湯の上で二十分間煮て
　　チーズ、ピミエントと玉子を切つたものを加へ、鹽、胡椒で味を附けてよく
　　混ぜ、チーズが溶ける迄溫めてパテ・シエル（パイ皮で作つた小さい丸形の
　　もの、一流の洋菓子店にあり）　　るか、又は溫い御飯を添えます。

No. 161　　クリームド・エツグスとアスパラガス

材料　クラステード　　　四個　　　　アスパラガス　　　十二本
　　　バター　　　　　　大匙三杯　　　メリケン粉　　　大匙三杯
　　　鹽　　　　　　　　小匙半杯　　　ミルク　　　　カツプ一杯半
　　　茹玉子の輪切り　　四個

作り方——バターを熱して溶し、メリケンを加へ、ミルクで混ぜながら延して、
　　ホワイト・ソースを作り、鹽、胡椒で味を附けます。クラステードの中に此
　　のホワイト・ソースで和へた玉子を入れ、上にアスパラガスを三本並べての
　　せ、好みにより卸したチーズを少量掛け、天火の中で數分間燒いてチーズに
　　色を附けます。

No. 162   CREAMED EGGS AND MUSHROOMS

⅛ Pound mushrooms
2 Tablespoons fat
2 Tablespoons flour
½ Teaspoons salt
Few grains

⅛ Teaspoon onion juice
11Cup milk
3 Hard-cooked eggs sliced
1 Tablespoon chopped parsley
1 Tablespoon chopped pimiento

Wash and scrape mushrooms and split into small pieces. Saute in fat until tender. In a separate pan heat the butter, add flour and then milk and make a white sauce, seasoning with salt and paprika. Add the sauted mushrooms, eggs, onion juice, parsley and pimento and serve hot on slices of toast or rice.

No. 162　　玉子こ松茸クリーム

材料	松茸	二十五匁	バター	大匙二杯
	メリケン粉	大匙二杯	鹽	小匙半杯
	パプリカ	少量	玉葱汁	小匙八分ノ一
	ミルク	カツプ一杯	茹で玉子の輪切り	三個
	パセリ微塵切り	大匙一杯	ビミェント微塵切り	大匙一杯

作り方――松茸の皮を取り細くさいて少量のバターで軟くいためます。別にバターを熱して溶し、メリケン粉を加へ、混ぜながらミルクを加へて延し、鹽とパプリカを加へてホワイト・ソースを作り、これに松茸、玉子、玉葱汁、パセリ及びビミェント等を加へます。これはトースト又は溫い御飯の上に掛けて皿に盛るのです。

No. 163   **CREAM OF WHEAT**

After cooking cream of wheat as directed on the box, it may be served hot or cold with cream and sugar, or with addition of seasonable fruit sliced and place over the top of the dish containing cream of wheat. For children serve cream of wheat decorated with raisins arranged to represent different forms, or add the raisins just before removing cereal from the fire. Also grated apple or fruit juice may be added to give flavor.

No. 164   **OATMEAL GRUEL**

¼ Cup oats   1½ Cups water
½ Teaspoon salt

Add the oats and salt to the boiling water and cook 4 to 5 hours in a double boiler. Strain and dilute with hot milk to the desired consistency of thin paste or jelly.

No. 165   **QUICK COOKING OATS**

¼ Cup quick cooking oats   ¼ Teaspoon salt
1 Cup boiling water

Add salt to the boiling water and add the oat flakes stirring continuously and cook over direct heat for about three minutes. Serve hot with cream and sugar. Raisins may be added while cooking if desired.

No. 166   **BREAKFAST FASTMEAL**

¼ Cup Fastmeal   ¼ Teaspoon salt
1 Cup boiling water

Add salt to boiling water and add the Fastmeal gradually while stirring. Cook over slow fire until it is the consistency desired. Remove from fire and serve with sugar and cream, or with fruit in season.

No. 163　　クリーム・オブ・ホキート

作り方――クリーム・オブ・ホキートの普通朝食用調理法はクリーム・オブ・ホキートの箱にくわしく書いて有りますからその通りに調理して、クリームと砂糖を添へます。クリーム・オブ・ホキートを皿に盛り、上に季節の果實の薄切りをのせても美味しく、又子供に與へる場合に上に乾葡萄で顔の型を作る様に並べるのも面白いものです。又火よりクリーム・オブ・ホキートを下す前に乾葡萄を加へて煮てもよく、火より下して林檎の卸したものを加へてもよいものです。

No. 164　　オートミールの重湯

材料　オート・ミール　　　カツプ四分ノ一　　鹽　　　　　　　　小匙半杯
　　　水　　　　　　　　　カツプ一杯半

作り方――水を沸騰させて、鹽とオートミールを加へ、二重鍋で湯煎にして四五時間煮て裏漉にし熱したミルクを適當に加へて好みの濃さにします。夏季ならば冷して果實シロツプ、炭酸等を加へて冷飲料としても滋養のあるものです。

No. 165　　朝食用オート・ミール

材料　オート・ミール（即席）カツプ四分ノ一　　熱湯　　　　　カツプ一杯
　　　鹽　　　　　　　　　小匙一杯

作り方――熱湯に鹽を加へて強火で沸騰させながらオート・ミールを徐々に加へ三分間以上煮て好みの固さにして火より下し、溫い內に砂糖とミルクを掛けて召し上るのです。煮て居る時に乾葡萄を加へると更に美味しくなります。

No. 166　　朝食用フアストミール

材料　フアストミール　　　カツプ四分ノ一　　熱湯　　　　　カツプ一杯
　　　鹽　　　　　　　　　小匙四分ノ一

作り方――熱湯に鹽を加へ、フアストミールを混ぜながら靜かに加へ、混ぜ續けながら火の上で望みの濃さになる迄煮て火より下し、砂糖とミルクを添へます。季節の果實の薄切りを上に盛る事、又は煮る時に中に乾葡萄を加へる事も結構です。

No. 167   RICE MUFFINS

1½ Cup cold boiled rice	1 Cup milk
2 Cups flour	3 Tablespoons melted shortening
6 Teaspoons baking powder	2 Tablespoons sugar
1 Teaspoon salt	1 Egg

Sift flour with baking powder and salt. Add sugar. Add rice to milk with beaten egg. Combine the mixtures, add melted shortening and stir slightly. Bake in greased muffin tins in oven at 370 degrees F. for about 15 to 20 minutes. Dates and raisins and nice fat prunes add much to cereal breads and muffins.

No. 168   POPOVERS

1½ Sups flour	1 Teaspoon sugar
¼ Teaspoon salt	1 Cup milk
2 Eggs	

Mix the flour, salt and sugar. Gradually add the milk and the well beaten eggs. Beat thoroughly. Have ready some small ramekins or iron muffin pans, well greased and piping hot. Fill them about half full of the batter and bake in a hot oven for 30 to 40 minutes. The heat should be reduced toward the end to prevent the popovers from becoming too brown.

No. 169   SWEDISH COFFEE CAKE

1 Cup milk	1 Compressed yeast cake
1/3 Cup shortening	2 Eggs
1/3 Cup sugar	4 Cups flour
1 Teaspoon salt	

Scald the milk and add the shortening, sugar, and salt. Allow the mixture to cool until lukewarm and add the yeast cake, broken in pieces. Stir until the yeast cake dissolves. Add one cupful of the flour and beat thoroughly. Cover with a towel and set in a warm place to rise. When light add the beaten eggs and the remaining flour.

The amount of flour used will vary slightly, but enough should be added to keep the dough from being sticky. Knead the dough on a floured board until smooth and elastic and allow to rise again. Shape into braids or buns, place in a well-greased pan and brush over the top with melted shortening. Allow to rise again until light, top each bun with a half cherry cr a whole nut, and bake in a hot oven of 400 degrees F., for 15 or 20 minutes.

No. 167　　ラ　イ　ス・マ　フ　エ　ン

材料　御飯　　　　　　　カツプ半杯　　メリケン粉　　　カツプ二杯
　　　ベーキング・パウ　　　　　　　　　鹽　　　　　　小匙一杯
　　　　ダー　　　　　小匙六杯　　　ミルク　　　　カツプ一杯
　　　溶したバター又は　　　　　　　　砂糖　　　　　大匙二杯
　　　　代用品　　　　大匙三杯　　　玉子　　　　　一個

作り方――メリケン粉、鹽、ベーキング・パウダーを篩ひ、砂糖を加へ、別に混
　　ぜた玉子にミルクと御飯を加へ、メリケン粉等に混ぜて加へ、最後に溶した
　　バターを入れ、油を塗つたマフエン用（小形）天パンに流し、中火の天火で
　　十五分乃至二十分燒きます。乾葡萄、デート、プルンズ等を入れてもよい。

No. 168　　　ポツプ・オーバー（パン代用）

材料　メリケン粉　　　カツプ一杯半　鹽　　　　　　　小匙四分ノ一
　　　玉子　　　　　　二個　　　　　砂糖　　　　　　小匙一杯
　　　ミルク　　　　　カツプ一杯

作り方――メリケン粉、鹽、砂糖を篩ひ、絶えず混ぜながら、ミルクと泡立てた
　　玉子を加へ、手早く混續けます。これより前に鐵のマフエン用天パン又は瀬
　　戸の小型のラミキン型に充分油を塗つて天火に入れてよく熱して置き、前の
　　材料がよく混ざつたらば、之に半分の所迄流し込み直に強火の天火に入れ、
　　十五分程たつたらば火力を少し弱めて、全部で四十分間燒きます。これは四
　　倍位にふくらむものです。燒けたらばすぐにバターを附けて召し上るので
　　す。

No. 169　　　スヱーデン式コーヒー・ケーク（標準）

材料　ミルク　　　　　カツプ一杯　　バター　　　　カツプ三分ノ一
　　　砂糖　　　　　　カツプ三分ノ一　鹽　　　　　小匙一杯
　　　乾燥イースト　　一個　　　　　玉子　　　　　二個
　　　メリケン粉　　　カツプ四杯

作り方――ミルクを熱し、砂糖、バター及び鹽を加へ、微温になる迄冷して、細
　　く割つたイーストを加へ、溶ける迄混ぜ、メリケン粉の篩つたものをカツプ
　　一杯加へて更によく混ぜ、タオルを器の上にかけて、室の温い所に置いて輕
　　くふくらませ、泡立てた玉子とメリケン粉の殘りを加へます。メリケン粉の
　　分量は多少違つても手に材料を取つてべとつかぬ程度に入れます。メリケン
　　粉を振掛けた板の上で手で充分こねて後、再び輕くふくらむ迄置きます。少
　　しづつちぎつて丸めてバンズ（小形のパン）にし、油を塗つた天パンに並べ
　　溶したバターを上に塗り、また暫らく置いてふくらませ、強火の天火で十五
　　分乃至二十分間燒きます。

No. 170   **MARMALADE BUNS**

Use the Swedish Coffee Cake recipe. Shape the dough into round buns about the size of an English walnut, place in a greased pan, and brush with melted shortening. Set aside to rise, and when light place a teaspoonful of marmalade on each bun. Bake as above.

No. 171   **COCOANUT BUNS**

Make the small buns as for marmalade buns and bake. When done cover with confectioners' sugar moistened with milk, and sprinkle with shredded cocoanut.

No. 172   **PRUNE FOLDS**

Follow the recipe for Swedish coffee cake. After kneading, roll the dough about one fourth inch thick and cut into four inch squares. Spread with cooked sweetened prunes, fold over diagonally, brush with shortening and allow to rise. Bake as Swedish coffee cake. The filling should be within half an inch of the edge, and the edges pinched together.

No. 173   **JAM ROULETTES**

Roll baking powder biscuit dough one-fourth inch thick and brush with melted butter. Spread with jam; roll up like a jelly roll. With a sharp knife cut into slices one-half inch thick. Place on a greased baking sheet, about two inches apart. Bake at 450 degrees F. for 10-12 minutes. To glaze, brush with a mixture of equal parts of sugar and milk just before removing from oven. These can be varied by substituting for the jam, grated cheese, deviled ham or any of the following mixtures: dates, figs, raisins, cherries, and nuts.

No. 17o　　　マーマレード・バンズ

作り方――スエーデン式コーヒー・ケークを作り、丸めて天パンに並べ、バターを溶して塗り、しばらく置いてふくらましたらば上にマーマレード（蜜柑のジヤム）を少しのせて焼くのです。

No. 171　　　ココナッツ・バンズ

作り方――スエーデン式コーヒー・ケークを焼き、上に粉砂糖を少量のミルクで混ぜた砂糖飾りを掛け、ココナッツを振掛けます。

No. 172　　　プルンズ・バンズ

作り方――スエーデン式コーヒー・ケークの材料を混ぜ合せ、最後に丸める代りに二分位の厚さに板の上で延し、直徑三寸位の丸形に切抜き、甘く軟く煮たプルンズ（西洋梅）を中に塗つて三日月形に半分に折り、合せ目を指でつまんで溶したバターで表面を塗り、しばらく置いてふくらませ、強火の天火で十五分間乃至二十分間燒きます。

No. 173　　　ジヤム・ビスケット（パン代用）

作り方――普通のベーキング・パウダーの材料を混合せ、メリケン粉を振つた板の上で二分位の厚さに延し、表面に少量の溶したバターを塗り、その上にジヤムを一面に敷き、海苔卷の様に卷き、三分の厚さの輪切りにします。次に之を油を少し塗つた天パンに間を離して並べ、強火の天火で十二分程燒きます。取り出して直に上にミルクに砂糖を少し加へたものを塗るとつやのあるビスケットが出來ます。

ジヤムの代りにくだいたチーズ、挽肉、果物を甘く煮たもの等を用ひてもよろしいのです。

No. 174   **GINGERBREAD**

½ Cup butter	1 Teaspoon cinnamon
½ Cup sugar	¼ Teaspoon salt
2 Eggs	1½ Cups flour
1 Teaspoon soda	½ Cup cold water
½ Cup molasses	1 Cup grated cocoanut
1 Teaspoon ginger	

Cream well butter and sugar, add eggs, beat all together. Dissolve soda in molasses and add to first mixture. Mix and sift remaining dry ingredients and add to first mixture alternately with the cold water. Stir in cocoanut. Pour into well greased pan and bake in moderate oven, of 325 degrees F. for 35 minutes.

No. 175   **BANANA NUT BREAD**

2/3 Cup sugar	1 Teaspoon soda
1 Cup evaporated milk	2 Cups cake flour
2/3 Teaspoon salt	½ Cup walnuts, finely broken
3 Large ripe bananas	2 Eggs

Force bananas through potato ricer, into a bowl with the sugar in it. Mix together and add milk, beaten eggs and salt. Beat all together. Sift flour and soda together two or three times. Then add to the mixture in bowl and put nuts on top of flour so they will become coated with flour as you stir all together thoroughly. Bake in buttered and floured bread tin at 350 degrees F., until a toothpick inserted in center comes out clean.

No. 176   **TUTTI FRUTTI ROLLS**

1½ Cups flour	2 Tablespoons nut meats, cut fine
3 Teaspoons baking powder	2 Tablespoons sugar
2 Tablespoons shortening	2 Tablespoons dates or figs, chopped fine
½ Cup milk	
1 Tablespoon melted butter	½ Teaspoon cinnamon

Sift the flour and baking powder and cut in the shortening as you would for biscuits. Then add the milk and pat out on floured board to one half inch thickness. Spread the surface with the melted butter and sprinkle over the dough the nuts, dates, cinnamon and sugar which have been first mixed. Roll up as you would a jelly roll and cut in one inch thicknesses. Put on a greased baking sheet and bake for 15 minutes in a hot oven.

No. 174　　　　ジンジヤー・ブレツド

材料	バター	カツプ半杯	砂糖	カツプ半杯
	玉子	二個	ソーダ	小匙一杯
	モラセズ（黒蜜）	カツプ半杯	粉生薑	小匙一杯
	粉ニツケ	小匙一杯	鹽	小匙四分ノ一
	メリケン粉	カツプ一杯半	冷水	カツプ半杯
	ココナツツ	カツプ一杯		

作り方――バターを煉り、砂糖を少しづつ加へて煉り續け、玉子を一寸混ぜて加
　へ、全部をよく攪混ぜ、これにモラセズにソーダを溶したものを入れます。
　メリケン粉、ニツケ、生薑及び鹽を篩ひ水と交互にバター等に加へ、ココナ
　ツツを入れて、油を塗つた天パンに流し、中火の天火で三十五分間燒きま
　す。

No. 175　　　　バナナと胡桃のパン

材料	砂糖	カツプ三分ノ二	クリーム	カツプ一杯
	鹽	小匙三分ノ二	熟したバナナ	三本
	ソーダ	小匙一杯	メリケン粉	カツプ二杯
	胡桃細く切つたもの	カツプ半杯	玉子	二個

作り方――バナナの皮をむき、裏漉にして砂糖と混ぜ、之にクリームと泡立てた
　玉子と鹽を加へて混ぜます。メリケン粉は一度篩つてから量り、ソーダと共
　に三度篩ひ、胡桃と混ぜて前のバナナ等に併せ、油を塗つた細長いパン用の
　天パンに流し中火の天火で燒きます。パンの中央に楊子を差込んだのに何も
　附着しなくなつたらば出來上つたのです。バターを添へパン代用に召し上る
　のです。

No. 176　　　　果實入リロール（卷パン）

材料	メリケン粉	カツプ一杯半	ベーキング・パウ	
	バター又は代用品	大匙二杯	ーダ	小匙三杯
	ミルク	カツプ半杯	溶したバター	大匙一杯
	胡桃微塵切り	大匙二杯	砂糖	大匙二杯
	乾無花果又はデー		粉ニツケ	小匙半杯
	ツ微塵切り	大匙二杯		

作り方――メリケン粉とベーキング・パウダーを篩ひ、バターを切り込み、ミル
　クを加へて混ぜ、メリケン粉を少量篩つて置いた板の上で三分の厚さに延し
　溶したバターを表面に塗り殘りの材料を上に振掛け、海苔卷きの様に卷き、
　五分の輪切りにして、油を塗つた天パンに間を置いて並べ強火の天火で十五
　分程燒きます。パン代用又はビスケツト代用としてお茶の時のお菓子になり
　ます。

No. 177   **CREAM SCONES**

2 Cups flour	2 Eggs
3 Teaspoons baking powder	½ Cup evaporated milk
½ Teaspoon salt	2 Tablespoons sugar
3 Tablespoons shortening	

Mix and sift the dry ingredients and cut in the shortening until well blended. Add the beaten eggs to the cream, and then mix to a dough with the dry ingredients. Do not knead, but pat out as you would biscuits. Cut in triangles or diamonds. Place in a greased pan, brush with milk, sprinkle with sugar, and bake in a hot oven of 400 degrees F.

No. 178   **QUEEN BISCUIT**

¼ Cup shortening	2/3 Cup flour
2/3 Cup currants or Chopped raisins	¼ Pound candied orange peel
½ Cup sugar	2 Eggs

Cream the shortening and sugar and add the well-beaten egg yolks. Sift the flour, shaking a little over the fruit, and add slowly to the shortening and sugar mixture. Add the fruit. Fold in the stiffly beaten whites, and pour into your tiniest muffin pans, which should be greased and floured. Bake in a moderate oven of 350 degrees F. for 15 or 20 minutes. If the cakes are inclined to run over the sides of the pans add a tablespoonful of flour to the dough. As different flours behave differently, it is well to make a test cake. This recipe makes 36 tiny biscuits.

No. 179   **CINNAMON TOAST**

Work four tablespoons butter until creamy, add slowly three tablespoons light brown sugar and one tablespoon cinnamon. Remove crusts from eight slices bread, spread with mixture, cut in strips and put in a hot oven, 450 degrees F., until mixture is melted.

No. 177　　　クリーム・スコンズ

材料　メリケン粉　　　　　カップ二杯　　　ベーキング・パウダ
　　鹽　　　　　　　　　小匙半杯　　　　　　一　　　　　　小匙三杯
　　バター又は代用品　　大匙三杯　　　　　玉子　　　　　　二個
　　クリーム　　　　　　カップ半杯　　　　砂糖　　　　　　大匙二杯

作り方——メリケン粉、　ーキング・パウダー、砂糖及び鹽を篩ひ、これにバタ
　ーを切込み、別に玉子を泡立ててクリームと併せたものをメリケン粉等に混
　込み、メリケン粉を振掛けた板の上で厚さ四分位に延し、四角、三角又はダ
　イヤモンド形に切り、天パンに並べ表面にミルクを塗り、砂糖を少し振り強
　火の天火で十五分間位燒きます。

No 178　　　クヰーン・ビスケット・パン

材料　バター　　　　　　カップ半杯　　　乾葡萄　　　　　カップ三分ノ二
　　砂糖　　　　　　　　カップ半杯　　　メリケン粉　　　カップ三分ノ二
　　蜜柑の皮の砂糖漬　　四分ノ一封度　　玉子　　　　　　二個

作り方——バターを煉り、砂糖を少量づつ加へて更に煉り續け、よく混ぜた玉子
　の黄味を加へ、メリケン粉を少量、乾葡萄と蜜柑の皮を細く切つた上に篩ひ
　殘りをバター等に加へ、乾葡萄と蜜柑の皮を加へ、よく泡立てた白味を折込
　み一番小型のマフエンの丸型天パンによく油を塗つた中に流し、中火の天火
　で十五分乃至二十分間燒きます。此のビスケットはメリケン粉の量が少いと
　天パンから溢れて流れますから、一個分だけ、先に燒いて見るのです。流れ
　出る様でしたら更に大匙一、二杯のメリケン粉を加へます。

No. 179　　　シナモン・トースト

作り方——大匙四杯バターを煉り大匙三杯の黒砂糖を加へて更に煉り、大匙一杯
　ニツケを加へます。白パンの端を切り取りニツケ等を上に塗り、一枚のパン
　を横四ツに切り、その儘又は天パンに並べ強火の天火で五分程燒き、おやつ
　の御菓子代りに用ひます。

No. 180   **FOUNDATION HOT CAKES**

2½ Cups flour	2 Cups milk
4 Teaspoons baking powder	1 Egg
1 Teaspoon salt	2 Tablespoons shortening
1 Tablespoon sugar	

Sift together, flour, baking powder, salt, sugar and add to this the egg slightly beaten and milk. Lastly add the melted shortening. The milk may be substituted with two cups sour milk, or two cups of milk to which two tablespoons of vinegar have been added, the baking powder omitted and one teaspoons of soda added. Mix hot cake batter quickly and pour by spoonfuls onto hot greased grindle and cook until the underside is brown, and many small holes appear on the surface. Turn and brown the other side. They should not be turned more than once.

No. 181   **CHEESE HOT CAKES**

Measure the dry ingredients used for standard griddle cakes into a bowl. Add two-thirds of a cupful of snappy American grated cheese and mix until the cheese is fairly well distributed. Add the wet ingredients as for the standard griddle cakes, mix and bake as usual.

No. 182   **COOKED CEREAL HOT CAKES**

Assemble the ingredients for standard griddle cakes, but use only two cupfuls of flour. Add one cupful of cooked rice or one cupful of cooked Fastmeal or rolled oats to the wet ingredients. Finish as for standard griddle cakes. Serve with butter and syrup.

No. 183   **BACON OR HAM HOT CAKES**

To the dry ingredients for standard griddle cakes, add one cupful of cold boiled ham which has been chopped finely, or else one cupful of bacon fried until crisp. For the ham griddle cakes decrease the salt to one half teaspoonful. Finish as for standard griddle cakes and serve with tomato or cheese sauce or with syrup.

No. 18o　　　　ホ　ツ　ト・ケ　ー　キ

材料　メリケン粉　　　　カツプ二杯半　　　ベーキング・パウダ
　　　鹽　　　　　　　小匙半杯　　　　　　一　　　　　　　小匙四杯
　　　砂糖　　　　　　大匙一杯　　　　　ミルク　　　　　カツプ二杯
　　　玉子　　　　　　一個　　　　　　溶したバター又は
　　　　　　　　　　　　　　　　　　　　サラダ油　　　大匙二杯

作り方——メリケン粉、ベーキング・パウダー、鹽及び砂糖を篩ひ、玉子を一寸
　　泡立てたのをミルクと混ぜて、メリケン粉等に加へ、最後に油を入れます。
　　ホツト・ケーキの場合はメリケン粉にミルクをぜる時手早くして、少し位塊
　　りがあつてもよいのです。又ベーキング・パウダーの代りにソーダ小匙一杯
　　を用ひ、これにミルクの代りに腐つたミルク又はミルクカツプ二杯に西洋酢
　　大匙二杯加へて作つた腐つたミルクを使ふと尚輕いホツト・ケーキが出來ま
　　す。フライパンを熱して油を底にひたひたに入れ、ホツト・ケーキの素大匙
　　一杯を流し、火力を減じて下側が狐色になり表面にぶつぶつ穴が出來る迄燒
　　き、 かへして他の側を狐色に燒き上げるのです。 上にバターと蜜をかけま
　　す。以下の變りホツト・ケーキは此の素の作り方を土臺にしたものです。

No. 181　　　チ ー ズ・ホ ツ ト・ケ ー キ

作り方——メリケン粉等を篩つた中に卸したチーズカツプ三分ノ二を加へます。
　　その先は普通のホツト・ケーキの作り方通りです。

No. 182　　　ラ イ ス・ホ ツ ト・ケ ー キ

作り方——普通のホツト・ケーキのメリケン粉の分量をカツプ二杯にして、ミル
　　クの方にカツプ一杯の御飯を加へ、後は普通の通りに致します。御飯の代り
　　に煮たオート・ミール、フアストミール等を同じ樣に使つてもよいのです。

No. 183　　　ハム(ベーコン)・ホツト・ケーキ

作り方——普通のホツト・ケーキのメリケン粉等を篩つた中にハムをカツプ一杯
　　微塵切りにして（又は挽肉を）加へます。ベーコンの場合は細く切つたフラ
　　イパンで燒いて加へるのです。

No. 184   BANANA HOT CAKES

Fairly ripe bananas will give the best flavor for these. Assemble the wet and dry ingredients for a standard recipe of griddle cakes, and to the wet ones add two large bananas sliced rather thinly. Finish as for plain griddle cakes. Serve with syrup or lemon sauce.

No. 185   PINEAPPLE HOT CAKES

These make an easily prepared and delicious dessert course. They are prepared just like standard griddle cakes, except that instead of two cupfuls of milk, two-thirds of a cupful of pineapple juice, one and one-third cupfuls of milk and one cupful of pineapple pulp are used. Mix these with the beaten egg and melted shortening and then add this combination to the dry ingredients.

Place one griddle cake on the serving plate, cover generously with pineapple sauce, place over this another cake and sift over the top of it confectioner's sugar.

For the pineapple sauce, thicken a mixture of one cupful of pineapple juice and half a cupful of the pulp with two tablesoonfuls of flour; cook until nicely thickened and serve piping hot.

No. 186   FRENCH PANCAKES

½ Cup flour	¼ Teaspoon salt
3 Tablespoons powdered sugar	½ Cup milk
	1 Egg

Sift flour with sugar and salt. Add milk, stir until perfectly smooth, add egg and beat thoroughly. Cook on hot griddle, roll up and baste in hot orange sauce or spread with compote of fruit before rolling.

No. 187   ORANGE SAUCE FOR FRENCH PANCAKES

3 Tablespoons butter	1 Orange
½ Cup powdered sugar	

Cream butter and add the powdered sugar gradually, lastly add the juice and grated rind of one orange. Other fruit may be used instead of oranges.

No. 184　　　バナナ・ホツト・ケーキ

作り方——バナナ二本を極く薄い輪切りにして普通のホツト・ケーキのミルク等
　　に加へ後は普通に致します。
　　バナナの代りに林檎の薄切りを一個半分使つても結構です。

No. 185　　　パイナツプル・ホツト・ケーキ

作り方——普通のホツト・ケーキのミルクをカツプ二杯の代りにカツプ一杯三分
　　ノ一に減らしてパイナツプル汁カツプ三分ノ二とパイナツプル微塵切りカツ
　　プ一杯を使ふのです。此のパイナツプル・ホツト・ケーキ二枚の間にパイナ
　　ツプル汁カツプ一杯とパイナツプル微塵切りカツプ半杯を大匙二杯のメリケ
　　ン粉でどろどろに固めたソースを掛けると美味しいデザートになります。

No. 186　　　フランス風パン・ケーキ

材料	メリケン粉	カツプ半杯	粉砂糖	大匙三杯
	鹽	小匙四分ノ一	牛乳	カツプ半杯
	玉子	一個		

作り方——メリケン粉を砂糖と共に篩ひ、牛乳を加へてよく攪混ぜ、玉子を泡立
　　てて加へ混合せます。熱したフライパンに薄く油を塗り前の材料を大匙一杯
　　程流して、兩面を狐色に焼きます。片面に次のオレンヂ・ソース又はフルー
　　ツ・ソースを塗り、海苔巻の様に巻き、上に粉砂糖を掛けて召上るのです。
　　朝食用又は食後のデザートとして好適のケーキです

No. 187　　　オ　レ　ン　ヂ・ソ　ー　ス

材料	バター	大匙三杯	粉砂糖	カツプ半杯
	蜜柑	一個		

作り方——バターを充分に煉り、粉砂糖を段々に加へ、最後に蜜柑一個分の汁及
　　び皮を卸したものを加へます。蜜柑の代りに他の果物を使つてもよろしい。

No. 188   HAWAIIAN FRENCH TOAST

2 Eggs	8 Slices stale bread
½ Teaspoon salt	8 Slices bacon
1 Cup pineapple juice	8 Slices pineapple

Beat the egg and add to the pineapple juice with the salt and allow the bread to soak in this mixture for a few minutes. Heat frying pan and cook bacon, then fry bread in the bacon fat, and after the bread is fried, fry the sliced pineapple in the same fat. Put the slices of pineapple on top of the fried bread and top the pineapple with a piece of bacon.

No. 189   FRENCH DOUGHNUTS

2 Eggs	2 Cups flour
½ Cup sugar	2 Teaspoons baking powder
½ Cup evaporated milk	Grated rind and juice of 1 orange

Beat eggs, add sugar, and continue beating. Add cream, then add flour and baking powder which have been sifted together. Last add the juice and rind of orange. Drop from spoon and fry in deep fat.

No. 190   SOUTHERN APPLE FRITTERS

1 Cup milk	¼ Teaspoon salt
2 Eggs	Dash cinnamon
2 Tablespoons sugar	2 Cups flour
2 Tablespoons butter	2 Teaspoon baking powder
4 Chopped apples	

Beat the eggs into the milk, add sugar, butter, salt and cinnamon. Mix thoroughly, then stir in flour and baking powder which has been sifted, stir in the apples, chopped fine. Fry in deep fat and sprinkle with powdered sugar.

No. 191   RICE FRITTERS

2 Cups boiled rice	¼ Teaspoon vanilla
3 Eggs	½ Teaspoon nutmeg
½ Cup sugar	3 Teaspoons baking powder
½ Teaspoon salt	6 Tablespoons flour

Beat the eggs lightly and add to the rice with vanilla and nutmeg. Sift sugar, salt, baking powder and flour and add to the first mixture. Drop by spoonfuls into hot deep fat frying oil. Fry until golden brown and sprinkle with powdered sugar, or unsugared use with chicken.

No. 188　　　ハワイ式フレンチ・トースト

材料　玉子　　　　　　　　二個　　　　鹽　　　　　　　小匙半杯
　　　パイナツプル罐詰汁　カツプ一杯　二日位經つた古い
　　　ベーコン　　　　　　八切れ　　　　パン　　　　　八枚
　　　パイナツプル　　　　八切れ

作り方——玉子を輕く泡立てて、鹽と一緒にパイナツプルの汁に加へ、この中に
　　三分の厚さに切つたパンを漬けます。フライパンを熱して、ベーコンを燒き
　　その油で、汁に漬けたパンを燒き、後、同じフライパンで輪切りのパイナツ
　　プルを一寸燒き、パイの上にパイナツプルを置き、ベーコンを添えます。

No. 189　　　フランス式ドーナツツ

材料　玉子　　　　　　　　二個　　　　砂糖　　　　　　カツプ半杯
　　　クリーム　　　　　　カツプ半杯　上等メリケン粉　カツプ二杯
　　　ベーキング・パウダ　　　　　　　オレンヂ　　　　一個
　　　　ー　　　　　　　　小匙二杯

作り方——玉子はよく泡立て、砂糖を加へて再びよく混ぜ、クリームを加へます
　　別にメリケン粉とベーキング・パウダーを篩つたものを前の材料に混ぜ、之
　　にオレンヂの汁及び卸した皮を加へ、熱した油の中に大匙一杯づつ落して揚
　　げるのです。

No. 19o　　　林　檎　フ　リ　ツ　タ　ー

材料　ミルク　　　　　　　カツプ一杯　玉子　　　　　　二個
　　　砂糖　　　　　　　　大匙二杯　　バター　　　　　大匙二杯
　　　林檎細く切つたもの　四個　　　　鹽　　　　　　　小匙四分ノ一
　　　ニツケ　　　　　　　小匙八分ノ一　上等メリケン粉　カツプ二杯
　　　ベーキング・パウ
　　　　ーダ　　　　　　小匙二杯

作り方——玉子を泡立て、ミルクに加へ、砂糖とバターを煉つた中に加へ、鹽と
　　ニツケを入れます。別にメリケン粉とベーキング・パウダーを篩つたものを
　　加へて林檎を入れ、熱した油の中に落して輕く揚げ粉砂糖を振掛けます。

No. 191　　　ラ　イ　ス　・　フ　リ　ツ　タ　ー

材料　軟い御飯　　　　　　カツプ二杯　玉子　　　　　　三個
　　　砂糖　　　　　　　　カツプ半杯　鹽　　　　　　　小匙半杯
　　　ヴアニラ　　　　　　小匙四分ノ一　ナツメグ　　　　小匙半杯
　　　ベーキング・パウダ　　　　　　　メリケン粉　　　大匙六杯
　　　　ー　　　　　　　　小匙三杯

作り方——冷した御飯に玉子を少し泡立てゝ混込み、ヴアニラ、ナツメグを加へ
　　て後、ベーキング・パウダー、砂糖、鹽及びメリケン粉を篩つたものを加へ
　　て混ぜ、熱した揚物油の中に大匙一杯づつ落して揚げ、粉砂糖を振掛けます
　　粉砂糖を掛けないで鶏料理の附合せにしても結構です。

No. 192   JIFFY CAKE

1/3 Cup shortening	½ Teaspoon salt
1 1/3 Cups brown sugar	1 Teaspoon cinnamon
2 Eggs (save 1 white for icing)	¼ Teaspoon nutmeg
½ Cup milk	½ Teaspoon cloves
½ Teaspoon lemon extract	¼ Teaspoon ginger
1¾ Cups flour	1 Cup chopped raisins
3 Teaspoons baking powder	

Cut raisins with scissors or chopper. Put all ingredients together and beat thoroughly until smooth. Bake in a shallow pan rubbed with fat, in a moderate oven of 350 degrees F., for 25 to 30 minutes. Sprinkle with powdered sugar while warm or ice with seven minute icing.

No. 193   SEVEN MINUTE ICING

¾ Cup granulated sugar	1 Egg white
⅛ Teaspoon cream of tartar	3 Tablespoons hot water

Place all ingredients in top of double boiler, have water boiling in lower part. Beat until thick enough to spread on cake. Add one-half teaspoon of vanilla. It will be necessary to cook this icing about seven minutes.

No. 194   SPICED CAKE

½ Cup shortening	½ Teaspoon soda
1 Cup brown sugar	½ Teaspoon baking powder
1 Whole egg	½ Teaspoon cloves
1 Egg yolk	½ Teaspoon cinnamon
1 1/3 Cups cake flour	½ Cup sour milk
¼ Teaspoon salt	

Cream shortening and add the brown sugar gradually. Add to the creamed mixture one whole egg and the yolk well beaten. Sift the flour once before measuring then sift together flour, soda, salt, baking powder, cloves, cinnamon and add alternately with sour milk to the first mixture. Pour into greased and floured pan. Bake 35 minutes in a moderate oven of 350 degrees F.

No. 192　　　スパイス（香料）ケーキ（其一）

材料	バター	カツプ三分ノ一	黒砂糖	カツプ一杯三分ノ一
	玉子（白味一個は砂		ミルク	カツプ半杯
	糖飾りに用ひる爲		レモン・エツセンス	小匙半杯
	別にして置く）二個		メリケン粉	カツプ一杯四分ノ三
	ベーキング・パウ		鹽	小匙半杯
	ダー	小匙三杯	ニツケ	小匙一杯
	ナツメグ	小匙四分ノ一	クローブ	小匙半杯
	生姜粉	小匙四分ノ一	乾葡萄	カツプ一杯

作り方──乾葡萄を半分に切つて少量のメリケン粉でまぶし、他の材料を全部並べた順に混合せ、よく混ざる迄手早く混ぜバターを塗つた淺い天パンに入れて中火の天火で二十五分乃至三十分間燒きます。燒き上げましたらば直に上に粉砂糖を振掛けるか又は次の砂糖飾りをケーキの上に塗ります。

No. 193　　　七分間アイシング

材料	グラニユ糖	カツプ四分ノ三	クリーム・オブ・ター	
	玉子の白味	一個	ター又はベーキン	
	湯	大匙三杯	グ・パウダー	小匙八分ノ一
	ヴアニラ	小匙半杯		

作り方──砂糖、クリーム・オブターター、白味及び湯を二重鍋の上の部に入れ、沸騰して居る湯の上で絕えず玉子攪拌器で混ぜながら七分程煮でどろどろに固め小匙半杯のヴアニラを加へてケーキの上に塗るのです。

No. 194　　　スパイス（香料）ケーキ（其二）

材料	バター又は代用品	カツプ半杯	黒砂糖（花見砂糖）	カツプ一杯
	玉子	一個	玉子の黄味	一個
	メリケン粉	カツプ一杯三分ノ一	鹽	小匙四分ノ一
	ソーダ	小匙半杯	ベーキング・パウ	
	クローブ	小匙半杯	ダー	小匙半杯
	ニツケ粉	小匙半杯	腐つたミルク	カツプ半杯

作り方──バターを煉り、砂糖を徐々に加へて煉り續け、玉子一個と黄味一個をよく泡立てたものを加へます。メリケン粉、鹽、ベーキング・パウダー、クローブ、ニツケ、ソーダ等を篩ひ、ミルクと交互に前のバター等に混合せ、油を塗り、メリケン粉を少し振つた天パンに流します。普通のケーキにする場合はこれを中火の天火で三十五分間燒けばよろしいのです。ベークト（天火で燒いた）砂糖飾りを上に掛ける場合は、材料を全部天パンに流したらばその上に砂糖飾りを掛けて中火の天火で三十五分間燒くのです。

No. 195   **BAKED ICING**

1 Egg white   ¼ Cup broken nut meats
½ Cup brown sugar

Beat egg whites until they hold a point when the beater is pulled out of them.   Add brown sugar, beating it in. Spread on top of cake batter, sprinkle on the nuts and bake in a moderate oven, 350 degrees F., until the cake is done, which will be in approximately 35 minutes if it is in a pan eight inches square. Make twice the recipe for a larger cake.

No. 196   **BEST EVER DEVIL'S FOOD**

½ Cake bitter chocolate   1 Cup sour milk
2/3 Cup granulated sugar   2 Cups cake flour
½ Cup milk   1 Teaspoon soda dissolved in a
3 Eggs   little hot water
1 Cup granulated sugar   1 Teaspoon vanilla
½ Cup butter

Cream the butter and one cup of granulated sugar, add the egg yolks well beaten, the sour milk and then the sifted flour. Mix well, then add the soda, blend thoroughly. Combine the chocolate, sweet milk and the first granulated sugar and dissolve to a paste over a low flame, and add to the first mixture, together with the vanilla. Now fold in the beaten whites of three eggs. Bake in a moderate oven. The batter must be thin. Frost with a marshmallow or seven-minute icing.

No. 197   **CHOCOLATE ROLL**

½ Cup powdered sugar   3 Rounded tablespoons cocoa
2 Rounded tablespoons cake   3 Eggs
   flour

Sift together dry ingredients. Separate eggs. Beat yolks five minutes. Beat whites until stiff. Fold yolks into whites. Fold dry ingredients into eggs. Grease baking pan and line bottom with well greased oil paper. Bake in very slow oven 20 or 25 minutes. Turn onto wet cloth twice the size of pan, remove paper, cover with remaining half of wet cloth and roll like jelly roll, the wet cloth being inside of cake. Let stand. When ready to serve, unroll cake, remove from cloth, spread with whipped cream sweetened to taste and flavored with vanilla. Roll again, slice into individiual servings and serve with following chocolate sauce.

No. 195　　ベークド・アイシング（焼きケーキ砂糖飾り）

材料　玉子の白味　　　　　　　一個　　　　　　　黒砂糖（花見砂糖）　　カツプ半杯
　　　胡桃細く切つたもの　カツプ四分ノ一

作り方——玉子の白味を充分形を保つ迄泡立て、砂糖を泡立て續けながら加へ、
　　ケーキの生の材料の上に塗り、上に胡桃を振掛け、中火の天火で三十五分間
　　燒きます。

No. 196　　　チヨコレート・ケーキ

材料　料理用ビター・チヨ　　　　　　グラニユ糖　　カツプ三分ノ二
　　　　レコート　　　　　半角　　　ミルク　　　　　カツプ半杯
　　　玉子　　　　　　　　三個　　　グラニユ糖　　　カツプ一杯
　　　バター又は代用品　カツプ半杯　腐敗したミルク　カツプ一杯
　　　上等メリケン粉　　カツプ二杯　ソーダ（少量の湯に
　　　ヴアニラ　　　　　小匙一杯　　　溶して用ふ）　　小匙一杯

作り方——先づ初の三つの材料を併せ、湯煎にして溶します。次にバターを煉り
　　砂糖を少量づつ加へて煉り續け、之に充分混ぜた玉子の黄味を入れ、腐敗し
　　たミルクと次に篩つたメリケン粉を加へます。之に少量の湯に溶したソーダ
　　を加へてよく混合せ、前に作つて置いたチヨコレート等を加へ、最後に充分
　　泡立てた白味を折込み、油を塗つた天パンに五分位の厚さに流し込んで中火
　　の天火で燒きます。好みにより上に白いアイスイングを塗つても結構です。

No. 197　　　チヨコレート・ロール・ケーキ

材料　粉砂糖　　　　　カツプ半杯　　上等メリケン粉　大匙山盛り二杯
　　　ココア　　　　大匙山盛り三杯　玉子　　　　　　　三個

作り方——メリケン粉と粉砂糖とココアを篩ひます。玉子は白味と黄味を分け、
　　先づ白味が固まる迄攪拌器で泡立て、次に黄味を攪拌器で五分間泡立て白味
　　に黄味を折込み、前の材料を静に加へます。四角の淺い天パンに油を充分塗
　　り、底に油を塗つたパラフイン紙を敷き、前の材料を流し込み、弱火の天火
　　で二十五分程燒き、ぬれた布の上に取出し、底の油を塗つた紙を取り、上に
　　もぬれた布を一枚のせ、布をかぶせた儘海苔卷の様に卷き、そのまゝ数時間
　　置きます。召し上る前に一度卷いたものを延し、泡立てたクリームに粉砂糖
　　を少し加へて甘くしたものを塗り、再び布を取つて卷き、一寸位の厚さに切
　　り、その儘ケーキとして又は次のソースを掛けてデザートとして召上るので
　　す。

No. 198   **CHOCOLATE SAUCE**

2 Squares chocolate	1 Tablespoon cornstarch
1 Cup sugar	⅛ Teaspoon salt
½ Cup milk	1 Teaspoon vanilla

Mix dry ingredients. Add liquids. Cook until thickened, stirring constantly.

No. 199   **BURNT SUGAR LAYER CAKE**

1½ Cups sugar	½ Cup milk
½ Cup butter	2 Teaspoons baking powder
3 Eggs	½ Cup cold water
¼ Teaspoon salt	3 Tablespoons burnt sugar
2½ Cups flour	1 Teaspoon vanilla

Cream sugar and butter. Add well beaten eggs. Then the milk and water mixed. Stir well. Then add flour and baking powder sifted together. Last add burnt sugar and vanilla. Bake in three layers about 40 minutes in moderate oven.

No. 200   **BURNT SUGAR FILLING**

2½ Cups powdered sugar	1 Tablespoon burnt sugar
2 Tablespoons melted butter	1/3 Cup evaporated cream

Add the melted butter and cream to the powdered sugar and beat in the burnt sugar. Spread between layers and on top of the cake.

No. 201   **ICE WATER CAKE**

2 Cups sugar	6 Teaspoons baking powder
½ Cup butter	4 Egg whites
1½ Cups ice water	¼ Teaspoon salt
3 Cups flour	1 Teaspoon vanilla

Cream the sugar and the butter. Sift flour and measure, add salt. Add alternately with ice water to sugar and butter mixture, fold in stiffly beaten egg whites, flavoring and baking powder . Bake at 350 degrees F.

No. 198　　　　チョコレート・ソース

材料　料理用ビター・チョ		砂糖	カツプ一杯
コレート	二角	ミルク	カツプ半杯
コンスターチ	大匙一杯	鹽	小匙八分ノ一
ヴアニラ	小匙一杯		

作り方——チョコレートを細く切り、砂糖、鹽、コンスターチと合せ、ミルクを
　加へ、火に掛けて混ぜながらどろどろに固まる迄に煮て火より下し、ヴアニ
　ラを加へます。溫くても冷くてもよい。他のプデングにも使用出來る美味し
　いソースです

No. 199　　　焦し砂糖のケーキ

材料　砂糖	カツプ一杯半	バター又は代用品	カツプ半杯
玉子	三個	鹽	小匙四分ノ一
上等メリケン粉	カツプ二杯半	ミルク	カツプ半杯
ベーキング・パウダ		冷水	カツプ半杯
一	小匙二杯	焦した砂糖	大匙三杯
ヴアニラ	小匙一杯		

作り方——バターを煉り、砂糖を少しづつ入れて煉り續け、よく混ぜた玉子を加
　へ、冷水とミルクを入れ、之にメリケン粉とベーキング・パウダーを篩つた
　ものを加へます。之に手早く混ぜながら焦した砂糖を流し込みます。（焦し
　た砂糖がブツブツ固まりますがこれは差支へありません）。之を三枚の油を
　塗つた天パンに流し込み、中火の天火で四十分位燒きます。

No. 2oo　　　ケーキのソースと砂糖飾り

材料　粉砂糖	カツプ二杯半	溶したバター	大匙二杯
焦した砂糖	大匙一杯	クリーム	カツプ三分ノ一位

作り方——粉砂糖とクリームと溶したバターを混ぜ、焦した砂糖を手早く混ぜな
　がら加へ、ケーキの間と上に塗ります。

No. 2o1　　　冷　水　の　ケ　ー　キ

材料　砂糖	カツプ二杯	バター又は代用品	カツプ半杯
氷水	カツプ一杯半	上等メリケン粉	カツプ三杯
ベーキング・パウダ		玉子の白味	四個
一	小匙六杯	鹽	小匙四分ノ一
ヴアニラ	小匙一杯		

作り方——バターを煉り砂糖を少しづつ加へて更に煉り續けます。別にメリケン
　粉と鹽を篩ひ、氷水と交互にバター等に加へ、之に充分泡立てた白味にヴア
　ニラとベーキング・パウダーを加へたものを折込み、中火の天火で燒きます
　經濟的なケーキです。

No. 202 AN OLD FASHIONED FRUIT CAKE

1 Pound flour (4 cups)	1 Pound candied cherries
1 Pound butter	1 Dozen eggs
1 Pound sugar	1 Tablespoon allspice
¼ Pound candied orange peel	1 Tablespoon cloves
3 Pounds seeded raisins	1 Tablespoon nutmeg
2 Pounds currants	1 Tablespoon cinnamon
1 Pound figs	1 Cup molasses
1 Pound dates	1 Pint brandy
1 Pound prunes	1 Glass tart jelly
1 Pound walnuts	2½ Teaspoons soda

Cream the butter and add the sugar gradually and next the beaten egg yolks. Sift the dry ingredients and add to the first mixture alternately with the molasses. Then add brandy, jelly, and soda which has first been dissolved in a little warm water. Chop the dried fruit fine and coat with flour, then add to the other ingredients and fold in the beaten egg whites. Grease loaf pans and put in oiled paper. Bake for two and a half hours in a very slow oven. Ice with a thin frosting and set away until ready for use in a tightly covered tin.

No. 203 TUTTI FRUTTI ANGEL FOOD

1 Cup cake flour	¼ Teaspoon almond extract
10 Egg whites	¼ Cup candied cherries
¼ Teaspoon salt	¼ Cup candied pineapple
¾ Teaspoon cream of tartar	¼ Cup cocoanut
1¼ Cup sugar	¼ Cup chopped almonds
1 Teaspoon vanilla	

Sift flour, measure, then sift again four times. Beat egg whites and salt on a large platter with a flat wire whisk beater. When foamy add cream of tartar and continue beating until the eggs are stiff enough to hold up in peaks. Fold in sugar gently, about two tablespoons at a time, until all is used add flour. Fold in the fruit, finely chopped, cocoanut and nuts. Bake in an ungreased anged food pan, with heat at 250 degrees F., increase after 30 minutes to 325 degrees F. Remove from oven and invert pan for one hour before removing from pan.

No. 2o2　　　本格的クリスマス・ケーキ

材料　上等メリケン粉　　カツプ四杯(一封度)バター　　　　　一封度
　　　砂糖　　　　　　　　一封度　　　　オレンヂ皮の砂糖
　　　種子を取つた乾葡萄　三封度　　　　　漬　　　　　　四分ノ一封度
　　　カラント(小さい乾　　　　　　　　　乾無花果　　　　一封度
　　　　葡萄の一種)　　　二封度　　　　デーツ　　　　　一封度
　　　プルンズ　　　　　　一封度　　　　胡桃　　　　　　一封度
　　　櫻桃砂糖漬　　　　　一封度　　　　玉子　　　　　　十二個
　　　オール・スパイス(香　　　　　　　　クローブ　　　　大匙一杯
　　　　料)　　　　　　大匙一杯　　　　ナツメグ　　　　大匙一杯
　　　粉ニツケ　　　　　大匙一杯　　　　モラセズ(黑蜜)　カツプ一杯
　　　ブランデー酒　　　カツプ二杯　　　カラント又はプラ
　　　ソーダ　　　　　　小匙二杯半　　　　ム・ゼリー(瓶詰の
　　　　　　　　　　　　　　　　　　　　　デエリー)　　　一瓶

作り方——バターを煉り、少しづつ砂糖を加へて煉りつづけ、玉子の黄味を混ぜ
て加へ、メリケン粉、クローブ、ナツメグ、ニツケ、オールスパイス等を篩
つてモラセズと交互に之に加へ、ブランデー酒、ゼリー、及び少量の湯で溶
したソーダを加へます。乾果實、砂糖漬等を細く切りメリケン粉をまぶして
前の材料に入れ、最後に泡立てた白味を加へ、油を塗つた天パンに油を塗つ
た紙を敷き、その上に流して極く弱火の天火で二時間程燒きます。此の分量
では三、四個の小さいケーキに分けた方がよく燒けます。此のケーキはクリ
スマスの一月位前に燒き密閉出來る罐に入れて、仕舞つて置くと味がよくな
ります。

No. 2o3　　　果實入りエンゼル・フード・ケーキ

材料　上等メリケン粉　　カツプ一杯　　　玉子白味　　　　十個
　　　鹽　　　　　　　小匙四分ノ一　　　クリーム・オブ・ター
　　　砂糖　　　　カツプ一杯四分ノ一　　　ター　　　　小匙四分ノ三
　　　ヴアニラ　　　　　小匙一杯　　　　アーモンド(香料)エ
　　　櫻桃砂糖漬　　　カツプ四分ノ一　　　ツセンス　　　小匙四分ノ一
　　　パイナツプル砂糖漬　カツプ四分ノ一　ココナツツ　　カツプ四分ノ一
　　　アーモンドの微塵切
　　　　り　　　　　　カツプ四分ノ一

作り方——メリケン粉は一度篩つてから量り、更に四度篩ひます。別に玉子の白
味を鹽と一緒に輕く泡立てクリーム・オブ・ターターを入れ、砂糖を大匙二杯
位づつ加へながら靜かに泡立てつづけ、篩つたメリケン粉を少しづつ入れ、
櫻桃、パイナツプル、ココナツツ、胡桃等を細く切つて入れ、油をぬらぬ中
央に穴のある天パンに入れて弱火の天火で三十分間燒き、火力を少し強めて
燒き上げ、天パンに入れた儘倒に網の上に置いて一時間冷し、のち、ナイフ
で靜に天パンから取出します。

No. 204   **AMBROSIA CAKE**

2 Cups sugar	6 Egg whites
½ Cup butter	3 Cups cake flour
1 Cup milk	3 Teaspoons baking powder

Beat sugar and butter thoroughly, then add alternately the milk and flour, having the baking powder sifted with the flour. Add the beaten whites. Bake in two oblong layers and put together with the following lemon filling. Bake the cake in a moderate oven of 350 degrees F., from 25 to 30 minutes.

No. 205   **LEMON FILLING**

Juice of 2 lemons	¼ Cup butter
Grated rind of 1 lemon	½ Cup sugar
3 Egg yolks	

Mix all ingredients well and cook until thick. Place between layers. The top and sides of the cake may be covered with any boiled icing or with lemon icing.

No. 206   **EMERGENCY CAKE**

1¾ Cups cake flour	2/3 Cup milk
¼ Teaspoon salt	1 Egg
2½ Teaspoons baking powder	1 Teaspoon flavoring
1/3 Cup shortening	

Sift the flour once before measuring. Sift, flour, salt and baking powder together. Measure one third cup softened shortening and fill the cup with milk. Add these with the unbeaten egg to the flour mixture, add flavoring and beat well for two or three minutes. Pour into greased and floured pan and bake. Baking time, 25 to 35 minutes, at 350 degrees F. or moderate oven.

No. 2o4　　レ　モ　ン・ケ　ー　キ

材料　砂糖　　　　　　　　カツプ二杯　　　バター又は代用品　カツプ半杯
　　　ミルク　　　　　　　カツプ一杯　　　玉子の白味　　　　六個
　　　上等メリケン粉　　　カツプ三杯　　　ベーキング・パウダ
　　　　　　　　　　　　　　　　　　　　　　ー　　　　　　　小匙三杯

作り方——バター煉り、砂糖を徐々に加へて煉り續け、別にメリケン粉とベーキ
　　ング・パウダーを篩つて、ミルクと交互に前の材料に混込みます。之に玉子
　　の白味を充分に泡立てて折込み、油を塗つた二個の四角の天パンに流して中
　　火の天火で二十五分乃至三十分間燒き、天パンより取出して冷し、ケーキ二
　　枚の間に次のソースを敷き、重ねて上と周圍にアイスイング（砂糖飾り）を
　　塗ります。

No. 2o5　　ケ　ー　キ・ソ　ー　ス

材料　レモン　　　　　　　二個　　　　　　レモン皮おろしたも
　　　玉子の黄味　　　　　三個　　　　　　の　　　　　　　　一個
　　　バター　　　　　　　カツプ四分ノ一　砂糖　　　　　　　カツプ半杯

作り方——レモンの汁をしぼり、外皮を卸します。之にバターを煉り、砂糖を加
　　へ、黄味を混ぜたものを併せ、どろどろになる迄火の上で煮て冷して用ひま
　　す。

No. 2o6　　エ　マ　ー　ジ　エ　ン　シ　ー・ケ　ー　キ

材料　上等メリケン粉　カツプ一杯四分ノ三　鹽　　　　　　　小匙半杯
　　　砂糖　　　　　　　　カツプ一杯　　　ベーキング・パウダ
　　　バター又は代用品　カツプ三分ノ一　　ー　　　　　　　小匙二杯半
　　　ミルク　　　　　　カツプ三分ノ二　　玉子　　　　　　一個
　　　ヴアニラ又は他のエ
　　　ツセンス　　　　　小匙一杯

作り方——此のケーキは、一番手輕で普通の家にある材料のみを用ひた標準ケー
　　キです。後述の砂糖飾り又は他の砂糖飾りを用ひてもよく急ぎの場合にすぐ
　　燒けるケーキです。先づメリケン粉、ベーキング・パウダー、鹽及び砂糖を
　　篩ひます。別にミルク、バター（此の場合カツプにミルクを量りバターをカ
　　ツプのミルクに加へて、ミルクが丁度カツプに一杯のところ迄來ればバター
　　がカツプ三分ノ一加はつた事になります。これは手輕な量り方です）玉子（泡
　　てずその儘）とヴアニラを混ぜ、前のメリケン粉等に混ぜながら加へ、玉子
　　攪拌器で三分間材料を全部混ぜ、之を油を塗りメリケン粉を少量篩つた天パ
　　ンに流し、中火の天火で二十五分乃至三十五分間燒き、次の砂糖飾りを用ひ
　　る場合はその儘天パンに入れて置き、溫い間に砂糖飾りを掛けて再び燒きま
　　す。普通の場合は燒けたらば天パンより取出し、網の上で冷し、その儘、又
　　は他の砂糖飾りを掛けて供します。

No. 207   **BROILED ICING**

3 Tablespoons melted butter	2 Tablespoons cream or top milk
5 Tablespoons brown sugar	½ Cup shredded coconut

Mix all ingredients together and spread on top of cake while it is still warm. Place very low under the broiler with flame turned down about 375 degrees F. Broil until icing bubbles all over the surface and becomes brown, but use care that it does not burn. This amount will cover a cake baked in a pan eight inches square.

No. 208   **DATE NUT LOAF**

½ Cup sugar	¾ Teaspoon baking powder
2 Eggs	1 Package dates
½ Cup flour	½ Pound walnuts

Beat the egg yolks, add the sugar, and mix thoroughly. Sift the baking powder and flour together, sift a little of this over the fruit, and add the remainder to the egg mixture. Stir in the fruit, and fold in the well-beaten egg whites last. Pour into a greased loaf pan measuring eight by four inches at the bottom and three inches deep, and bake for one hour in a moderate oven of 350 degrees F. Do not attempt to slice the loaf until it has stood in a covered pan overnight.

No. 209   **PINEAPPLE CAKE**

4 Egg whites	2 Teaspoons baking powder
½ Cup butter or shortening	½ Cup milk
1½ Cups sugar	½ Cup pineapple juice
2½ Cups flour	1 Teaspoon vanilla
½ Teaspoon salt	

Cream the shortening and add the sugar a little at a time. Sift the flour, baking powder and salt and add to the creamed mixture alternately with the milk. Add pineapple juice, and vanilla and lastly the well beaten egg whites. Pour into two well greased layer cake pans and bake in a moderate oven of 350 degrees F. for 35 minutes. When baked remove pan and cool on wire cooler. Fill between layers with pineapple chopped fine and cooked to a thick paste with sugar and lemon juice and finish top of cake with seven minute icing.

No. 2o7　　　グリルで燒く砂糖飾り

材料　溶したバター　　　　大匙三杯　　　黑砂糖（花見砂糖）　　大匙五杯
　　　生クリーム　　　　　大匙二杯　　　ココナツツ　　　　　カツプ半杯

作り方——材料全部を混合せ、ケーキがまだ溫い間に上に塗り、グリルのオブン
　　（上から火が出る天火）の火からなるべく離れた所に置き、砂糖が全部ブツ
　　ブツ煮立ち、狐色に色が附く迄焦げぬ樣注意して燒きます。

No. 2o8　　　デーツ・胡桃・ローフ

材料　砂糖　　　　　　　カツプ半杯　　　玉子　　　　　　　　二個
　　　メリケン粉　　　　カツプ半杯　　　ベーキング・パウダ
　　　デーツ（乾果實）　一包　　　　　　—　　　　　　　　　小匙四分ノ三
　　　胡桃　　　　　　　半封度

作り方——玉子の黃味を混ぜ砂糖を加へて更によく混ぜます。メリケン粉とベー
　　キング・パウダーを篩ひ、その少量をデーツ、胡桃等にまぶし、殘りを玉子
　　等に加へ、之に胡桃、デーツを細く切つたものを加へ、よく泡立てた白味を折
　　込み、小型の四角の大パンに油を塗つた中に入れ、中火の大火で燒き上げ、
　　一晚蓋をしてその儘置き、召上る時に薄く切ります。

No. 2o9　　　パイナツプル・ケーキ

材料　玉子の白味　　　　　　　　　　　バター又は代用品　　カツプ半杯
　　　砂糖　　　　　　　カツプ一杯半　　上等メリケン粉　　カツプ二杯半
　　　鹽　　　　　　　　小匙半杯　　　ベーキング・パウダ
　　　ミルク　　　　　　カツプ半杯　　　—　　　　　　　　小匙二杯
　　　パイナツプル汁　　カツプ半杯　　　ヴアニラ　　　　　小匙一杯

作り方——バターを煉り砂糖を少しづつ加へて更に煉り、別にメリケン粉、ベー
　　キング・パウダー及び鹽を篩つたものをミルクと交互に加へてよく混ぜ、パ
　　イナツプル汁を加へ、ヴアニラを入れ、最後によく泡立て〻置いた白味を靜
　　かに折込み、油を塗つた二枚の天パンに流して中火の天火で三十五分間燒き
　　ます。燒けたならば天パンより取出して冷し、二枚の間にパイナツプルの微
　　塵切りを砂糖と少量のレモン汁とで煮詰めたものをはさみ、上に砂糖飾りを
　　つけます。

No. 210   **APRICOT CAKE**

¼ Cup butter   1½ Cups cake flour

¼ Cup sugar   1 Teaspoon baking powder

3 Eggs

Work the butter into the flour, with which the sugar and baking powder have been sifted. Beat eggs and add to the mixture. Bake slowly and let cool. Spread the following apricot mixture over the top of the baked cooled cake and bake for 15 minutes longer.

1 Pound cooked chopped   ½ Cup sugar

Apricots   ½ Cup chopped almonds

5 Egg whites   1 Lemon rind grated

Soak the apricots over night and then cook over slow fire in the same water in which they have been standing, sweeten to taste just before removing from the fire. Chop the apricots and spread over the top of the cooled cake, then top with a meringue made by beating the whites of eggs and adding the sugar, chopped almonds and lemon rind. Spread over apricots and bake in a medium oven for 15 minutes.

No. 211   **APPLE SAUCE CAKE**

½ Cup butter   *½ Teaspoon cloves

1½ Cup sugar   *½ Teaspoon nutmeg

1 Egg   ¼ Teaspoon salt

1 Cup raisins   1 Teaspoon vanilla

1 Cup apple sauce,   2 Cups flour

  unsweetened   1 Teaspoon soda

1 Teaspoon cinnamon   1 Tablespoon hot water

Cream the fat and sugar. Add rest of ingredients and beat two minutes. Pour into greased loaf pan and bake 40 minutes in moderately slow oven. Cool and cover with following caramel frosting.

* Ingredients not absolutely necessary.

No. 21o　　杏子のケーキ

ケーキ

材料	バター又は代用品	カップ四分ノ一	砂糖	カップ四分ノ一
	玉子	三個	メリケン粉	カップ一杯半
	ベーキング・パウダ ー	小匙一杯		

作り方——メリケン粉、ベーキング・パウダー及び砂糖を篩ひ、バターを切り込み、玉子を泡立てゝ加へ、油を塗つた天パンに流し弱火の天火で三十分程焼いて天パンより取出して冷します。上に次のものをのせます。

ケーキ飾り

材料	乾杏子	百二十匁	玉子の白味	五個
	砂糖	カツプ半杯	アーモンド又は胡桃	
	レモン皮の卸したも の一個分		微塵切り	カツプ半杯

作り方——杏子は一晩かぶる程の水に漬けて置き、のち、弱火で杏子が柔くなり水が殆んど無くなる迄ゆで、砂糖を適當に入れます。此の樣にして茹でた杏子を細く切り、焼いて冷したケーキの上に塗り、別に白味を充分に泡立て、砂糖と胡桃とレモン皮の卸したものを折込んで杏子の上に盛り、弱火の天火の中で十五分間燒き ます。

No. 211　　　林檎のソースのケーキ

材料	バター又は代用品	カツプ半分	砂糖	カツプ一杯半
	玉子	一個	乾葡萄	カツプ一杯
	林檎のソース(甘く ないもの)	カツプ一杯	粉ニツケ	小匙一杯
	ナツメグ	小匙半杯	クローブ	小匙半杯
	ヴアニラ	小匙一杯	鹽	小匙四分ノ一
	ソーダ	小匙一杯	上等メリケン粉	カツプ二杯
			熱湯	大匙一杯

作り方——バターを煉り砂糖を少しづゝ加へて煉り續け、林檎のソースと泡立てた玉子を加へ、メリケン粉、ニツケ、クローブ、ナツメグ及び鹽を篩つたものと湯に溶したソーダを加へ、最後にヴアニラを入れ、細長いパン用の天パンに油を塗つた中に流し、中火の天火で四十分間燒き、天パンより取出して冷します。此の儘又は上と周圍に次のキラヤメル・アイスイングを掛けて召上るのです。

No. 212   CARAMEL NUT ICING

2 Egg whites   1 Teaspoon vanilla
2½ Cups brown sugar   *1 Cup chopped walnuts
5 Tablespoon water

Place the egg whites, sugar and water in a double boiler. Beat well with rotary egg beater until thoroughly blended. Place over rapidly boiling water, beating constantly, for seven minutes, or until the mixture will stand in peaks . Add the vanilla after removing from fire and beat until thick enough to spread. Sprinkle nuts over frosting.

* Ingredient not absolutely necessary.

No. 213   APPLE CHEESE CAKE

3 Cups cake flour   1 Egg, beaten
2 Teaspoons baking powder   3 Apples
½ Teaspoon salt   ½ Cup sugar
4 Tablespoons shortening   1 Teaspoon cinnamon
½ Cup grated cheese   Bits of butter
2/3 Cup milk

Sift the flour with the baking powder and salt. Work in the shortening as in making biscuits, then add the cheese and mix lightly. Add the milk to the egg and stir into the dry ingredients only until mixed but not smooth. Place in a deep layer cake pan which has been oiled and spread evenly. Pare and skin the apples and arrange over the cake with the slices overlapping each other. Sprinkle with the sugar and cinnamon, dot with butter and bake in a hot oven, 450 degrees F., for 10 minutes, then reduce heat to 400 degrees F. and bake until apples are tender. Serve warm, cut into slices and eat with butter or serve with top milk as a pudding. Serves 10 to 12.

No. 214   MERINGUES GLACEES (KISSES)

1 Egg white   ⅛ Teaspoon vanilla
3 Tablespoons fine granu-   1 Tablespoon sugar
   lated sugar

Beat the egg white until stiff, add gradually the first sugar and beat until mixture will hold its shape. Add vanilla and fold in the sugar. Shape with pastry bag and tube on wet board covered with paper. Bake 50 minutes in slow oven or at 250 degrees F.

No. 212　　　キヤラメル・アイスイング

材料　玉子の白味　　　　二個　　　　黒砂糖（花見砂糖）カツプ二杯半
　　　冷水　　　　　　　大匙五杯　　　ヴアニラ　　　　　小匙一杯
　　　胡桃の微塵切り　　カツプ一杯

作り方——白味、砂糖、冷水を二重鍋の上に入れ、全部混ざる迄玉子攪拌器で混
　　ぜ、のち、沸騰して居る湯の上にのせ、七分間絶えず泡立てながら煮ます。
　　火より下してヴアニラを加へ、ケーキの上に塗るによい程度に固まる迄泡立
　　て續け、ケーキに塗り、上に好みにより微塵切りの胡桃を振掛けます。

No. 213　　　林檎とチーズのケーキ

材料　上等メリケン粉　　カツプ三杯　　　ベーキング・パウダ
　　　鹽　　　　　　　　小匙半杯　　　　—　　　　　　　小匙二杯
　　　バター又は代用品　大匙四杯　　　　チーズ卸したもの　カツプ半杯
　　　ミルク　　　　　　カツプ三分ノ二　玉子泡立てたもの　一個
　　　林檎　　　　　　　三個　　　　　　砂糖　　　　　　　カツプ半杯
　　　粉ニツケ　　　　　小匙一杯　　　　バター　　　　　　少量

作り方——メリケン粉とベーキング・パウダーと鹽を篩込み、バターを切り込み、
　　チーズを加へて輕く混ぜます。泡立てた玉子とミルクを併せ、前の材料に手
　　早く加へて混ぜ（此の時には全部がなめらかにならないでもよいので、少し
　　ぶつぶつの固りが有る程度でよい）　油を塗つた天パンに流し、上を平にし
　　て、林檎を薄く切つたものを少し重ね合せながら表面全部に並べ、砂糖とニ
　　ツケを振掛けます。此の上にバターを小さくちぎつて點々と置きます。強火
　　の天火で十分燒いて後、火力を少し減じて上の林檎が柔くなる迄燒きますこ
　　れは溫いうちにその儘バターを添えてか又はデザーとして、ミルクを掛けて
　　召し上るのです。

No. 214　　　キツセズ（メラング・ケーキ）

材料　玉子の白味　　　　一個　　　　グラニユ糖　　　大匙四杯
　　　ヴアニラ　　　　　小匙八分ノ一

作り方——玉子の白味をよく泡立て、之に砂糖大匙三杯を一杯位づつ静かに加へ
　　ヴアニラを入れて、殘りの砂糖を折込みます。別に薄い板を水でぬらした上
　　に紙を敷きその上に前の玉子の白味等をいろいろの形にしぼり出して、弱火
　　の天火で五十分間程燒きます。此のキツセズを大匙一杯位の大きさにして燒
　　き、二個の間にアイスクリームをはさんでも面白いデザートが出來ます。

No. 215   **CRUMB CAKE**

2 Cups flour	1 Teaspoon baking powder
¾ Cup shortening	¼ Teaspoon salt
1 Cup sugar	1 Cup evaporated milk
1 Teaspoon soda	1 Egg
½ Teaspoon cloves	1 Cup nuts
1 Teaspoon cinnamon	

Cut the shortening into the flour and sugar until the mixture is about the consistency of bread crumbs. Reserve three quarters cupful of these crumbs. To the remaining crumbs add the soda, cloves, cinnamon, baking powder, and salt, and mix thoroughly. Stir in the cream and the well-beaten egg, add the chopped nuts, and spread in a greased baking pan eight inches square. Sprinkle with the reserved crumbs and bake in a moderate oven of 350 degrees F. When done cut in square and serve warm.

No. 216   **COCOANUT MACAROONS**

2 Egg whites	¼ Teaspoon salt
¾ Cup sugar or	½ Teaspoon vanilla
1 Cup brown sugar	1 Cup finely shredded cocoanut

When the egg whites are partially beaten begin adding the sugar in two tablespoonful portions, beating after each addition. Just before the last portion, add salt and vanilla. Fold in the cocoanut. Take up heaping teaspoonfuls and push onto a well-greased baking sheet. Bake in a slow oven of 275 degrees F. until dry on the surface, or from 20 to 30 minutes. To test, lift one from the pan and let it stand for a minute. If it holds its shape, take from oven and remove macaroons while still warm.

No. 215　　　　パ　ン　粉　ケ　ー　キ

材料	メリケン粉	カツプ二杯	バター	カツプ四分ノ三
	砂糖	カツプ一杯	ソーダ	小匙一杯
	クローブ粉	小匙半杯	ニツケ	小匙一杯
	ベーキング・パウダ		鹽	小匙四分ノ一
	一	小匙一杯	クリーム	カツプ一杯
	玉子	一個	胡桃細く切つたもの	カツプ一杯

作り方——メリケン粉と砂糖を混ぜ、この中にバターを切り込んで手でもみ、パン粉の様にざらざらにします。こはをカツプに四分ノ三杯別にして、殘りのメリケン粉等に、ソーダ、クローブ、ニツケ、ベーキング・パウダー及び鹽を加へ、よく混ぜてクリームとよく混ぜた玉子を加へ、胡椒を入れて油を塗つた天パンに敷き、別にして置いたメリケン粉等を上に掛振け、中火の天火で中迄燒ける迄燒き、四角に切り溫い間に召上るのです。

No. 216　　　　コ　コ　ナ　ツ　ツ・マ　カ　ロ　ン

材料	玉子の白味	二個	白砂糖カツプ四分ノ三（又は黒砂
	鹽	小匙四分ノ一	糖カツプ一杯）
	ヴアニヲ	小匙半杯	ココナツツ　　カツプ一杯

作り方——玉子の白味を泡立てて、少し形を保つ程度に泡立つたらば砂糖を大匙二杯づつ加へながら更に泡立てつづけます。最後の砂糖を加へる前に鹽とヴアニラを加へるのです。此の後、ココナツツを靜かに折込み、油を塗つた天パンに小匙山盛一杯づつ盛り、弱火の天火で二十分乃至三十分間燒きます。燒き上つたのを知るには一個を天火より取出し、二、三分間置いて冷してみて固つて形を保てば燒き上つたのです。天火より取出し、溫い間に天パンから取つて冷します。

No. 217   **CORNFLAKE KISSES**

1 Egg White	½ Cup shredded coconut or
½ Cup sugar	Chopped nuts
¼ Teaspoon salt	1 Cup cornflakes
½ Teaspoon vanilla	

Follow directions given for coconut macaroons.

No. 217　　　　コーンフレークス・キッセズ

材料　玉子の白味　　　　　一個　　　　　　砂糖　　　　　　カツプ半杯
　　　鹽　　　　　　　　小匙四分ノ一　　　ヴアニラ　　　　小匙半杯
　　　ココナツツ又は胡桃　カツプ半杯　　　コーンフレークス　カツプ一杯

作り方——玉子の白味を泡立てて少し形が附く樣になつた時、砂糖を大匙二杯づ
　つ加へて泡立てつゞけ、最後の砂糖を加へる前に鹽とヴアニラを入れます。
　後、ココナツツとコーンフレークスを靜に加へ、油を塗つた天パンに小匙山
　盛り一杯づつ落して中火の天火で二、三十分間燒きます。天火より一個取出
　してみて數分間冷して後、形を保つ樣でしたらば燒けたのです。天火より出
　して天パンから取つて冷します。

No. 218   **PLAIN DROPPED COOKIES**

½ Cup shortening	½ Teaspoon vanilla
1 Cup sugar	2 Cups flour
1 Egg	2 Teaspoons baking powder
4 Tablespoons milk	¼ Teaspoon salt

Let the shortening stand in a warm room for a while then cream and add sugar, egg, milk and vanilla. Mix thoroughly. Sift together the flour, baking powder and salt. Stir the flour into the other mixture and drop by teaspoonfuls on a well greased sheet. Bake on the top shelf in a moderate oven of 375 degrees F., until firm to the touch and delicately brown in color or for eight to 12 minutes. Remove the cookies from the pan while hot with a spatula. Place on a wire rack to cool. Do not heap warm cookies on top of one another. Store cooled cookies in a tightly covered tin box or stone crock.

No. 219   **SPICE COOKIES**

Sift half a teaspoonful of cinnamon, mace, or nutmeg—or a quarter of a teaspoonful of cinnamon and a quarter of a teaspoonful of either mace or nutmeg—with the flour in the recipe for plain dropped cookies. Omit the flavoring extract.

No. 220   **ORANGE COOKIES**

Substitute orange juice for milk in the recipe for plain dropped cookies. In place of the flavoring use the grated rind of half an orange.

No. 221   **COCOA AND NUT DROPS**

2 Eggs	¼ Teaspoon salt
2/3 Cup sugar	1 Teaspoon vanilla
½ Cup cocoa	1 Cup flour, sifted
½ Cup chopped walnut meats	1½ Teaspoons baking powder

Beat eggs well and add other ingredients in order given. Mix thoroughly. Drop by teaspoon on buttered tin. Bake in moderate oven for 10 minutes. Oven temperature 350 degrees F.

No. 218　　標準ドロップ(匙より落した)ビスケット

材料　バター又は代用品　　カツプ半杯　　砂糖　　　　　　カツプ一杯
　　　玉子　　　　　　　　一個　　　　　ミルク　　　　　大匙四杯
　　　ヴアニラ　　　　　　小匙半杯　　　メリケン粉　　　カツプ二杯
　　　ベーキング・パウダ　　　　　　　　鹽　　　　　　　小匙四分ノ一
　　　ー　　　　　　　　　小匙二杯

作り方——バターを煉り、砂糖を加へて更に煉り續け、玉子一個をミルクと混ぜ
　　たものとヴアニラを加へ、全部をよく混ぜます。次にメリケン粉、鹽及びベ
　　ーキング・パウダーを篩ひ、前の材料に加へます。天パンによく油を塗つた
　　上に前の材料を小匙に一杯づつ一寸以上間を置いて落し、中央の天火の上の
　　段で八分乃至十二分間燒き、溫い間に網の上に取り出して冷し、罐に入れて
　　置きます。此の分量で三十個程出來ます。

No. 219　　香料入リドロツプ・ビスケツト

作り方——標準のドロツプ・ビスケツトのヴアニラを省き、メリケン粉を篩ふ時
　　に小匙半杯のニツケ又はナツメグ或はメースを加へるか或は小匙四分ノ一づ
　　つのニツケとメース又はナツメグを加へます。

No. 22o　　オレンヂ・ドロツプ・ビスケツト

作り方——標準のドロツプ・ビスケツトのミルクの代りにオレンヂ汁を用ひ、ヴ
　　アニラの代りに卸したオレンヂ皮を何れも同分量代用するのです。

No. 221　　ココア・ドロツプ・ビスケツト

材料　玉子　　　　　　　二個　　　　　砂糖　　　　　カツプ三分ノ二
　　　ココア　　　　　　カツプ半杯　　胡桃の微塵切り　カツプ半杯
　　　鹽　　　　　　　　小匙四分ノ一　ヴアニラ　　　　小匙一杯
　　　上等メリケン粉　　カツプ一杯　　ベーキング・パウダ
　　　　　　　　　　　　　　　　　　　ー　　　　　　　小匙一杯半

作り方——玉子を充分泡立て、他の材料と並べた順に加へ、油を塗つた天パンに
　　小匙二杯位づつ落し、中火の天火で十分程燒きます。

No. 222   **PEANUT COOKIES**

½ Cup shortening

1½ Cups sugar

4 Tablespoons milk

1 Teaspoon vanilla

¼ Teaspoon salt

2 Eggs

1 Cup chopped roasted peanuts

3½ Cups flour

2 Teaspoons baking powder

Cream shortening and sugar. Add milk, vanilla, salt and eggs. Beat two minutes. Add rest of ingredients. Drop portions of dough three inches apart on greased baking sheets. Flatten cookes with knife. Bake 12 minutes in moderate oven.

No. 223   APRICOT AND PEANUT DROP COOKIES

1 Cup dried apricots

1 Cup peanuts

2 Tablespoons lemon juice

1½ Cups condensed milk

Wash the dried apricoats and put through the meat chopper and mix with condensed milk. Chop peanuts fine and add to the first mixture together with lemon juice. Drop by teaspoonfuls on greased baking sheet and bake in a moderate oven for 20 minutes.

No. 224   ROLLED SUGAR COOKIES

½ Cup shortening

¾ Cup sugar

1 Egg

1 Tablespoon milk

1 Teaspoon vanilla

1 Teaspoon baking powder

3 Cups flour

Let the shortening stand in a warm room until soft, then cream and add sugar, egg, milk and vanilla and mix thoroughly. Sift one cup of flour with the baking powder and add to the first mixture, then add the remaining flour until the dough is stiff enough to roll after chilling. The quantity of flour differs according to the type of flour used. Chill dough, roll very thin, cut into rounds with a cookie cutter, lift the rounds onto a greased baking sheet with a spatula. Sprinkle with sugar, bake in a hot even of 425 degrees F. until delicately browned or for about five minutes.

No. 222　　　ピーナツツ・ビスケット

材料	バター又は代用品	カツプ半杯	砂糖	カツプ一杯半
	ミルク	大匙四杯	ヴアニラ	小匙一杯
	鹽	小匙四分ノ一	玉子	二個
	ピーナツツ（つぶしたもの）	カツプ一杯	上等メリケン粉	カツプ三杯半
			ベーキング・パウダー	小匙二杯

作り方——バターを煉り、砂糖を少量づつ加へて煉り續け、之にミルク、ヴアニラ、鹽及び玉子を加へます。之を二分間よく攪拌ぜ、他の材料を加へて、油を塗つた天パンに大匙一杯づつ間をあけて並べ、表面をナイフで平にして中火の天火で十二分燒きます。

No. 223　　　杏子・ピーナツツ・ビスケット

材料	乾杏子	カツプ一杯	落花生	カツプ一杯
	レモン汁	大匙二杯	コンデンス・ミルク	カツプ一匙半

作り方——乾杏子はよく洗つて挽肉器で挽き、コンデンス・ミルクとよく混合せます。落花生は微塵切りにして、前のコンデンス・ミルクに入れ、レモン汁を加へます。これを油を塗つた天パンに小匙一杯づつ落し、中火の天火で二十分間燒きます。燒けたらば直に天パンより取り出してさまします。

No. 224　　　ロールド（棒で延した）ビスケット

材料	バター又は代用品	カツプ半杯	砂糖	カツプ四分ノ三
	玉子	一個	ミルク	大匙一杯
	ヴアニラ	小匙一杯	ベーキング・パウダー	小匙一杯
	メリケン粉	カツプ三杯位		

作り方——バターを煉り砂糖を加へて更に煉り續け、一寸泡立てた玉子にミルクとヴアニラを加へたものを入れて充分混ぜます。メリケン粉をカツプ二杯とベーキング・パウダーを篩つてバター等に加へ、殘りのカツプ二杯のメリケン粉を別に篩つて出來るだけばらばらにならぬ樣にして加へ、一塊にして冷して後、麵棒でメリケン粉を篩つた板の上で薄く延し、ビスケット切りで丸形に切り、油を塗つた天パンに並べ、上に砂糖を少量振掛け強火の天火で五分間燒きます。

No. 225   **CINNAMON ROLLED COOKIES**

Follow the recipe for rolled sugar cookies with the following changes. When the cookies are on the baking sheet, sprinkle them with a mixture of sugar and cinnamon (one teaspoon cinnamon to three tablespoons granulated sugar) and bake as rolled sugar cookies.

No. 226   **ROLLED MOLASSES COOKIES**

1 Cup molasses	½ Teaspoon salt
½ Cup shortening	1½ Teaspoons soda
3¼ Cups flour	1 Tablespoon ginger

Heat the molasses to the boiling point, put the shortening into a large mixing bowl and pour the molasses over the shortening. Sift the flour salt, soda and ginger together. Add dry ingredients to the molasses mixture and mix thoroughly. Chill and roll very thin, then cut into rounds with a cookie cutter. With a spatula, lift the cookies onto a greased baking sheet. Bake on the top shelf in a hot oven of 425 degrees F. for about five minutes.

No. 227   **HARD-BOILED EGG COOKIES**

1 Cup butter t	Rind of one lemon
1 Cup sugar	2½ Cups flour
2 Raw egg yolks	6 Hard-boiled egg yolks

Cream butter and add sugar gradually then the beaten raw egg yolks. Add the flour and the lemon rind and make a stiff dough. The hard-boiled egg yolks are put through a ricer and added to the dough. The addition of the hard-boiled eggs makes these keep a long time.

No. 225   シナモン・ロールド・ビスケツト

作り方——標準ロールド・ビスケツトを作り、天パンに並べたらば上に砂糖大匙三杯にニツケ大匙一杯を併せたものを振掛けて焼くのです。

No· 226   モラセズ（黒蜜）ビスケツト

材料	モラセズ(黒蜜)	カツプ一杯	バター又は代用品	カツプ半杯
	メリケン粉	カツプ三杯四分一	鹽	小匙半杯
	ソーダ	小匙一杯半	生姜粉	大匙一杯

作り方——モラセズを沸騰點迄熱して、バターの上に流し、バターを溶し、メリケン粉、ソーダ、鹽及び生姜を篩つたものを加へて混ぜ、冷して後、メリケン粉を篩つた板の上で極く薄く延し、丸形に切ります。それを油を塗つた天パンに入れ、強火の天火で五分間燒きます。

No. 227   茹玉子のビスケツト

材料	バター又は代用品	カツプ一杯	砂糖	カツプ一杯
	玉子の黄味	二個	レモンの皮の卸した	
	上等メリケン粉	カツプ二杯半	もの	一個分
	茹玉子の黄味	六個		

作り方——バターを煉り、砂糖を少しづつ加へながら煉り續け、一寸混ぜた黄味と卸したレモン皮を加へ、更にメリケン粉を篩つて加へます。之に黄味を茹で裏漉にしたものを入れ、板の上で薄く延し、丸形に切つて強火の天火で十二分程燒きます。此のビスケツトは作つてから一週間以上置ても美味しさが變りません。

No. 228   COCOANUT AND WALNUT SQUARES

½ Cup butter

½ Cup brown sugar

1 Cup cake flour

1 Cup brown sugar

2 Eggs

1 Teaspoon vanilla

½ Teaspoon salt

½ Teaspoon baking powder

2 Tablespoons cake flour

1½ Cups cocoanut

1 Cup nut meat

Mix the one cup of flour and half cup of brown sugar and cut in half cup of butter and mix well until it is of a crumbly mass . Pat into a shallow pan and bake for 10 minutes in a moderate oven at 375 degrees F. Next mix one cup brown sugar, salt, baking powder, two tablespoons flour and sift. Add eggs beaten and the flavoring together with the nuts. Pour this mixture over the baked first mixture and bake for 20 minutes in a moderate oven, cool and cut into squares or bars.

No. 229   BUTTER SCOTCH BARS

½ Cup flour

½ Teaspoon salt

1 Teaspoon baking powder

¼ Cup shortening

1 Cup brown sugar

1 Egg

1 Teaspoon vanilla

½ Cup nuts, chopped

Sift the flour, salt and baking powder together. Melt the butter in a saucepan large enough to serve as a mixing bowl. Remove from the stove, stir in the brown sugar the unbeaten egg, the vanilla and the nuts. Stir in the dry ingredients. Spread the mixture in a shallow pan which has been greased and lined on the bottom with a piece of heavy waxed paper, the layer of batter should not be more than three quarters of an inch thick. Bake in a moderate oven of 350 degrees F. for about 30 minutes, or until the surface will spring back when pressed lightly with the forefinger. Remove from the pan to a wire rack, peel off the waxed paper, when cool cut in strips about four inches by one inch, or else in squares.

No. 228　　　ココナツツと胡桃のビスケツト

材料	バター又は代用品	カツプ半杯	黒砂糖（花見砂糖）	カツプ半杯
	上等メリケン粉	カツプ一杯	玉子	二個
	黒砂糖（花見砂糖）	カツプ一杯	鹽	小匙半杯
	ヴアニラ	小匙半杯	ベーキング・パウダ	
	上等メリケン粉	大匙二杯	―	小匙半杯
	ココナツツ	カツプ一杯半	胡桃微塵切り	カツプ一杯

作り方――初めに黒砂糖とメリケン粉をバタの中に煉り込み、天パンの底に平に塗附け、中火の天火で十分間燒きます。別に殘りのメリケン粉と鹽、ベーキング・パウダー及び黒砂糖を篩ひ、之に攪拌した玉子、胡桃及びココナツツを加へ、前の燒いた材料の上に流し込み、中火の天火で二十分間燒き冷して後、細長く切ります。

No. 229　　　バター・スコツチ・バー・ビスケツト

材料	メリケン粉	カツプ半杯	鹽	小匙半杯
	ベーキング・パウダ		バター又は代	
	―	小匙一杯	用品	カツプ四分ノ一
	黒砂糖（花見砂糖）	カツプ一杯	玉子	一個
	ヴアニラ	小匙一杯	胡桃細く切つたもの	カツプ半杯

作り方――バターを溶して火より下し、砂糖を加へて混ぜ、攪拌しない儘の玉子とヴアニラと胡桃を加へます。次にメリケン粉、鹽及びベーキング・パウダーを篩ひ、前のバター等に併せます。別に淺い天パンに油を塗り、パラフイン紙を底に敷いて、その上に材料を五分の厚さに流し、中火の天火で三十分程燒きます。この時表面に指でふれてみて彈性があれば燒けたのです。天パンより取出し、網の上にのせ、パラフイン紙を取つて冷します。さめましたらば長さ三寸、幅八分位の細長い形に切ります。美味しいビスケツトです。

No. 230   DATE SQUARES

3 Cups flour	6 Tablespoons shortening
6 Teaspoons baking powder	½ Cup chopped dates
½ Teaspoon salt	¼ Cup milk

Mix flour, baking powder and salt. Cut in shortening with knife. Mixing with knife, add dates and milk. When soft dough forms, pat it out on floured board until one half inch thick. Cut in one and a half inch squares bake on greased baking pan 12 minutes in moderate oven. Serve warm with butter.

No. 231 BUTTERSCOTCH ICEBOX COOKIES

3½ Cups flour	2 Eggs, unbeaten
3 Teaspoons baking powder	2 Teaspoons vanilla
1 Cup shortening	1 Cup nuts, chopped
2 Cups brown sugar	

Sift the flour and baking powder. Cream the shortening and gradually stir in the sugar, eggs and vanilla. Mix well and stir in the flour mixture together with the nuts. This mixture will be a stiff dough. With floured hands shape the dough into rolls about two inches in diameter, wrap the rolls in heavy waxed paper, twisting the ends. The cylinders will settle to an elliptical shape on standing. Place the molded dough in an efficient refrigerator for at least several hours until it is very hard. Remove the chilled dough from its wrappings, place on a molding board covered with heavy waxed paper, cut into slices about one eighth inch thick. Place on a baking sheet, greasing is not necessary because of the large quantity of shortening in the dough. Bake on the top shelf in a moderate oven of 375 degrees F. for 10 to 15 minutes.

No. 232   TWO-OF-A-KIND COOKIES

Two-of-a-Kind Cookies. Remove about half of the butterscotch-cookie dough to another bowl. To the first half, add half a cupful of chopped nut meats; to the other half add one ounce (one square) of chocolate, melted. Shape and chill each half separately. The two kinds of cookies may or may not be baked at the same time.

No. 23o　　　デート・ビスケット

材料　メリケン粉　　　　　カップ三杯　　　　ベーキング・パウダ
　　　鹽　　　　　　　　　小匙半杯　　　　　—　　　　　　小匙六杯
　　　バター又は代用品　　大匙六杯　　　　デーツ細く切つた
　　　ミルク　　　　　　　カップ四分一位　　もの　　　　　カップ半杯

作り方——メリケン粉、ベーキング・パウダー及び鹽を篩ひ、バターを切り込み
デーツとミルクを加へて混ぜ、メリケン粉を少量篩つた板の上で五分の厚さ
に延し、一寸四方の角に切り、油を塗つた天パンに間を置いて並べ、中火の
天火で十二分燒きます。バターを添へ溫い間にパン代用として召し上るも
の。

No. 131　　　冷藏庫バター・スコツチ・ビスケット

材料　メリケン粉　　　　　カップ三杯半　　　ベーキング・パウダ
　　　バター　　　　　　　カツプ一杯　　　　—　　　　　　小匙三杯
　　　黑砂糖　　　　　　　カツプ二杯　　　　玉子　　　　　二個
　　　ヴアニラ　　　　　　小匙二杯　　　　胡桃細く切つたもの　カツプ一杯

作り方——メリケン粉とベーキング・パウダーを篩ひ、別にバターを煉り、砂糖
を少しづつ加へて更に煉り續け、玉子をその儘一個づつ加へて混ぜ、ヴアニ
ラを入れて後、メリケン粉等を胡桃と共に加へて混ぜ合せます。手にメリケ
ン粉をつけ前の混ぜ合せた材料と大形のソーセージの樣に數本の細長い形に
丸め、パラフイン紙に包んで冷藏庫に數時間入れて冷し、よく固りましたら
ば取り出してパラフイン紙を取り、よく切れるナイフで薄く切り、天パンに
（油を塗る必要はありません）並べて中火の天火で十分乃至十五分間燒きま
す。此のビスケットは成るべく燒きたてのものが美味しいのですが、パラフ
イン紙に包んだ儘、冷藏庫に入れて置けば一週間位は大丈夫ですから入用の
際に時々取出して數枚切つて燒くとよいのです。此の分量で五、六十枚のビ
スケツトが出來ます。

No. 232　　　二　色　ビ　ス　ケ　ツ　ト

作り方——前述のバタースコツチ・ビスケツトを作る時、材料を半分宛に分けて
その一方はカツプ半杯の微塵切りの胡桃を加へそのまゝ、他の半分の材料に
は料理用ビター・チョコレート一角を溶したものを加へるのです。冷藏庫に
入れる方法や燒方は前の通りですが、この樣にすると同一の材料で二種類の
異つたビスケツトが出來ます。

No. 233   **SHIOSEMBEI WITH MERINGUE**

1 Cup sugar	½ Teaspoon vanilla
⅛ Teaspoon cream of tartar	1 Cup chopped raisins or walnuts
½ Cup water	30 Japanese shiosembei
1 Egg white	

Dissolve the sugar and cream of tartar in the water and bring to boil, then simmer until a little amount dropped in cold water reaches the soft ball stage. Beat the white of egg and continue beating while pouring the cooked mixture over it. Continue beating until the mixture holds its shape, then add vanilla and chopped nuts or raisins and place one teaspoonful of mixture on each shiosembei. Bake in a slow oven for 25 minutes until the surface is dry.

No. 233　　鹽 煎 餅 メ ラ ン グ

材料　砂糖　　　　　　カツプ一杯　　　クリーム・オブ・ター
　　　水　　　　　　　カツプ半杯　　　　ター　　　　小匙八分ノ一
　　　玉子の白味　　　一個　　　　　　ヴアニラ　　　　小匙半杯
　　　胡桃又は乾葡萄の　　　　　　　　鹽煎餅直經一寸位の
　　　微塵切り　　　　カツプ一杯　　　もの　　　　　　三十枚位

作り方——砂糖とクリーム・オブ・ターターを水に溶して沸騰させ、その少量を水
　　に落して指先で丸められる程度のかたさになる迄煮詰めます（十分位）。　白
　　味をよく泡立て、泡立てつゞけながら熱した蜜を掛け、更に泡立てつゞけて
　　形を保つ硬さにして、胡桃又は乾葡萄とヴアニラを加へ、小匙に山盛り一杯
　　づつを鹽煎餅の上に盛り、弱火の天火で二十五分程、表面がすつかり乾く迄
　　燒きます。

No. 234　　SIMPLE HOMEMADE PIE CRUST

1½ Cups flour	½ Cup shortening
4 Tablespoons ice water (about)	½ Teaspoon salt

Sift the flour, salt and add the shortening which is well chilled and hard. Cut in thoroughly with two knives, until the mixture is like meal. Add the ice water a little at a time, adding just sufficient to moisten the ingredients together. The less water used the shorter the crust. Take out the dough on to a slightly floured board and roll out thin with a rolling pin and arrange in pie pan.

No. 235　　HOT WATER PIE CRUST

1½ Cups flour	½ Cup shortening
½ Teaspoon salt	½ Teaspoon baking powder
¼ Cup hot water	

Sift the flour, baking powder and salt . Add the shortening to the hot water and stir and melt the shortening, then add to the flour and mix thoroughly. Chill dough made in this way in the refrigerator thoroughly and use as standard pie crust.

No. 236　　OIL PIE CRUST

1½ Cups flour	1/3 Cup salad oil
1 Teaspoon baking powder	1/3 Cup cold water
½ Teaspoon salt	

Sift flour, baking powder and salt together into bowl, leaving hollow in center. Beat oil with water till it looks like French dressing and pour in center, then mix with flour to dough. Pat or roll out to square or round size of baking pan use as any other pie crust.

No. 234　　家　庭　用　パ　イ　皮

材料　メリケン粉　　　　　カツプ一杯半　　氷入り冷水　　　大匙四杯位
　　　バター又は代用品　　カツプ半杯　　　鹽　　　　　　小匙半杯

作り方——メリケン粉と鹽を篩ひ、之によく冷して固めたバターを切り込み、充
　　分混ざつたらば、ナイフ等で混ぜながら冷水を少しづゝ加へて、全部が一塊
　　に丸められる固さにします。此の時加へる冷水の分量が少い程美味しいパイ
　　皮が出来ますから成るべく少しで間に合せる様にします。メリケン粉を少量
　　振つた板の上で薄く（二分位）に延して、パイ用の天パンの底に敷きます。

No. 235　　　熱　湯　パ　イ　皮

材料　メリケン粉　　　　　カツプ一杯半　　鹽　　　　　　　小匙半杯
　　　熱湯　　　　　　　　カツプ四分ノ一　バター又は代用品　カツプ半杯
　　　ベーキング・パウダ
　　　ー　　　　　　　　　小匙半杯

作り方——メリケン粉とベーキング・パウダーと鹽を篩ひます。器に熱湯を入れ、
　　バターを加へて搔混ぜながらよく溶し、前のメリケン粉とベーキング・パウ
　　ダーと鹽を混ぜたものを一度に加へ、よく混ぜ合せて一塊にして冷藏庫の中
　　で充分冷し、前と同様に延して用ひます。

No. 236　　　オ　イ　ル・パ　イ　皮

材料　メリケン粉　　　　　カツプ一杯半　　ベーキング・パウダ
　　　鹽　　　　　　　　　小匙半杯　　　　ー　　　　　　　小匙一杯
　　　サラダ油　　　　　　カツプ三分ノ一　冷水　　　　　　カツプ三分ノ一

作り方——メリケン粉、ベーキング・パウダーと鹽を篩ひ、中央に穴をあけて、
　　その中にサラダ油と冷水をどろどろに混ざる迄玉子攪拌器で混ぜたものを加
　　へて、メリケン粉等と手早く充分混ぜ合せ、普通のパイ皮と同様に延して燒
　　きます。

No. 237   **CREAM FRUIT PIE**

Pie crust	1 2/3 Cups scalded milk
½ Cup flour	3 Eggs
½ Cup sugar	1½ Cups berries
⅛ Teaspoon salt	6 Tablespoons granulated sugar
1/3 Cup milk	

Line a pie plate with pastry having a fluted rim, prick well, and bake 10 minutes in a hot oven of 500 degrees F. Meanwhile measure and combine flour, sugar, salt and one third cup of milk. Add the scalded milk, while stirring constantly and cook in the top of a double boiler for 15 minutes. Pour this mixture gradually over three beaten egg yolks while stirring. Return to the double boiler and cook three minutes. Chill thoroughly, then pour into the baked pastry shell and top with one and a half cup sweetened strawberries or other fruit. Top with meringue made from the egg whites and six tablespoons sugar, and bake in a slow oven of 300 degrees F. for 15 minutes.

No. 238   **PRUNE CREAM PIE**

½ Pound prunes	¼ Cup butter
½ Cup sugar	¼ Cup orange marmalade or
½ Cup prune juice	candied orange peel
½ Cup molasses	4 Egg yolks
2/3 Cup grated coconut	

Cook prunes with as little water as possible, using three tablespoons molasses to sweeten. Make syrup of sugar and prune juice. Add molasses, prunes and cocoanut. Cook 10 minutes. Remove from fire and add other ingredients and fill pie. Bake 30 to 40 minutes in moderate oven, 350 degrees, F. Add meringue made with two egg whites and 4 tablespoons confectioner's sugar.

No. 237　　　クリーム・フルーツ・パイ

材料　パイ皮　　　　　　一個分　　　　メリケン粉　　　カツプ半杯
　　　砂糖　　　　　　　カツプ半杯　　鹽　　　　　　小匙八分ノ一
　　　冷ミルク　　　　　カツプ三分ノ一　沸騰させたミル
　　　玉子　　　　　　　三個　　　　　　　グ　　　　カツプ一杯三分ノ二
　　　莓又は他の果物　　カツプ一杯半　砂糖　　　　　　大匙六杯

作り方——パイ皮を薄く延し、パイ用の天パンに敷き、周圍を切取りふちを飾り
ます。別にメリケン粉と砂糖と鹽を併せ、冷ミルクと充分混ぜ、これに熱し
たミルクを加へ、二重鍋の湯の上で十五分間時々混ぜながら煮ます。玉子の
黄味を充分混ぜた上にミルク等を掛け、攪拌して、二重鍋の中で更に三分間
煮て冷します。パイ皮は底をフォークでつゝき強火の天火で十分位燒きます
此のパイ皮に前のミルク等を流し、上に果物を並べ、更にその上に泡立てた
白味に砂糖を加へたものを盛り、再び天火に入れて弱火で十五分間燒いて白
味を狐色に燒き上げます。

No. 238　　　プルンズ・クリーム・パイ

材料　乾プルンズ（西洋梅）半封度　　砂糖　　　　　　カツプ半杯
　　　プルンズの煮汁　　カツプ半杯　モラセズ（黒蜜）　カツプ半杯
　　　ココナツツ　　　　カツプ三分ノ二　バター　　　カツプ四分ノ一
　　　マーマレード（蜜柑　　　　　　　玉子の黄味　　　四個
　　　ヂヤム）　　　　　カツプ四分ノ一

作り方——プルンズに水を少し加へ、一晩漬けて置き、軟く煮てモラセズで甘く
します。別にプルンズをゆでた時の汁と砂糖を併せ十分間煮て蜜を作り、こ
れにモラセズ、プルンズ及びココナツツを入れ十分間煮ます。火より下して
他の材料を加へ、パイ皮を敷いたパン天パンに流し、三十分間強火の天火で
燒き、上に白味二個を泡立て、大匙四杯の粉砂糖を折込んだメラングを上に
盛り、再び天火に入れて上を狐色に燒きます。

No. 239   **GINGER ORANGE CREAM PIE**

18 Ginger snaps (1⅛ cups   1 Tablespoon sugar
    crumbs)   1/3 Cup butter

Roll snaps fine and mix with sugar and softened butter. Press mixtrue firmly against sides and bottom of buttered pie plate, building the sides up well, about one quarter of an inch above top of pie plate, to allow for shrinking. Bake 10 minutes in a hot oven of 425 degrees F. When cold fill with following filling:

No. 240   **ORANGE CREAM FILLING**

¾ Cup sugar   2 Cups scalded milk
1/3 Cup flour   1 Teaspoon vanilla
⅛ Teaspoon salt   2 Oranges
2 Eggs

Mix sugar, flour, and salt. Add eggs, slightly beaten and pour gradually on scalded milk. Cook 15 minutes in double boiler, stirring constantly until thickened. Cool and add flavoring. Drain orange pieces which have been cut in small pieces, arrange in pie shell, and pour custard over the top with whipped cream and garnish with crumbs.

No. 241   **STRAWBERRY AND BANANA PIE**

3 Eggs   ½ Teaspoon vanilla
4 Tablespoons sugar   1 Banana
¼ Teaspoon salt   1 Cup strawberries
2 Cups milk

Add sugar, salt, and milk to eggs which have been slightly beaten. Pour into a pie shell which has been baked to a light brown. Bake in a slow oven of 300 degrees F., about 30 minutes or until a silver knife, run into the center, comes out clean. Just before serving, arrange starwberries and sliced bananas on top of pie. Garnish with a mound of whipped cream.

No. 242   **FUDGE TOP PIE**

Make a custard pie according to the strawberry recipe. When cold, cover with the following mixture of two tablespoons evaporated milk and one cup powdered sugar together. Add one square unsweetened chocolate, melted, one teaspoon vanilla and two tablespoons butter, melted.

No. 239　　ジンジヤー・オレンヂ・クリーム・パイ

材料　ジンジヤー・ビスケ　　　　　　　　砂糖　　　　　　　　大匙一杯
　　　ツト　　　　　十八個位　　　バター　　　　　カツプ三分ノ一

作り方――ジンジヤー・ビスケツト（一名ジンジヤー・スナツプ）を棒でくづし
　てパン粉の様にして（此の時カツプ一杯半あればよい）砂糖と混ぜ、軟くし
　たバターを加へます。パイ用の天パンにバターを塗り底と側面に此のパイ皮
　を指でおさへて入まれす。これは焼く時に縮みますから周圍のパイ皮は天パ
　ンより二分位上に出して置きます。これを強火で十分間焼き、次のクリーム
　を中に盛ります。

No. 24o　　　オ　レ　ン　ヂ・ク　リ　ー　ム

材料　砂糖　　　　　　カツプ四分ノ三　メリケン粉　　カツプ三分ノ一
　　　鹽　　　　　　　小匙八分ノ一　　玉子　　　　　　二個
　　　沸騰したミルク　カツプ二杯　　　ヴアニラ　　　　小匙一杯
　　　オレンヂ　　　　二個

作り方――メリケン粉と砂糖と鹽を篩ひ、玉子を混ぜたものを加へて熱したミル
　クを混ぜながら掛け、二重鍋の湯の上で十五分間混ぜながら煮てどろどろに
　し、火より下して冷し、ヴアニラを入れます。別にオレンヂは皮をむき、薄
　い輪切りにして前のパイ皮の上に並べ、オレンヂ・クリームを掛けます。此
　の上に泡立てたクリームを盛つても結構です。

No. 241　　　苺　と　バ　ナ　ナ　の　パ　イ

材料　玉子　　　　　　三個　　　　　　砂糖　　　　　　大匙四杯
　　　鹽　　　　　　　小匙四分ノ一　　ミルク　　　　　カツプ二杯
　　　ヴアニラ　　　　小匙半杯　　　　バナナ　　　　　一本
　　　苺　　　　　　　カツプ一杯

作り方――玉子を混ぜ、砂糖と鹽とミルクを加へて更に混ぜ、焼いたパイ皮の中
　に流して弱火で三十分間程焼き、中のカスタードが軟く固りましたらば取出
　して冷します。召し上る少し前に輪切りのバナナと苺で上を飾り、泡立てた
　クリームを所々に盛つて置きます。

No. 242　　　チ　ヨ　コ　レ　ー　ト　飾　リ　パ　イ

作り方――前の苺とバナナのパイの材料でカスタードを焼き、苺とバナナの代り
　に次の材料を混合せて上に盛るのです。クリーム大匙二杯に粉砂糖カツプ一
　杯を混合せて料理用ビター・チヨコレート一角を溶したものとバター大匙二
　杯溶したもの及びヴアニラ小匙一杯を加へ、カスタード・パイの焼上つたも
　のの上に掛けます。

No. 243   **CUSTARD FRUIT PIE**

Pie crust	2 Cups milk
3 Eggs	2 Cups sweetened fruit
½ Cup sugar	1 Cup whipping cream
⅛ Teaspoon salt	½ Teaspoon vanilla

Line a pie plate with pastry having a fluted rim. Prick well and bake in a hot oven of 500 degrees F. for 10 minutes. Meanwhile beat three eggs and add sugar, salt, milk and turn into the baked pastry shell and bake in a slow oven of 350 degrees F. for 30 minutes, or until a silver knife inserted in the center of the pie comes out clean. Remove and cool the pie. Then arrange two cups of halved sweetened strawberries or other fruit over the custard and top with whipped and flavored cream.

No. 244   **BURNT SUGAR PIE**

1 Baked piecrust	1 Cup sugar
2 Cups milk	1 Tablespoon butter
½ Cup sugar	4 Tablespoons cornstarch
3 Eggs	1 Teaspoon vanilla

Scald the milk in a double boiler. Melt the half cup of sugar in a frying pan, stirring all the time. When caramelized, add to hot milk and dissolve. Beat egg yolks, add one cup of sugar and butter. Stir cornstarch which has been dissolved in a little cold water into hot milk, then egg mixture and add a pinch of salt. Stir and cook until thick and smooth. Take from fire, add vanilla and pour into baked crust. Top with meringue and sprinkle with coconut if desired.

No. 245   **DE LUXE LEMON PIE**

1 Cup coarse soft bread crumbs	1 Large lemon, juice and rind
1 Cup hot water	4 Eggs
¼ Cup butter	1/16 Teaspoon soda
¾ Cup sugar	¼ Teaspoon salt

Pour one cup boiling water on crumbs, butter, sugar and salt. Add flavoring and beaten egg yolks. Fold in beaten whites of two eggs and soda. Pour on uncooked crust bake in a hot oven of 450 degrees F., 30 minutes. Make a meringue as follows.

No. 243　　果實のカスタード・パイ

材料　パイ皮　　　　　　　　一個分　　　玉子　　　　　　　　三個
　　　砂糖　　　　　　　　カップ半杯　　鹽　　　　　　小匙八分ノ一
　　　ミルク　　　　　　　　カップ二杯　　苺　　　　　　　カップ二杯
　　　泡立てクリーム　　　カップ一杯　　ヴアニラ　　　　　小匙半杯

作り方——パイ皮を極く薄く延し、パイ用天パンの底に敷き、周圍を切り取りふ
　　ちを飾りフォークで表面を所々つついて、強火の天火で十分間燒きます。別
　　に泡立てた玉子に砂糖を加へ、鹽を入れ、熱したミルクを掛け、燒いて置い
　　たパイ皮の中に流し、弱火の天火で三十分間燒き、ナイフをさして何も附着
　　しなくなつたらばカスタードが燒けたのです。取り出して冷し、上に苺を薄
　　く切り、好みにより砂糖を加へてのせ、上に泡立てたクリームにヴアニラで
　　味をつけたものを盛ります。苺の代りに他の軟い果物を用ひても宜しい。

No. 244　　焦した砂糖のパイ

材料　ミルク　　　　　　　カップ二杯　　砂糖　　　　　　カップ半杯
　　　玉子　　　　　　　　　　三個　　　砂糖　　　　　　カップ一杯
　　　バター　　　　　　　　大匙一杯　　コンスターチ　　　大匙四杯
　　　ヴアニラ　　　　　　　小匙一杯

作り方——ミルクを二重鍋の上部に入れて、湯の上で熱します。砂糖カップ半杯
　　をフライパンに入れて溶し、混ぜながら茶色に焦して、熱したミルクに加へ
　　て溶します。玉子の黃味を充分泡立て、砂糖とバターをねり合せたものを加
　　へて混ぜ、別にコンスターチは少量の水と混ぜて後、混ぜながら熱したミル
　　クに加へ、此のミルクを前の玉子の黃味等の上に掛けます。再び以上の材料
　　を二重鍋で混ぜながら煮てどろどろにして、火より下し、ヴアニラを入れ、
　　燒いて置いたパイ皮に流し込み、上に白味を充分泡立てて砂糖大匙三杯加へ
　　たものを盛り、天火に入れて、上を狐色に色附けます。此の時好みにより白
　　味の上にココナツツを振掛けてい燒ても結構です。

No. 245　　スペシヤル・レモン・パイ

材料　生パン粉　　　　　　カップ一杯　　熱湯　　　　　　　カップ一杯
　　　バター　　　　　　カップ四分ノ一　砂糖　　　　　カップ四分ノ三位
　　　レモン　　　　　　　　大一個　　　玉子　　　　　　　　四個
　　　ソーダ　　　　　小匙十六分ノ一　　鹽　　　　　　小匙四分ノ一

作り方——パン粉に熱湯を掛け、バタ、砂糖、鹽を加へ、レモン汁とレモン皮の
　　卸したもの及び玉子の黃味を泡立てたものを入れ、白味二個分を充分泡立て
　　ゝソーダと共に入れ、パイ天パンに薄くパイ皮を敷いた上に流し込み、強火
　　の天火で三十分間燒き、次のメラングを上に盛り、再び弱火の天火で色が上
　　に附く迄燒きます。

No. 246   **MERINGUE**

2 Egg whites, slightly beaten	1/3 Cup sugar
	1/16 Teaspoon baking powder

Beat the eggs to which add the sugar gradually and then the baking powder. Pile on top of pie and bake in a slow oven of 300 degrees F. until brown.

No. 247   **RHUBARB AND PINEAPPLE PIE**

2 Cups rhubarb	3 Egg whites
2 Cups canned pineapple	6 Tablespoons sugar
2 Tablespoons flour	1 Baked Pie shell
2 Cups sugar	

Use canned crushed pineapple or cut in small pieces canned sliced pineapple. Cook the rhubarb and pineapple together until the rhubarb is soft, combine the sugar and flour and blend together, add to the fruit and cook at simmering point for five minutes with constant stirring. When cool fill a baked pie shell and cover with meringue and serve cold.

No. 248   **ENGLISH DEEP DISH APPLE PIE**

Pie crust	1 Tablespoon butter
6 to 8 tart, juicy apples	¼ Cup water
1 Cup sugar	1 Teaspoon cinnamon

Invert an egg cup in center of a baking dish about three inches deep. Line sides of dish with strips of pie paste, letting paste come a little above edge of dish, but not over bottom. Fill with apples, pared, cored and cut in slices. Add sugar, spice and water, dot with bits of butter, cover with top crust and bake until apples are thoroughly cooked. Put in a 450 degree F. oven for 10 minutes, then reduce to 400 degrees for 30 minutes. When serving slip knife under cup to allow juice to mix with apples. Serve hot with hard sauce or plain cream.

No. 246　メ　ラ　ン　グ

材料　玉子の白味　　　　二個　　　　砂糖　　　　カツプ三分ノ一
　　　ベーキング・パウダ
　　　　ー　　　　　　　小匙十六分ノ一

作り方——白味を充分泡立てゝベーキング・パウダーと砂糖を折込みます。これ
　　を前のパイの焼けた上に盛り焼くのです。

No. 247　ルバーブミパイナツプルのパイ

材料　ルバーブ（西洋蕗の　　　　　　　　パイナツプル　　　カツプ二杯
　　　　様なもの）　　　カツプ二杯　　　メリケン粉　　　　大匙二杯
　　　砂糖　　　　　　　カツプ二杯　　　玉子の白味　　　　三個
　　　砂糖　　　　　　　大匙六杯　　　　パイ皮の焼いたもの　一個分

作り方——ルバーブの茎をよく洗ひ、一寸位に切り、パイナツプルと合せてルバ
　　ーブが軟くなる迄煮てメリケン粉と砂糖を混ぜたものを加へ、攪混ぜながら
　　五分間煮ます。冷してパイ皮の中に入れ、白味を充分泡立てゝ砂糖を加へた
　　ものを上に盛り、天火の中で上を狐色に焼きます。白味の代りに泡立た生ク
　　リームを盛つてもよいのです。

No. 248　深い天パンの林檎のパイ

材料　パイ皮　　　　　一個分　　　　林檎（料理用の青い
　　　砂糖　　　　　　カツプ一杯　　　物がよい）　　　六乃至八個
　　　バター　　　　　大匙一杯　　　水　　　　　　　カツプ四分ノ一
　　　ニツケ又はナツメグ　大匙一杯

作り方——天パンは二寸五分位の深さの物を選び、これに薄く延したパイ皮を周
　　圍丈に敷きます。（底にはパイ皮を敷きません）。上の方は少し天パンのふち
　　から出る程度の廣さにパイ皮を敷くのです。次に天パンの中央に深さと同じ
　　二寸五分位の湯呑茶椀をふせて入れます。林檎は皮と芯を取つて薄く切り、
　　これをパイ皮の中に時々砂糖を振掛けながら重ねて盛り、上に砂糖の残りと
　　水及びニツケを掛け、バターを點々と置き、残りのパイ皮を薄く延して上に
　　掛け、強火の天火で十分間焼き、後、火力を減じて三十分間（林檎が軟くな
　　り、パイ皮が焼ける迄）焼きます。天パンの中の茶椀の中に汁が吸込まれま
　　すから、ナイフで茶椀のふちを一寸持上げて汁を出してから一人附けの皿に
　　パイを取り出した方が汁が多くて美味しく出來ます。クリーム又はバターと
　　砂糖を煉つたソースを掛けても結構です。

No. 249   **GRAPE PIE**

2½ Cups grape pulp and skins 2 Tablespoons flour

¾ Cup sugar   3 Tablespoons melted butter

Wash fully the ripened grapes. Separate the pulp and skins. Cook the pulp slowly until soft, then rub through a sieve. Combine the sieved pulp and skins. Combine the sugar and flour and add to the grape mixture. Add the butter. Pour into a ten inch pie pan lined with pastry, cover with a top crust or with strips of pastry, and bake in a hot oven of 425 degrees F. for about 25 minutes.

No. 250   **GRAPE SKIN PIE**

2 to 2½ Cups grape skins 1 Cup sugar
 and juice drained from 1½ Tablespoons flour
 pulp

Wash the grapes and press out the pulp. Drain the juice from the pulp onto the skins and discard the pulp. Combine the sugar and flour and mix with the skins and juice. Place in a ten-inch pie pan lined with pastry and cover with a top crust. Bake slowly in a moderate oven of 360 degrees F.

No. 251   **GRAPE MERINGUE PIE**

2 Cups grape juice   ¾ Cup flour

1 Tablespoon lemon juice 1 Tablespoon butter

1 Cup sugar   3 Egg yolks

Combine the sugar and flour, and add the butter, beaten egg yolks, and lemon juice. Add this mixture to the hot grape juice (in a double-boiler top). Allow the mixture to cook until thickened. Pour into a baked pie shell and cover with meringue made from the egg whites. Brown lightly in a moderate oven of 350 degrees F.

No. 249　　　葡　萄　の　パ　イ

材料　葡萄の實と皮　　　　カツプ二杯半　　砂糖　　　　　　カツプ四分ノ三
　　　メリケン粉　　　　　大匙二杯　　　　溶したバター　　大匙三杯

作り方——葡萄は實と皮を別々にして、實の方を鍋に汁と共に入れて、弱火で軟
　　くなる迄煮て裏漉にします。裏漉にした實と皮を併せ、別に砂糖とメリケン
　　粉を併せたものを加へ、溶したバターを入れてよく混ぜます。別にパイ用の
　　天パンの底と側面に薄く延したパイ皮を敷き、葡萄の皮を入れて、上に五分
　　幅位に切つたパイ皮を網の樣に縱横に間を置いてのせ、強火の天火で二十五
　　分間燒きます。

No. 25o　　　葡　萄　の　皮　の　パ　イ

材料　葡萄の皮と汁　　　　カツプ二杯半　　砂糖　　　　　　　カツプ一杯
　　　メリケン粉　　　　　大匙一杯半

作り方——葡萄の皮と實を別々にして實の方の汁をよくしぼつて皮に加へ、これ
　　に砂糖とメリケン粉を混合せたものを加へ、パイ用の天パンにパイ皮を薄く
　　延して敷いた中に入れ、上にパイ皮をかぶせて、中火の天火でパイ皮が充分
　　燒ける迄燒きます。

No. 251　　　葡　萄　メ　ラ　ン　グ・パ　イ

材料　葡萄汁（瓶詰グレー　　　　　　　　レモン汁　　　　大匙一杯
　　　プ・ジュース）　　　カツプ二杯　　砂糖　　　　　　カツプ一杯
　　　メリケン粉　　　　　カツプ四分ノ三　バター　　　　大匙一杯
　　　玉子　　　　　　　　三個

作り方——砂糖とメリケン粉を併せ、玉子の黃味、溶したバター、レモン汁等を
　　加へます。別に二重鍋の湯の上で葡萄汁を熱した中に前の砂糖等を入れ、混
　　ぜながら湯の上でどろどろにかたまる迄混ぜ續けます。これを燒いて置いた
　　パイ皮の中に流し、白味を泡立てたものを上に盛り、中火の天火で燒いて色
　　を附けます。

No. 252   GREEN TOMATO PIE

3 Cups green tomatoes	¼ Teaspoon powdered cinnamon
1½ Cups granulated sugar	5 Tablespoons lemon juice
¼ Teaspoon salt	2 Tablespoons butter
5 Teaspoons grated lemon rind	Pie crust

Wash and slice thinly the green tomatoes. Mix together the sugar, salt, lemon rind, and cinnamon. Arrange the tomatoes in layers in a pastry lined pan, sprinkling each layer with the sugar mixture. Then add the lemon juice and dot with bits of butter. Cover with top crust and bake 35 to 40 minutes in a hot oven.

No. 253   FRUIT TARTS

Pie Crust

2 Cups cake flour	2/3 Cup shortening
1/3 Teaspoon salt	2 Tablespoons cold water (about)

Mix flour and salt. Cut in shortening and slowly add water. The exact amount of water cannot always be determined, so add it slowly. When stiff dough forms, roll it out until one-eighth inch thick. Cut into four-inch squares. Place portions of filling on squares. Fold corners over and press edges with side of fork. Prick top of each tart. Place two inches apart on greased baking pan. Bake 25 minutes in a moderate oven.

Filling

2/3 Cup chopped raisins	1 Tablespoon lemon juice
1/3 Cup chopped nuts	½ Teaspoon cinnamon
½ Cup chopped dates	¼ Teaspoon cloves
½ Cup sugar	⅛ Teaspoon salt
1 Tablespoon flour	2/3 Cup water

Blend sugar and flour . Add rest of ingredients. Cook slowly and stir constantly until filling thickens. Beat well and cool.

No. 252　　青　ト　マ　ト　の　パ　イ

材料　青トマト薄い輪切り	カツプ三杯	グラニュ糖	カツプ一杯半
鹽	小匙四分ノ一	卸したレモン皮	小匙五杯
ニツケ粉	小匙四分ノ一	レモン汁	大匙五杯
バター	大匙二杯	パイ皮	一個分

作り方——砂糖、レモン皮の卸したもの、鹽及びニツケを併せます。別にパイ皮をパイ用の天パンの底に薄く延して敷き、その上にトマトを並べ、砂糖等を振掛け、また一段トマトを敷き、砂糖を振掛け、これを繰返して、トマトを全部パイ皮の中に入れ、上からレモン汁を流し、バターを點々と置き、殘りのパイ皮を上にのせて強火の天火で三十分乃至四十分間燒きます。

No. 253　　　フ　ル　ー　ツ・タ　ー　ト

パイ皮

材料　上等メリケン粉	カツプ二杯	鹽	小匙三分ノ一
バター又は代用品	カツプ三分ノ二	氷水	大匙二杯位

作り方——メリケン粉と鹽を篩ひ、バターを冷して充分固くしたものを切り込み最後に氷水を少量づつ加へ、延すによい固さにします。之をメリケン粉を少量振つた板の上で一分位の厚さに延し、二寸五分の四角に切り、次のソースを中央にのせ、四隅で包んで上と横をフオークでつついて穴をあけ、油を塗つた天パンに並べ、中火の天火で二十五分間燒きます。

中に入れるソース

材料　微塵切り乾葡萄	カツプ三分ノ二	微塵切り胡桃	カツプ三分ノ一
微塵切りデーツ	カツプ半杯	砂糖	カツプ半杯
メリケン粉	大匙一杯	レモン汁	大匙一杯
粉ニツケ	小匙半杯	クローブ	小匙四分ノ一
鹽	小匙八分ノ一	水	カツプ三分ノ二

作り方——メリケン粉と砂糖を混ぜ、之に他の材料を加へ、火の上で混ぜながら少し固まる迄煮て後、火より下しよく混ぜて冷して使ひます。

No. 254   **TOAST PIE**

4 Slices toast	2 Egg whites
2 Teaspoons butter	3 Tablespoons sugar
4 Teaspoons sugar	1 Teaspoon lemon juice
1 Teaspoon cinnamon	½ Teaspoon grated lemon rind
2½ Cups apple sauce	

Spread the toast with two teaspoons butter and cover with a mixture of the sugar and cinnamon, then arrange in the bottom of a pie pan. Make a sweet apple sauce and pour over the toast. Beat the egg whites until stiff, add sugar, lemon juice and grated lemon rind and pile over the apple sauce. Bake in a low oven for 15 to 20 minutes. Serve immediately.

No. 254　　トーストのパイ

材料　トースト　　　　　四枚　　　　バター　　　　　小匙二杯
　　　砂糖　　　　　　　小匙四杯　　ニツケ　　　　　小匙一杯
　　　林檎のソース　　　カツプ二杯半　玉子白味　　　　二個
　　　砂糖　　　　　　　大匙三杯　　レモン汁　　　　小匙一杯
　　　レモン皮の卸したも
　　　　の　　　　　　　小匙半杯

作り方――トーストにバターを塗り砂糖とニツケを一緒にして塗ります。之をパイ天パンの底に並べます。別に林檎の芯を取り少量の水で柔く茹でて裏漉にかけ砂糖で甘くした林檎のソースを作り、之をトーストの上に掛けます。別に白味を泡立て、砂糖、レモン汁及びレモン皮の卸したものを加へて、林檎のソースの上に盛り、弱火の天火で十五分乃至二十分燒きます。これは直に召上るのです。

No. 255   **SPECIAL BAKED PRUNES**

2 Cups stewed unsweetened   1 Cup condensed milk
    prunes

To stew prunes, soak over night in water and cook the next morning in the same water, being careful not to boil too hard. Remove seeds and combine with the condensed milk and put in baking dish which has been greased. Bake in a moderate oven for 40 minutes. This dessert is good hot or cold and can be served with the following lemon sauce which is made with the remaining condensed milk.

Lemon Sauce.

Add one fourth cup of lemon juice to two thirds tin of condensed milk and mix well.

No. 256   **LEMON DELICACY**

2 Tablespoons butter   1 Cup milk
¾ Cup sugar   2 Tablespoons flour
Juice 1 lemon   2 Eggs
Grated rind ½ lemon

Cream butter, add sugar gradually and cream well together. Add well-beaten egg yolks, flour, lemon juice, and rind. Mix thoroughly. Add milk and fold in stiffly-beaten egg whites. Pour into greased baking dish. Set in pan of hot water and bake in a slow oven of 350 degrees F. about 45 minutes. A delicate crust will form on top, and the pudding will supply its own sauce.

No. 257   **CUSTARD SOUFFLE**

2 Tablespoons fat   ¼ Cup sugar
2 Tablespoons flour   ½ Teaspoon vanilla
½ Cup milk   2 Egg whites
2 Egg yolks

Melt fat, add flour, mix well and add milk gradually. Stir until smooth and thick, add egg yolks beaten until light, sugar and vanilla or other flavoring. Cool, fold in egg whites beaten stiff, turn into baking dish which has been buttered and bake in a hot oven, 400 degrees F., 10 to 20 minutes. Leave in the oven until served.

No. 255　　　プルンズ・プデイング

　　材料　茹でたプルンズ　　　カツプ二杯　　　コンデンス・ミルク　カツプ一杯
作り方——茹でて柔くしたプルンズ(西洋梅)(これは一晩水に漬け後弱火で煮る
　　のです)をほぐし、コンデンス・ミルクと混ぜ、油を塗つた天パンに流し中
　　火の天火で四十分燒きます。これは温いまゝでも冷してもよく、次のレモン
　　・ソースを一罐の残りのコンデンス・ミルクで作ると宜しい。ソースはカツプ
　　三分ノ二のコンデンス・ミルクにカツプ四分ノ一の レモン汁を入れよく混ぜ
　　ればよろしいのです。

No. 256　　　レモン・デリカセ・プデイング

　　材料　バター　　　　　　大匙二杯　　　砂糖　　　　　　カツプ四分ノ三
　　　　　レモン汁　　　　　一個分　　　　レモン皮の卸したもの　半個分
　　　　　ミルク　　　　　　カツプ一杯　　メリケン粉　　　　　　大匙二杯
　　　　　玉子　　　　　　　二個
作り方——バターを煉り、徐々に砂糖を煉込み、よく泡立てた玉子の黄味をレモン
　　汁とメリケン粉とレモン皮とともに加へ、混合せます。次にミルクを前の材
　　料に加へて、白味を泡立てたものを折込みます。バターを塗つた天パンに流
　　して之を水に入れた天パンの中に置き、弱火の天火で四十五分程燒き上が狐
　　色に燒ければよいのです。プデイングの下の方は軟いので プデイング・ソー
　　スは必要ありません。

No. 257　　　カスタード・スフレー

　　材料　バター　　　　　　大匙二杯　　　メリケン紛　　　　　大匙二杯
　　　　　ミルク　　　　　　カツプ半杯　　玉子の黄味　　　　　二個
　　　　　砂糖　　　　　　　カツプ四分ノ一　ヴアニラ　　　　　小匙半杯
　　　　　玉子の白味　　　　二個

作り方——バターを熱して溶し、メリケン粉を加へて混ぜ、ミルクを徐々に混ぜな
　　がら加へて延し、ホワイト・ソースを作り、これに黄味をよく泡立て 砂糖と
　　ヴアニラを加へたものを混合せて冷します。玉子の白味はよく泡立て前のミ
　　ルク等が冷めたらば之に折込み、油を塗つた天パンに入れ強火の天火で十五
　　分乃至二十分間燒き、召し上る時迄火を消した天火に入れて置きます。これ
　　はフルーツ又は何かプデイング・ソースを掛けて召上るのです。

No. 258   BANANA CREME

2 Cups milk	Few grains salt
3 Egg yolks	½ Teaspoon vanilla
3 Tablespoons sugar	3 Bananas, sliced

Scald milk in double boiler. Remove from fire and pour over beaten egg yolks to which sugar has been added. Return to boiler and cook slowly, stirring constantly, until custard coats a spoon. Add salt. Cool slightly and add vanilla and bananas. Just before serving, cover top with meringue made by beating two egg whites stiff and adding four tablespoons sugar. Put in moderate oven (325 degrees F.) to brown the meringue.

Variation—Omit the bananas. Pour the plain custard into glass baking dish and chill. Before serving cover top with thin layer of apricot pulp and top with marshmallows. Place under broiler long enough to brown and melt marshmallows slightly.

No. 259   BANANA PUDDING

5 Bananas	2 Eggs
½ Lemon rind grated and juice	½ Cup sugar
	¼ Teaspoon salt
1½ Tablespoons butter	1½ Teaspoon vanilla
¾ Cup milk	½ Cup bread crumbs

Arrange a layer of sliced bananas in the bottom of a greased baking dish, dot with butter and sprinkle with lemon juice and bread crumbs. Repeat this several times and arrange all the bananas in the dish, having the bread crumbs on top. Heat milk to boiling point with the grated rind of lemon and pour over eggs which have been beaten with sugar and salt. Add vanilla to this mixture and pour over the bananas and bread crumbs and bake in a moderate oven for 20 minutes or until the custard is set.

No. 260   BAKED COFFEE CUSTARD

2 Cups milk	⅛ Teaspoon salt
2 Tablespoons ground coffee	¼ Teaspoon vanilla
¼ Cup sugar	2 or 3 eggs

Scald milk with coffee, strain through double cheesecloth and finish like baked custard.

No. 258　　バナナ・クリーム

材料	ミルク	カツプ二杯	玉子の黄味	三個
	砂糖	大匙三杯	鹽	極少量
	ヴアニラ	小匙半杯	薄切りのバナナ	三本
	玉子の白味	二個	砂糖	大匙四杯

作り方——黄味をよく泡立て、砂糖を加へて混ぜ、これに沸騰させたミルクを混ぜながら掛け、二重鍋に入れて湯の上で混ぜながら煮て、匙の表面に薄く皮がはる様になる迄煮て火より下し、鹽を加へ、少し冷してヴアニラとバナナを入れます。召上る少し前に白味をよく泡立て、砂糖を加へこれを前のミルク等の上に盛り一寸天火に入れて色を附けます。

此のプデングのバナナを取り冷してガラスの器に入れ、召し上る前に上に軟く甘く煮た乾杏子を一重その上にマシマロを並べて天火の中で手早く燒いて色附けても美味しいデザートです。

No. 259　　バナナ・プデイング

材料	バナナ	五本	レモン汁とレモン皮の卸したもの	半個分
	バター	大匙一杯半	ミルク	カツプ四分ノ三
	玉子	二個	砂糖	カツプ半杯
	鹽	小匙四分ノ一	ヴアニラ	小匙一杯半
	パン粉	カツプ半杯位		

作り方——バターを塗つた瀬戸引き天パンにバナナの輪切りを一段並べ、上にバターをちぎつて點々と置き、レモン汁を少し掛け、上全部にパン粉を振り掛けます。これを数度繰返してバナナを全部天パンに入れ、上にパン粉、バター、レモン汁をかけます。別にミルクにレモン皮の卸したものを入れて沸騰させ、混ぜて置いた玉子に砂糖と鹽を加へた上に掛けて混合せ、ヴアニラを加へ、バナナ等の上に流し、中火の天火で二十分間位燒いて固めるのです。

No. 260　　コーヒー・カスタード

材料	ミルク	カツプ二杯	コーヒー粉	大匙二杯
	砂糖	カツプ四分ノ一	鹽	小匙八分ノ一
	ヴアニラ	小匙四分ノ一	玉子	三個

作り方——ミルクにコーヒー粉を加へ、火に掛けて沸騰させ、布を通して漉します。別に玉子は白味、黄味がよく混ざる様に攪拌し、鹽、砂糖を加へて混ぜながら熱したミルクを掛け、ヴアニラを加へて、油を塗つた瀬戸引天パンに流し、別の天パンに湯を入れた中にカスタードを入れた天パンを置き、中火の天火で四十五分間燒きます。

No. 261   **BROWN BETTY**

1 Cup soft bread crumbs   1 Teaspoon cinnamon
2 Cups chopped sour apples   2 Tablespoon butter cut into
½ Cup sugar   small bits

Butter a deep dish and put a layer of chopped apples at the bottom, sprinkle with sugar, a few bits of butter and cinnamon. Cover with bread crumbs, then more apples. Proceed in this manner until the dish is full, having a layer of crumbs on top. Cover closely and bake 45 minutes having a layer of crumbs on top. Cover closely and steam or bake 45 minutes in a moderate oven, then uncover and brown quickly. Eat warm with sugar and cream or pudding sauce.

No. 262   **PEACH PUDDING SAUCE**

1 Cup canned peach syrup   2 Teaspoons sugar
2 Teaspoons butter   2 Teaspoons flour

Heat the syrup to the boiling point. Mix the flour, butter and sugar in equal quantities, add a little vanilla and cook this mixture in the hot peach juice. This is good for almost any pudding.

No. 263   **TOPSY-TURVY PUDDING**

¼ Cup fat   ¼ Cup fat
¾ Cup sugar   ½ Cup sugar
1 Egg   ¼ Cup almonds or walnuts
1½ Cups flour   ⅛ Teaspoon salt
½ Teaspoon salt   1 Cup dried apricots soaked over-
2 Teaspoons baking powder   night in
½ Teaspoon ginger   3 Cups water
½ Cup apricot juice

Blend fat with sugar and egg until fluffy. Add sifted dry ingredients alternately with one half cup apricot juice. Beat one minute.

Caramel: Melt fat slowly in heavy skillet. Add sugar. Stir until melted. Remove from heat. Put a nut meat in hollow of each apricot. Place apricots, with round sides up, on caramel. Pour in batter. Bake in moderate oven (350 degrees F.) 30 minutes. While hot, turn out upside-down on plate. Serve warm—plain or with cream.

No. 261　　　　ブラウン・ベテイ

料材　柔いパン粉　　　　　カツプ一杯　　　林檎（料理用に少し　　カツプ二杯
　　　　　　　　　　　　　　　　　　　　　　青いのがよい）
　　　砂糖　　　　　　　　カツプ半杯　　　ニツケ　　　　　　　小匙一杯
　　　バター　　　　　　　大匙二杯

作り方——林檎は皮をむき、一寸位の薄切れにして置きます。バターを塗つた天
　パンの底に林檎を一段並べ、砂糖を振掛け、バターを小さく切つたものを點
　々と置き、ニツケを振掛けます。上に一面にパン粉を敷き、此の上に再び林
　檎を並べ、バター、ニツケ、砂糖、パン粉を掛ける事をくり返します。一番
　上にパン粉を掛けます。御飯蒸しに入れて蓋をして四十五分間蒸して後、取
　出し蓋を取つて強火の天火の中で上に色を附ける様に燒きます。蒸さずに初
　めから蓋をして燒いてもよい。溫い間にクリームを掛けるか又は次のソース
　を掛けて召し上るのです。

No. 262　　　　プデイング・ソース

材料　桃罐詰の汁　　　　カツプ一杯　　　バター　　　　　　　小匙二杯
　　　砂糖　　　　　　　小匙二杯　　　　メリケン粉　　　　　小匙二杯

作り方——桃の汁カツプ一杯につき他の材料を上記の割合に量り、バターの中に
　砂糖とメリケン粉を煉り込みます。桃の汁を火に掛け、沸騰したらば煉り合せ
　たバター等を入れ、混ぜながら全部がどろどろになる迄煮ます。最後にヴア
　ニラを少量加へて香をよくします。いろいろのプデングによいソースです。

No. 263　　　　倒さまプデイング

材料　バター又は代用品　カツプ四分ノ一　砂糖　　　　　　　カツプ四分ノ三
　　　玉子　　　　　　　一個　　　　　　上等メリケン粉　　カツプ一杯半
　　　鹽　　　　　　　　小匙半杯　　　　ベーキング・
　　　粉生姜　　　　　　小匙半杯　　　　パウダー　　　　　小匙二杯
　　　乾杏子の煮汁　　　カツプ半杯　　　バター又は代用品　カツプ四分ノ一
　　　砂糖　　　　　　　カツプ半杯　　　鹽　　　　　　　　小匙八分ノ一
　　　胡桃又はアーモン　　　　　　　　　乾杏子　　　　　　カツプ一杯
　　　　ド　　　　　　　カツプ四分ノ一　冷水　　　　　　　カツプ三杯

作り方——バターをカツプ四分ノ一煉り、砂糖を加へて更に煉り續け、一寸泡立
　てた玉子を加へて混ぜます。メリケン粉、鹽、粉生姜 及びベーキング・パウ
　ダーを篩ひ、杏子の汁と交互に前の砂糖等に加へ（杏子の汁とは杏子を一晩
　水に漬けて置いた汁の事です）、 一分間程此の材料を攪混ぜます。別にケー
　キ用の鐵の天パンにカツプ四分ノ一のバターを入れて火の上で溶し、砂糖カ
　ツプ半杯を加へて溶ける迄混ぜて熱します。火より下して此の中に一晩水に
　漬けて置いた杏子の種子の所に胡桃一個を入れたものを胡桃を下にして並べ
　此の上に前のメリケン粉等を流し、中火の天火で三十分間位燒きます。これ
　は溫い間に倒さまに天パンより皿に取出します。皿にのせると杏子と胡桃が
　上になつて美しいプデイングになります。

No. 264   COTTAGE PUDDING

1 Egg

½ Cup sugar

1 Cup flour

1 Teaspoon baking

¼ Teaspoon salt

1/3 Cup milk

3 Tablespoons melted shortening

½ Teaspoon lemon extract

½ Teaspoon vanilla

Beat egg and add sugar while beating. Add flour sifted with baking powder and salt. Then add milk, melted shortening and flavorings. Mix thoroughly and bake in greased pan in a moderate oven, 350 degrees F., for 25 minutes. Serve with any pudding sauce.

No. 265   BUTTERSCOTCH SAUCE

2 Tablespoons butter

¾ Cup brown sugar

1/3 Cup evaporated milk or
cream

Melt butter in saucepan, add brown sugar and stir over the fire and boil one minute. Add cream or evaporated milk and leave low heat until melted.

No. 266   FRUIT SHORTCAKE

1½ Cups flour

½ Teaspoon salt

3½ Teaspoons tartrate or

1½ Teaspoons combination baking powder

4 Tablespoons shortening

½ to ¾ Cup milk

Put flour in sifter over mixing bowl, add salt and baking powder and sift into bowl. Add shortening, working it in with pastry mixer or knife, then add liquid, stirring with a knife. Turn onto floured board, knead for 20 seconds, shape in sheet five-eighths inch thick. Put on greased sheet and bake 12 minutes in a hot oven, 425 degrees F. Split, spread with butter and put fruit (cut in small pieces and sweetened) between and on top.

No. 264　　　　　コテーヂ・プデイング

材料　砂糖　　　　　　　　カツプ半杯　　　玉子　　　　　　　　一個
　　　メリケン粉　　　　　　カツプ一杯
　　　ベーキング・パウダー　小匙一杯　　　　鹽　　　　　　　　小匙四分ノ一
　　　ミルク　　　　　　　　カツプ三分ノ一　溶したバター　　　大匙三杯
　　　レモン・エツセンス　　小匙半杯　　　　ヴアニラ　　　　　小匙半杯

作り方——玉子を泡立て、砂糖を少しづゝ加へ、メリケン粉、鹽及びベーキング・
　パウダーを篩つたものを加へ、次にミルクと溶したバターを混込み、ヴアニ
　ラとレモン・エツセンスを入れてよく攪混ぜ、　油を塗つた天パンに流して中
　火の天火で二十五分間燒き次のソース又は他のプデイング・ソースを掛けて
　供します。

No. 265　　　　　バター・スコツチ・ソース

材料　バター　　　　　　　大匙二杯　　　　黒砂糖(花見砂糖)　カツプ四分ノ三
　　　クリーム　　　　　　　カツプ三分ノ一

作り方——バターを熱して溶し、砂糖を加へて一分間煮て、クリームを入れ弱火
　の上で砂糖がすつかり溶ける迄煮ます。

No. 266　　　　　フルーツ・シヨート・ケーキ

材料　上等メリケン粉　　　カツプ一杯半　　　鹽　　　　　　　　小匙半杯
　　　ベーキング・パ　　　　　　　　　　　　バター又は代用品　大匙四杯
　　　ウダー　　　　　　　　小匙三杯半　　　ミルク　カツプ半杯乃至四分ノ三

作り方——メリケン粉、鹽及びベーキング・パウダーを篩ひバターを　これによく
　混ざる迄切込み、ミルクを混ぜながら加へ、メリケン粉を篩つた板の上に取
　出し、十回程こねて四ツに分け丸形に固め、油を塗つた天パンに並べ、強火
　の天火で十二分程燒きます。取り出して横半分に割り、バターを塗り、豫め
　薄く切つて、砂糖を掛けて置いた果實をケーキの間と上に掛けます。その上
　に泡立てた生クリームを盛ると尚美味しくなります。

No. 267   **CRUMB TORTE**

6 Eggs, beaten well

1 Cup sugar

6 Tablespoons dry bread crumbs

1 Cup chopped dates

1 Cup chopped nut meats

1 Teaspoon baking powder

Blend all the above ingredients and bake in a one layer tin for 30 minutes. Have the oven at moderate heat, about 350 degrees F. Serve with whipped cream.

No. 268 **SCALLOPED APPLES WITH SWEET POTATOES**

3 Large sweet potatoes

2 Apples

½ Cup sugar

1/3 Cup butter

Steam the sweet potatoes and peel, then cut in a quarter of an inch slices. Wash apples and cut in slices without removing the skins. Arrange in greased baking dish first a layer of sweet potatoes and then a layer of apples alternately, sprinkling with sugar and dotting with butter each layer. When all ingredients have been arranged in layers cover and bake in a moderate oven for 30 minutes. Then remove cover and bake 30 minutes longer basting with the liquid in the dish.

No. 269   **DELICIOUS BAKED APPLES**

6 Firm apples

1 Cup sugar

1½ Cups water

6 Teaspoons sugar

Core and peel six firm apples about one third of the way down from the stem and arrange in a shallow, covered saucepan and pour over them a syrup made by boiling sugar and water together for six minutes. Cover tightly and simmer gently until the apples are nearly tender when tested with a toothpick, basting them frequently with the syrup. Then arrange the apples in buttered, individual, heat proof dishes. Fill the cavity of each with one teaspoon of sugar and sprinkle some sugar over the surface. Place under the broiler heat or in a hot oven of 400 degrees F. and cook until the sugar has melted and the apples are glazed. Baste once or twice with some of the syrup in which the apples were cooked. Serve hot or cold, with or without cream.

No. 267　　　　　パン粉のデザート

材料　よく泡立てた玉子　　六個　　　　砂糖　　　　　　　　カツプ一杯
　　　パン粉　　　　　　　大匙六杯　　デーツ細く切つたもの　カツプ一杯
　　　胡桃細く切つたもの　カツプ一杯　ベーキング・パウダー　小匙一杯
作り方──玉子を泡立てた中にベーキング・パウダー、砂糖、及びパン 粉を混合
　　せ、他の材料を次々に加へ油を塗つた一枚の天パンに入れ、中火の天火で三
　　十分間程燒きます。泡立てたクリームを掛けて召上ると宜しい。

No. 268　　　　甘藷こ林檎のスカロツプ

材料　甘藷（大）　　　　三本　　　　林檎　　　　　　　　二個
　　　砂糖　　　　　　　カツプ半杯　バター　　　　　　カツプ三分ノ一
作り方──甘藷を蒸して皮を取り、三分の厚さの輪切りにします。林檎は洗つて
　　芯を取り其儘薄輪切りにします。天パンの底に甘藷と林檎を一段づつ並べ、
　　砂糖を振掛け、バターを點々と置きます。これを繰返して全部材料を天パン
　　に入れ中火の天火で蓋をして三十分燒き、のち、蓋を取り時々汁を上に掛け
　　ながら又三十分燒きます、これはデザート用の料理です。

No. 269　　　　手早いベークト・アツプル

材料　林檎　　　　　　　六個　　　　砂糖　　　　　　　　カツプ一杯
　　　水　　　　　　　　カツプ一杯半　砂糖　　　　　　　小匙六杯
作り方──林檎六個の芯を拔き上から三分の一位の所迄皮をむき、淺い鍋に入れ
　　ます。砂糖カツプ一杯と水カツプ一杯半を六分間沸騰させてシロツプを作り
　　林檎の上に掛け鍋の蓋をして火に掛けて時々上から煮汁を掛けながら林檎が
　　軟くなる迄煮ます。林檎を取出し、天パンに入れ芯の處に小匙一杯の砂糖を
　　入れ上に餘分の砂糖を振掛け強火の天火の中で砂糖が溶ける迄燒きます。燒
　　く時天パンの中の汁を時々上から掛けます。温いまゝ又は冷してクリームを
　　掛けて召上るのです。

No. 270   **SPANISH CREAM**

2 Sheets gelatine

1½ Cups milk

2 Egg yolks

¼ Cup sugar

½ Teaspoon salt

½ Teaspoon vanilla

2 Egg whites

2 Tablespoons sugar

¼ Teaspoon vanilla

Heat the milk in the top of the double boiler, and add the gelatine which has been soaked in cold water and squeezed. Dissolve the gelatine in the hot milk, then pour this over the egg yolks which have been beaten with salt, and sugar, stirring constantly while doing so. Place in top of double boiler again and cook for two minute stirring constantly. Add vanilla. Beat white of eggs and add two tablespoons sugar and half teaspoon of vanilla. Pour the hot milk over the egg whites and pour into jelly molds and chill.

No. 271   **PRUNE DELIGHT**

2 Sheets gelatine

1½ Cup coffee

½ Cup sugar

1 Tablespoon cocoa

1 Cup prunes, chopped

¼ Cup walnut meats

½ Teaspoonful vanilla

½ Cup evaporated milk or cream, whipped

Few grains salt

Soak gelatine in cold water about five minutes drain well and dissolve in hot coffee. Add sugar and cocoa and stir until dissolved. Cool and when it begins to stiffen add vanilla, chopped prunes and nuts broken in pieces. Fold in the whipped evaporated milk or whipped cream. Turn into wet mold, chill and when firm unmold and garnish with stuffed prunes and whole nut meats. Serve with sweetened and flavored whipped cream or whipped evaporated milk.

No. 270　　　　スパニツシユ・クリーム

材料　ゼラチン紙	二枚	ミルク	カツプ一杯半
玉子の黄味	二個	砂糖	カツプ四分ノ一
		ヴアニラ	小匙半杯
鹽	小匙半杯	玉子の白味	二個
砂糖	大匙二杯	ヴアニラ	小匙四分ノ一

作り方——ミルクを二重鍋で熱し、水に五分間程漬けて置いたゼラチン紙をしぼ
つて之に加へて溶します。玉子の黄味を泡立てて鹽と砂糖を加へたものに前
の熱したミルクを混ぜながら加へ、再び二重鍋の上で混ぜながら二分間程煮
てヴアニラを加へます。次に玉子の白味を充分泡立て、ヴアニラと砂糖を加
へ前の玉子とミルクを熱い儘上から流して冷します。

No. 271　　　　プルンズのジエリー

材料　ゼラチン紙	二枚	コーヒー汁	カツプ一杯半
ココア	大匙一杯	砂糖	カツプ半杯
プルンズ(西洋梅)軟く煮て甘くしたもの	カツプ一杯	胡桃細く切つたもの	カツプ四分ノ一
ヴアニラ	小匙半杯	泡立て用クリーム	カツプ半杯
鹽	少量		

作り方——コーヒー汁を熱し、水に十分程漬けてしぼつたゼラチン紙を加へて火
より下し混ぜて溶します。之に砂糖とココアを加へて混ぜて溶し、冷します
少しかたまつたらば細くほぐしたプルンズと胡桃とヴアニラを入れ、泡立て
たクリームを折込み、水でぬらしたジエリー型に流して固めます。泡立てた
クリームを別に添えます。

No. 272   **APRICOT JELLY**

2 Cups stewed dried apricots	1 Cup milk
4 Sheets gelatine	1 Teaspoon lemon flavoring
2 Eggs well beaten	1 Cup sugar
¼ Teaspoon salt	

Boil milk, add salt, lemon flavoring and gelatine which has been soaked in water for 10 minutes and squeezed. Then remove from the fire immediately, stir and dissolve gelatine. Beat egg thoroughly and pour the hot mixture over the eggs beating continuously. Combine the stewed apricots and the sugar and pour the egg and gelatine mixture over these. Pour all into jelly molds which have been dipped in water and chill thoroughly. Unmold when hard and serve with cream.

No. 273   **STRAWBERRY CHANTILLY**

2 Cups strawberries	5 Tablespoons powdered sugar
2 Egg whites	1 Tablespoon sherry

Wash and stem berries and cut in halves. Sprinkle generously with sugar and set in refrigerator. Beat egg whites until stiff, add 5 tablespoons sugar and beat thoroughly. Sprinkle sherry over berries and mix them lightly with the egg whites. Pile in parfait glasses and chill thoroughly. Garnish with whole strawberries.

No. 274   **JAM DESSERT**

2 Cups dried crumbs	Whipped cream
1 Cup tart jam	1 Tablespoon sugar

This is a delicious Danish pudding. Crumble bits of graham or rye bread to make fine crumbs. Add sugar to the crumbs and heat them in slow oven until they dry. Cool and mix with any kind of jam, perferably a tart jam like apricot or plum. Mold, chill and serve with whipped cream.

No. 272　　杏子ジエリー・プデイング

材料　煮た乾杏子　　　　カツプ二杯　　　ゼラチン紙　　　四枚

　　　玉子泡立てたもの　二個　　　　　　鹽　　　　　　　小匙四分ノ一

　　　ミルク　　　　　　カツプ一杯　　　レモン・エツセンス　小匙一杯

　　　砂糖　　　　　　　カツプ一杯

作り方――ミルクを沸騰させ、鹽とレモン・エツセンスを加へ、之に水に漬けて
　しぼつたゼラチン紙を加へ、火より下して混ぜて溶します。これを充分泡立
　てた玉子の上に絶えず混ぜながら掛けます。別に砂糖と茹でて細く切つた杏
　子を併せ、玉子とミルク等をこれに加へます。之を水でぬらしたジエリー型
　に流し、冷して固めるのです。召し上る時にはクリームをかけます。

No. 273　　　　シヤンテイリー

材料　苺　　　　　　　　カツプ二杯　　　玉子の白味　　　二個

　　　粉砂糖　　　　　　大匙五杯　　　　シエリー酒　　　大匙一杯

作り方――苺を洗つて半分に切り、砂糖を好みの分量だけ振掛けて冷藏庫に入れ
　て冷します。別に白味をよく泡立て、粉砂糖を加へて更に泡立てシエリー酒
　を掛けた苺を輕く白味と混ぜガラスの器に盛つて冷して召上るのです。

No. 274　　　　パン粉のモールド

材料　黒パン粉　　　　　カツプ二杯　　　ジヤム　　　　　カツプ一杯
　　　泡立てた生クリーム　　　　　　　　砂糖　　　　　　大匙一杯

作り方――黒パンの切端等を乾燥させてパン粉にして、砂糖と混ぜて弱火の天火
　ですつかり水分が無くなる迄燒いて冷します。次に杏子かプラムのジヤムの
　様に酸味の強いジヤムと混ぜ、ゼリー型に入れ冷藏庫に入れて充分冷し、型
　より取出して泡立クリームを掛けます。

No. 275   PINEAPPLE DESSERT

The top of a pineapple is cut off and the center scooped out and chopped fine. Strawberries, peaches, grapes, dates, or any fruits in season are mixed with the chopped pineapple and then flavoured with honey. The pineapple shell is filled with the mixture and chilled for at least an hour before serving, so that it will be ice-cold. A perfect accompaniment to be passed with this dessert is cottage cheese.

No. 276   STRAWBERRY TORTE

1 1/3 Cups flour	5 Tablespoons milk
1 1/3 Teaspoons baking powder	½ Teaspoon almond flavouring
½ Cup shortening	4 Egg whites
½ Cup sugar	⅛ Teaspoon cream of tartar
4 Egg yolks	1 Cup sugar

Sift the flour, baking powder together. Work the shortening until soft and add the half cup of sugar and beat until fluffy, using an electric beater if you have one. Add the egg yolks one at a time, beating briskly after each addition. Then add alternately the sifted flour and the milk. Lastly stir in the almond flavoring. Spread this mixture in two eight inch layer cake pans lined with waxed paper and oiled, having mixture higher on sides than in the middle. Beat the egg whites until stiff, add cream of tartar and beat well, then beat in one cup of sugar. Spread evenly on top of the two layers of batter. Bake in a slow oven of 250 degrees F., for 25 minutes, then increase heat to 350 degrees F., and bake 20 minutes longer. Cool and put fresh strawberries combined lightly with plain whipped cream between the layers. Serve cut in wedges. Whipped cream sweatened and flavored with three tablespoons confectioner's sugar and a few drops of almond extract, is a good mixture to use.

No. 277   CUMQUAT CREAM

Cut one half cup cumquats in thinnest possible slices crosswise. Add one half cup water, bring to boiling point and cook gently 15 minutes or until cumquat is tender. Add two tablespoons of sugar. Beat one half cup cream until stiff, fold in cumquat mixture to taste and serve between layers of cake or Kasutera.

No. 275　　パイナツプルのデザート

作り方——生の冷したパイナツプルの上を二寸位の厚さに切り取り中をえぐり取り汁をきつて置きます。季節の生果實又は罐詰の果實等數種を、えぐり取つたパイナツプルを四角に切つたものと取混ぜ、蜂蜜を掛けて甘くし、冷して前のパイナツプルの皮に盛ります。

No. 276　　　　苺　ト　ル　ト

材料	上等メリケ		ベーキング・	
	ン粉	カツプ一杯三分ノ一	パウダー	小匙一杯三分ノ一
	バター又は代用品	カツプ半杯	砂糖	カツプ半杯
	玉子の黄味	四個	ミルク	大匙五杯
	アーモンド・エツセンス	小匙半杯	玉子白味	四個
	クリーム・オブ・ター		砂糖	カツプ一杯
	ター	小匙八分ノ一		

作り方——バターを煉り砂糖を加へて充分煉り續け、これに泡立て器で混ぜながら玉子の黄味を一個づつ加へます。後、ミルクと交互にメリケン粉とベーキング・パウダーを篩つたものを加へ、アーモンド・エツセンスを入れます。これを直徑八吋位の丸形のケーキの天パン二枚に流し、周圍が中央より少し高くなる様に上をナイフでなで、次のものを上に盛ります。玉子の白味四個をよく泡立て、クリーム・オブ・ターターを小匙八分ノ一入れて混ぜ砂糖カツプ一杯を泡立てながら加へます。初めは弱火の天火で二十五分間燒き、次に火を少し強くして(中火)二十分間燒き、取出して冷し、二枚の間に苺を泡立てたクリームと混ぜたものを輕く盛るのです。　これはショート・ケーキの様に切つて召上るのです。

No. 277　　　　金柑クリーム

作り方——金柑カツプ半杯を出來るだけ薄く輪切りにし、水をカツプ半杯かぶせ十五分間煮立てて大匙二杯の砂糖を加へます。生クリームカツプ半杯をよく泡立て、此の中に煮た金柑の冷したものを折込み、二三日經たケーキ、カステラ等に掛けるとデザートになります。

No. 278   RHUBARB SAUCE WITH RAISINS

1½ Cups rhubarb   ½ Cup sugar
½ Cup raisins

Wash rhubarb well and cut in two inch lengths and put in the sauce pan with the raisins and as little water as possible. Cook over low fire until the rhubarb becomes tender and add the sugar and cook five minutes. Serve cold

No. 279   GRAPE-JUICE BLANC MANGE

1 Pint grape juice   ½ Cup cold water
4 Tablespoon cornstarch   ¼ Cup sugar

Bring grape juice to the boiling point. Meanwhile mix the cornstarch and water to a smooth paste, then stir into hot grape-juice and add sugar. Cook over hot water, stirring constantly for seven to 10 minutes. Cool partially, then pour into sherbet cups and chill. Serve with cream.

No. 280   FIG MOUSSE

1½ Cups sliced fresh figs   ¼ Cup confectioners' sugar
½ Cup sugar   1 Cup fresh cream

Peel and slice fresh figs and cover them with the half cup of sugar. Let stand until the sugar has dissolved. Add confectioners' sugar to cream which has been whipped. Cover the bottom of a mold with a layer of whipped cream. Next place a layer of sliced figs over the cream. Continue this alternation until the mold is filled, ending with cream. Cover tightly. Pack the mold in ice and salt, using two parts of finely cracked ice to one of coarse rock salt.

No. 281   CARAMEL CREAM

2 Eggs   2 Cups milk
3 Tablespoons brown sugar   ½ Teaspoon vanila
1 Teaspoon cornstarch

Beat the eggs with the brown sugar and the cornstarch. Meanwhile bring the milk to the boiling point in a double boiler. Pour in the egg mixture slowly, beating all the time and cook gently till thick, stirring constantly. This will take about five minutes. Add vanilla, pour into serving dishes and cool. Sprinkle with brown sugar and set under the flame of the broiler oven to melt the sugar. Chill and serve with cream.

No. 278　　ルーバーブご乾葡萄のソース

材料　ルバーブ（西洋蕗の様　　　　　　　乾葡萄　　　　　カツプ半杯
　　　　　なもの）　　カツプ一杯半

　　砂糖　　　　　　カツプ半杯

作り方——ルバーブの茎を充分洗つて一寸位の長さに切り、乾葡萄と共に鍋に入
　れ焦げつかぬ程度に少量の水を加へて、ルバーブが軟くなる迄煮て砂糖を加
　へ五分間煮て冷して召上るのです。

No. 279　　グレープ・ジユース・プデイング

材料　グレープ・ジユーズ・　　　　　　コーンスターチ　　　大匙四杯
　　　（葡萄汁）　　カツプ二杯

　　冷水　　　　　カツプ半杯　　砂糖　　　　　　カツプ四分ノ一

作り方——コンスターチと水をよく混合せ、沸騰して居る　グレープ・ジユースに
　混ぜながら加へ砂糖を加へ、二重鍋の湯の上で絶えず混ぜながら七分乃至十
　分間煮て冷し、ガラスの皿に流し、充分冷してクリームを掛けて召上る簡單
　なデザートです。

No. 280　　無 花 果 の ム ー ス

材料　無花果輪切り　　カツプ一杯半　　砂糖　　　　　　カツプ半杯

　　粉砂糖　　　　カツプ四分ノ一　泡立てクリーム　　カツプ一杯

作り方——皮をむいた無花果を輪切りにして砂糖を掛け、砂糖が溶ける迄燒きま
　す。別にクリームを泡立て粉砂糖を少しづつ加へて更に泡立て續けます。密
　閉出來る罐の底に泡立てクリームを入れ、その上に無花果を入れこれを交互
　に繰返して材料を詰め蓋をして、氷二に鹽一の割合で混ぜた細く碎いた氷の
　中に二時間うめて置きますと美味しいムース（アイスクリームの一種）が出
　來ます。

No. 281　　キ ヤ ラ メ ル・ク リ ー ム

材料　玉子　　　　　　二個　　　　　黒砂糖　　　　　大匙三杯

　　コンスターチ　　小匙一杯　　ミルク　　　　　カツプ二杯

　　ヴアニラ　　　　小匙半杯

作り方——玉子と黒砂糖とコンスターチを一緒にして充分泡立て、これを煮立て
　たミルクに混ぜながら加へ、絶えず混續けながら弱火で五分間程煮ます。火
　より下し、ヴアニラを加へて器に流して冷します。冷めたらば上に黒砂糖を
　振掛けてグリルで上から火を當て〻砂糖が溶ける迄燒き、よく冷して召上る
　のです。

No. 282   **SHERRY CRUMB**

2 Cups thin custard   1½ Cups stale cake crumbs
Sherry

Cool custard, add crumbs and sherry to taste. Put in sherbet glasses and chill thoroughly.

The secret of the pudding is to have it cold. If the cake crumbs are plain, add a few chopped nuts and maraschino cherries. Raisin or nut cake, macaroons crumbled are particularly good.

No. 283   **ORANGE REFRIGERATOR PUDDING**

1¼ Cups condensed milk   ½ Cup orange juice
1/3 Teaspoon grated lemon   ½ Teaspoon vanilla
   rind   2 Tablespoons blanched almonds,
5 Tablespoons lemon juice   chopped
1 Teaspoon orange rind   Sponge cake

Add to condensed milk the fruit juices and rind, vanilla and almonds chopped fine, and mix carefully. Cut thin slices of sponge cake, or split lady fingers, place a layer in a brick mold lined with oiled paper, cover with orange mixture, put in another layer of the sponge cake and orange and continue until mixture is used. Let stand 24 hours in refrigerator Turn out on platter and serve.

No. 284   **CHOCOLATE ICE BOX PUDDING**

½ Pound sweet chocolate   4 Egg whites
4 Egg yolks   Lady fingers or stale cake cut
½ Teaspoon vanilla   in strips

Chop the chocolate and melt over hot water add, vanilla and whipped egg whites. Split lady fingers and place round side down in a cake tin in which has been lined with parafine paper. Pour half the chocolate mixture over these and put in another layer of lady fingers Then pour the remaining chocolate mixture in and top with lady fingers Put a sheet of parafine paper over the top and put in the refrigerator for several hours. It is best to let this stand in the refrigerator over night. Remove paper and serve.

No. 282　　　　　シエリー・クランム

作り方——これはケーキが少し古くなつてかたくなつたものの利用法の一つです
　が、このケーキをカツプに一杯半程ぼろぼろにくづして置き、別に作つて冷
　して置いた薄いカスタードカツプ二杯と混ぜ、シエリー酒を大匙三杯程加へ
　て全部を冷してシヤムペングラスに盛るのです。

No. 283　　　　　オレンヂ冷藏庫プデイング

材料	コンデンス・ミルク	カツプ一杯四分ノ一	卸したレモン皮	小匙三分ノ一
	レモン汁	大匙五杯	卸した蜜柑の皮	小匙一杯
	蜜柑汁	カツプ半杯	ヴアニラ	小匙半杯
	アーモンドの繊切り	大匙二杯	カステラ	

作り方——コンデンス・ミルクに果實の汁と皮を加へ、ヴアニラと　アーモンドを
　輕く混ぜ込みます。カステラは三分位の厚さに切ります。四角の深い天パン
　にハラフイン紙を敷き底にカステラを並べ、上にミルク等を掛け、再びカス
　テラを敷きこれを繰返して材料を全部交互に入れ上にパラフイン紙を敷き冷
　藏庫に二十四時間以上入れて置き　取出して五分の　厚さに切つて皿にのせま
　す。

No. 284　　　　　チヨコレート冷藏庫プデイング

材料	甘い板チヨコレート	半封度	玉子の黄味	四個
	ヴアニラ	小匙半杯	玉子の白味	四個
	レデイス・フインガー（お菓子）又はカステーラ			

作り方——チヨコレートを細く切り湯の上で溶します。玉子の黄味をチヨコレー
　トに加へて混ぜヴアニラを入れ、白味をよく泡立てゝ折込みます。レデイス・
　フインガーを用ひる時はこれを半分に割り丸い方を内側にしてパラフイン紙
　を敷いた天パンの内側と底に並べます。カステラは二分位の薄切れにして同
　様に並べます。この中にチヨコレート等を半分流し、　その上にレデイス・フ
　インガー又はカステラをまた一段並べ、殘りのチヨコレート等を流しまた上
　にカステラ等を並べパラフイン紙をかぶせて冷藏庫に數時間入れて置きます
　（一晩位置くと尚よい）。パラフイン紙を取つて皿に取出します。

No. 285   **GRAPE ICE**

2 Cups grape juice	Juice 2 oranges
1 1/3 Cups sugar	3 Cups water
Juice 2 lemons	Whites 2 eggs

Boil the sugar and water together for five minutes. Add the fruit juices, mix thoroughly, and cool and freeze in the trays of a mechanical refrigerator or in an ice-cream freezer. When partially frozen stir in the stiffly beaten egg whites. Serves 8 or 10.

No. 286   **THREE AND ONE SHERBET**

3 Oranges, juice	3 Cups sugar
3 Lemons, juice	3 Cups water
3 Bananas, crushed	1 Pint fresh cream
1 Can pineapple, crushed	1 Cup milk

Mix in order given, adding cream and milk last and stirring constantly, freeze at once. This makes one gallon.

No. 287   **LEMON VELVET**

4 Lemons and grated rind of 2	1 Pint fresh cream
4 Cups sugar	3 Cups milk

Mix sugar and lemon juice and rind. Then add the cream and milk. Freeze immediately or it will curdle.

No. 288   **GINGERALE ICE CREAM**

For the Ice Cream in Ginger Ale, make one and a half pints of vanilla ice cream and arrange in six tall glasses. Then fill the glasses with ginger ale and serve. Serves 6.

No. 285　　葡　萄　ア　イ　ス

材料　葡萄汁（瓶詰グレープ・　　　　　砂糖　　　　カツプ一杯三分ノ一
　　　　ジュース）　　カツプ二杯

　　レモン汁　　　　　二個分　　　オレンヂ汁　　　二個分

　　冷水　　　　　カツプ三杯　　玉子の白味　　　二個

作り方──砂糖と水を五分間煮て冷し、果實汁を加へ、アイスクリーム凍結機で
　　凍らせ、少しかたまつて來たらばよく泡立てた玉子の白味を加へ、廻轉させ
　　ながら凍らせます。

No. 286　　四色シヤーベット

材料　オレンヂ汁　　　三個分　　　レモン汁　　　　三個分
　　バナナ裏漉にした　　　　　　　パイナツプル
　　　もの　　　　　三個　　　　微塵切り　　　小一罐
　　砂糖　　　　カツプ三杯　　冷水　　　　カツプ三杯
　　クリーム　　　カツプ三杯

作り方──材料を並べた順に混ぜ合せ、最後に混ぜながらクリームを加へ、すぐ
　　にアイスクリーム凍結機で凍らせます。此の分量で二十人前位出來ます。

No. 287　　レモン・ベルベット

材料　レモン　　　　四個　　　レモン皮おろしたもの　二個分
　　砂糖　　　　カツプ四杯　　生クリーム　　　カツプ二杯
　　ミルク　　　カツプ三杯

作り方──レモンは四個分の汁をしぼり、二個分の皮をおろして混合せ、之に砂
　　糖を加へます。最後にクリームとミルクを加へ、直にアイスクリーム凍結機
　　で凍らせます。混ぜ合せてから時間を置くとクリームが離れてしまひますか
　　ら用意して置いてすぐ凍らせるのです。

No. 288　　ジンヂヤエール・アイスクリーム

作り方──細長いガラスのコツプにヴアニラのアイスクリームを大匙二杯程入れ
　　上に冷したジンヂヤエール（生薑味の炭酸水）を流します。夏のデザートのア
　　イスクリームの變つた召し上り方です。

No. 289   **SPICED LEMONADE**

2 Cups water
1 Cup lemon juice
½ Cup orange juice
¼ Teaspoon cloves
2 Cups sugar

Mix the water, cloves, and sugar. Put over the fire bring to boiling point slowly and boil two minutes. Cool. Add fruit juices and enough cold water to give the desired strength. Serve in tall glasses with cracked ice. Garnish with whole strawberries, if desired.

No. 290   **COFFEE EGGNOG**

1 Egg
1½ Teaspoons sugar
½ Cup milk
½ Cup strong coffee

Separate white and yolks of egg. Beat yolk, add sugar and beat until creamy. Add the milk and coffee. Beat the white of egg until foamy and fold in lightly. Serve at once.

No. 291   **FRENCH CHOCOLATE**

2½ Squares chocolate, cut
    in pieces
½ Cup cold water
¾ Cup sugar
Dash of salt
½ Cup cream, whipped
6 Cups hot milk

Combine chocolate and water and cook over direct heat four minutes, stirring constantly. Beat with rotary egg beater until smooth, add sugar and salt, return to fire, and cook four minutes longer. Cool. Fold into cream. Place one rounding tablespoon of chocolate mixture in each serving cup and pour hot milk over it, filling cup. Stir well to blend Serves eight.

No. 292   **CHOCOLATE MILK SHAKE**

2 Squares bitter chocolate
¼ Cup sugar
1 Cup boiling water
3 1/3 Cups milk

Chop the chocolate and put over hot water to melt, then add sugar and boiling water and place over direct heat and boil for one minute. Add this mixture to cold milk and shake well, this is best done by putting it in a wide mouthed bottle and shaking well. Pour into glasses filled with chopped ice and if desired serve with whipped cream.

No. 289　　　スパイスド・レモネード

材料　冷水　　　　　　カツプ二杯　　　レモン汁　　　　　　カツプ一杯
　　　オレンヂ汁　　　　カツプ半杯　　　クローブ(香料)　　小匙四分ノ一
　　　砂糖　　　　　　　カツプ二杯

作り方――冷水、クローブ、砂糖を混ぜ、火に掛けて二分間沸騰させて冷します
　　　オレンヂとレモン汁を加へ適宜に水を加へて好みの味にして氷を入れて飲む
　　　のです。

No. 290　　　コーヒー・エツグ・ノツグ

材料　(一人前)玉子　　一個　　　　　　砂糖　　　　　　　　小匙一杯半
　　　ミルク　　　　　　カツプ半杯　　　濃厚コーヒー液　　　カツプ半杯

作り方――玉子の白味と黄味を分け、黄味を泡立てゝ砂糖を加へてよく混ぜコー
　　　ヒー液とミルクを加へ、別に玉子の白味を充分泡立てて之に折込み直に召し
　　　上るのです。

No. 291　　　フレンチ・チヨコレート

材料　料理用ビター・チヨ　　　　　　　冷水　　　　　　　　カツプ半杯
　　　コレート　　　　　二角半
　　　砂糖　　　　　　　カツプ四分ノ三　塩　　　　　　　　　小匙八分ノ一
　　　ミルク熱したもの　カツプ六杯　　　泡立てたクリーム　　カツプ半杯

作り方――チヨコレートを細く切り、水と併せて火の上で絶えず混ぜながら四分
　　　間煮て玉子攪拌器で滑かになる迄混ぜ砂糖と塩を加へ、再び火の上で四分間
　　　煮て冷します。召上る前に泡立てたクリームにチヨコレート等を折込み器に
　　　盛ります。熱したミルクを水差の様なものに入れ召上る時茶椀の中にチヨコ
　　　レート等を大匙山盛り一杯入れ、上からミルクを掛け一杯にして混ぜて飲む
　　　のです。

No. 292　　　チヨコレート・ミルク・シエーク

材料　料理用ビター・　　　　　　　　　砂糖　　　　　　　　カツプ四分ノ一
　　　チヨコレート　　　二角
　　　熱湯　　　　　　　カツプ一杯　　　ミルク　　　カツプ三杯三分ノ一

作り方――湯煎にして細く切つたチヨコレートを溶し、砂糖と熱湯を加へ、火の
　　　上に掛けて一分間沸騰させ、冷ミルクに充分混ぜながら(瓶に入れ振り混ぜ
　　　てもよい)加へます。冷して氷の上に流し好みにより上に泡立てクリームを
　　　浮せて飲むのです。

No. 293 . **MARTINI COCKTAIL**

DRY

2/3 Dry gin
1/3 French vermouth
Angostura bitters added if
    required

MEDIUM

1/3 Dry gin
1/3 French vermouth
1/3 Italian vermouth

SWEET

2/3 Italian vermouth
1/3 Dry gin
Dash of gomme syrup

Place ingredients in tall glass in which chopped ice has been filled. Stir with a spoon strain and pour into cocktail glasses.

No. 294 **MANHATTAN COCKTAIL**

Dash of Angostura bitters   1/3 Italian vermouth
2/3 Canadian club whisky

Mix well in cocktail shaker containing chopped ice and strain into glasses and serve with maraschino cherry.

No. 295 **SIDE-CAR COCKTAIL**

1/3 Cointreau   1/3 Lemon juice
1/3 Brandy

Mix ingredients in shaker containing chopped ice and strain into cocktail glasses.

No. 296 **DUBONNET COCKTAIL**

1/3 Bacardi   Juice of half a lemon
1/3 Dubonnet   1 Teaspoon grenadine

Add ingredients to shaker containing ice and shake well. Serve in cocktail glasses.

No. 293　　　　マーテニー・カクテール

ドライ(辛口)

　材料　ドライ・ジン　　　三分ノ二　　　　フレンチ・ベルモツト　三分ノ一

　　　　アンゴラストラー・
　　　　　ビター　　　　　數滴

ミデイアム(普通)

　材料　ドライ・ジン　　　三分ノ一　　　　フレンチ・ベルモツト　三分ノ一

　　　　イタリアン・
　　　　　ベルモツト　　　三分ノ一

スキート(甘口)

　材料　イタリアン・　　　　　　　　　　ドライ・ジン　　　　三分ノ一
　　　　　ベルモツト　　　三分ノ二

　　　　ゴム・シロツプ　　一滴

作り方——氷の破片を入れた大きなコツプに材料を入れ匙で攪混ぜてカクテール
　　グラスに注ぎます。

No. 294　　　　マンハツタン・カクテール

　材料　アンゴラストラ・　　　　　　　ウキスキー　　　　　三分の二
　　　　　ビター　　　　　一滴

　　　　イタリアン・
　　　　　ベルモツト　　　三分の一

作り方——氷を碎いてシエーカーの中に入れ、その上に材料を加へ振混ぜてグラ
　　スに注ぎます。マラスキノー・チエリーを添へる。

No. 295　　　　サイドカー・カクテール

　材料　コントロー　　　　三分の一　　　ブランデー　　　　　三分の一
　　　　レモン汁又はオレ
　　　　　ンヂ汁　　　　　三分の一

作り方——氷を碎いて入れたコクテール・シエーカーに材料を入れ、よく振混ぜ
　　漉し乍らグラスに注ぎます。

No. 296　　　　デユボネー・カクテール

　材料　バカデイ`　　　　　三分の一　　　デユボネー　　　　　三分の一
　　　　レモン汁　　　　　半個分　　　　グレナデイン　　　　小匙一杯

作り方——氷を入れたシエーカーに材料を入れ、よく振つて後、カクテール・グ
　　ラスに漉して注ぎます。婦人向きの甘口のものです。

No. 297 ALEXANDER COCKTAIL

1/3 Dry gin
1/3 Creme de cacao
1/3 Fresh cream

Add chopped ice to shaker and pour in the ingredients mix thoroughly and serve in sherry glasses.

No. 298 BACARDI COCKTAIL

Juice of ½ a lemon
Glass of bacardi
1 Teaspoon powdered sugar

Add all ingredients to shaker containing chopped ice and shake well before serving in cocktail glasses.

No. 299 BRONX COCKTAIL

1/3 Dry gin
1/3 French vermouth
1/3 Italian vermouth
Juice of ¼ Orange

Mix well in shaker containing chopped ice and strain into cocktail glasses and serve.

No. 300 CHAMPAGNE COCKTAIL

In a champagne glass put one lump of sugar saturated with Angostura bitters ,and one lump of ice fill the glass with champagne, squeeze a piece of lemon peel, on the top and serve.

No. 301 MILLION DOLLAR COCKTAIL

3 Dry gin
1½ French vermouth
3 Pineapple or orange juice
   or ½ and ½
White of 1 egg
½ Grenadine

Put ingredients into shaker which contains chopped ice and shake, then serve in a champagne glass and arrange piece of pineapple on the side of the glass.

No.297　　　アレキサンダー・カクテール

材料　ドライ・ジン　　　　三分ノ一　　　クリーム・デ・カカオ 三分ノ一
　　　生クリーム　　　　　三分ノ一

作り方——コクテール・シエーカー 又は大口の瓶に氷を細く碎いて入れ材料を同
　　分量に量つて加へ輕く振つて混ぜ、コクテール・グラス又はシエリー・グラス
　　に漉して注いで召上るのです。食前用の甘口の美味しいカクテールです。

No. 298　　　バカデイー・カクテール

材料　レモン（又はオレンヂ）汁　半個分　　　バカデイ　　カクテール・グラス
　　　粉砂糖　　　　　　　　　　小匙一杯　　　　　　　　　　一杯

作り方——レモン汁半個分又は同分量のオレンヂ汁とバカデイ、粉砂糖と碎いた
　　氷を入れたシエーカーに入れ、縦に充分振つて混ぜ、カクテール・グラスに
　　漉して流し召し上るのです、桃色の手輕な御婦人向きのカクテール

No. 299　　　ブロンクス・カクテール

材料　ドライ・ジン　　　　三分ノ一　　　フレンチ・ベルモツト 三分ノ一
　　　イタリアン・　　　　　　　　　　　オレンヂ汁　　　四分ノ一個分
　　　ベルモツト　　　　　三分ノ一

作り方——碎いた氷をシエーカー又は大形のコツプに入れ、材料を加へ匙で輕く
　　混ぜてから漉してグラスに流します。このカクテールは振らぬ方がよろしい
　　のです。マーテイニ・カクテールの甘口の物です。

No. 300　　　シヤンペン・カクテール

作り方——シヤンペン・グラスに角砂糖を一個入れ、アンゴストラ・ビターを角砂
　　糖に振掛け充分冷えたシヤンペンをグラス一杯に注ぎ、好みによりレモン皮
　　一片をしぼつて上に浮せます。このカクテールは盆にグラス、砂糖、ビター
　　スをのせ客にそれぞれ好みのビターを使はせて、シヤンペンを注いで進める
　　様にするとよい。

No. 301　　　ミリオンダラー・カクテール

材料　ドライ・ヂン　　　　三パート　　　フレンチ・
　　　　　　　　　　　　　　　　　　　　ベルモツト　　　一パート半
　　　パイナツプル　　　　　　　　　　玉子の白味　　　一個分
　　　又はオレンヂ汁　　　三パート
　　　グレナデイン　　　　半パート

作り方——氷を入れたカクテール・シエーカーに材料全部を入れ、充分振混ぜて
　　漉してシヤムペン・グラスに注ぎ、パイナツプルの一片をグラスの口にはさ
　　んで召上るのです。

No. 302   MINT JULEP

Crush mint leaves in bottom of a glass with two teaspoons of sugar Add two glasses of bourbon or rye whisky and pack the large glass with crushed ice. Stir well and garnish with sprigs of mint. There should be a thin coating of ice on the outside of the glass.

No. 303   GIN FIZZ

Into the shaker put some crushed ice, the juice of half a lemon and a liquer glass of dry gin. Then add one white of egg and a teaspoon of powdered sugar. Shake well, and pour into glass and fill the glass with tansan.

No. 304   GIN RICKEY

Put one lump of ice in a tumbler, cut a fresh lemon in half and squeeze the juice in the glass, and add one glass of dry gin, and fill up with tansan.

No. 305   GIN SLING

Put into glass some pieces of ice, one teaspoon of powdered sugar, six dashes of lemon juice and two liqueur glasses of dry gin. Stir this mixture well and pour into a tall glass and fill up with tansan. A little claret floated on the surface is an improvement.

No. 306   CHAMPAGNE CUP

Put two or three lumps of ice in a large jug and add one liqueur glass of brandy, one liqueur glass of maraschino, one liqueur glass of curacao, one bottle of champagne, and two bottles of tansan. Stir this well, decorate with fruit in season, and add two sprigs of fresh mint if available and a slice of cucumber peel.

No. 307   CLARET PUNCH

3 Tablespoons gomme syrup	1 Pineapple, sliced and quartered
1 Tablespoon of angostura bitters	2 Wineglasses brandy
3 Oranges, sliced	2 Bottles claret
3 Lemons, sliced	

Stir the above ingredients gently and add two bottles of tansan and serve in punch glases or cups.

No. 302　　　　ミント・ジユレツプ

作り方——細長いグラス一杯に細く碎いた氷を詰めます。別の器に薄荷の葉を三
　　四杯と砂糖小匙二杯を入れ、葉をつぶす樣にして混ぜて、ウキスキー・グラス
　　二杯のライ・ウキスキーを加へ、これを前の氷の上に流して、上に薄荷の葉を
　　一枝飾ります。グラスの外側に薄く氷がはつて夏向きの非常に冷い飲物です
　　但しウキスキーはライでなければなりません。スコツチ・ウキスキーでは 美
　　味しくありません。

No. 303　　　　　ジン・フイズ

作り方——シエーカーに 氷の碎いたものを入れ、レモン汁半個分、リキユール・
　　グラス一杯のドライ・ジン、玉子の白味一個分及び小匙一杯の粉砂糖を入れ、
　　振混ぜて大形コツプに漉して注ぎ、冷した炭酸を一杯になる迄注ぎます。

No. 304　　　　　ジ　ン・リ　キ

作り方——大形コツプに氷一片を入れ、レモン汁半個分とドライ・ジンを リキー
　　ル・グラスに一杯入れ、炭酸のコツプが一杯になる迄加へます。

No. 305　　　　　ジン・スリング

作り方——大形コツプに初め氷の破片を入れ、その上に粉砂糖小匙一杯、レモン
　　汁六滴、ドライ・ジンをリキユール・グラス二杯加へよく攪混せ、コツプが一
　　杯になる迄炭酸を注ぎます。

No. 306　　　　シヤンペン・カツプ

材料	角砂糖	三個	ブランデ	
	マラスキノー	リキユール	ー	リキユル・ーグラス一杯
		グラス一杯	キユラソ	
	シヤンペン	大瓶一本	ー	リキユル・ーグラス一杯
	炭酸	二本		

作り方——大きい水挿叉は器に角砂糖を入れ、氷の破片を加へ、他の材料を書き
　　並べた順に加へ、薄荷の枝叉は胡瓜の皮を薄く切つたもので飾ります。小さ
　　いコツプに器より注いで召上るのです。

No. 307　　　　クラレツト・パンチ

材料	ゴム・シロツプ	大匙三杯	アンゴストラー・ビター	大匙一杯
	オレンヂ薄輪切り	三個分	レモン薄輪切り	三個分
	パイナツプル		ブランデー	ワイン・グラス二杯
	賽の目切り	一個分		
	クラレツト	大瓶二本	炭酸	二本

作り方——氷を入れた器に炭酸以外の材料を入れ、靜に混ぜ、炭酸を注込み、小
　　さいコツプに注いで召上るのです。

No. 308   CHOCOLATE FUDGE

2 Cups sugar	2 Tablespoons butter
¾ Cup milk	1 Teaspoon vanilla
2 Squares bitter chocolate	Pinch cream of tartar

If cocoa is used four tablespoons. Mix the sugar, milk, chocolate which has been chopped fine and cook until a very soft ball is formed when tested in cold water. Remove from the fire, add the butter, vanilla and the cream of tartar and beat well. But let stand a few minutes first. Beat until creamy, then add a few drops of cream or hot water and knead carefully with spoon. When thick, pour in a well buttered plate and mark in squares. Nuts and marshmallows may be added.

No. 309   COFFEE CREAM FUDGE

2 Cups light brown sugar	2 Tablespoons butter
½ Cup triple strength coffee	⅛ Teaspoon salt
¼ Cup evaporated milk	1 Cup chopped walnuts

Mix the sugar, coffee and cream. Cook slowly, without stirring, until it boils. Boil more rapidly, stirring occasionally until syrup tests a soft but firm ball in cold water. Remove from fire, add butter and salt and cool to lukewarm. Beat until thick, add nuts, pour in buttered tin and cut in squares. This makes about 15 one and a half inch squares.

No. 310   FRUIT AND NUT FUDGE

1 Level teaspoon baking powder	½ Cup grated chocolate
2 Cups sugar	½ Cup chopped nut meats
½ Cup molasses	½ Cup chopped almonds
½ Cup evaporated milk	1 Teaspoon lemon extract
2 Tablespoons stoned and chopped dates	1 Teaspoon orange extract

Boil together seven minutes, molasses, cream and butter, stirring constantly. Add chocolate and boil five minutes, then add fruits, baking powder and nut meats, stir constantly until it boils, then cook slowly until it forms a soft ball when tried in water. Remove from stove and stir until creamy. Pour into flat pan to cool. Sufficient for 40 or 50 squares.

No. 308　　　チヨコレート・フアツヂ(キヤンデー)

材料　砂糖　　　　　　　カツプ二杯　　　ミルク　　　　　カツプ四分ノ三
　　　料理用ビター・　　　　　　　　　　バター　　　　　大匙二杯
　　　　チヨコレート　　二角
　　　ヴアニラ　　　　　小匙一杯　　　　クリーム・オブ
　　　　　　　　　　　　　　　　　　　　　ターター　　　少量

作り方——砂糖とミルクと細く切つたチヨコレートを混ぜ、火に掛けて（水に少
　量落したのが指先で丸められる固さになる迄）十分間位煮ます。火より下し
　バター、ヴアニラ及びクリーム・オブ・ターターを加へて　固まる迄混ぜ、油を
　塗つた皿に流し、冷して後四分角位に切ります。胡桃等は火より下してから
　入れても宜しい。

No. 309　　　コ ー ヒ ー ・ フ ア ツ ヂ

材料　黒砂糖(花見砂糖)　カツプ二杯　　　普通の三倍位濃い
　　　　　　　　　　　　　　　　　　　　　コーヒー　　　カツプ半杯

　　　クリーム　　　　　カツプ四分ノ一　バター　　　　大匙二杯

　　　鹽　　　　　　　　小匙八分ノ一　　胡桃微塵切り　　カツプ一杯

作り方——砂糖とコーヒーとクリームを併せ、火の上に掛け、混ぜずに一度沸騰
　させて後時々混ぜながら煮て少量を水に落したのが指先で丸められる位の固
　さになつたらば火より下し、冷して後よく混ぜて固まつて來たらば胡桃を入
　れ油を塗つた皿に流し、五分角に切つてキヤンデーにします。

No. 310　　　フルーツ・胡桃・フアツヂ

材料　ベーキング・パウダー　小匙一杯　　　砂糖　　　　　　カツプ二杯

　　　モラセズ(黒蜜)　　　カツプ半杯　　クリーム　　　　カツプ半杯

　　　バター　　　　　　　カツプ半杯　　デーツ細く切つ
　　　卸した料理用ビター・　　　　　　　　たもの　　　　大匙二杯
　　　　チヨコレート　　　カツプ半杯　　胡桃細く切つたもの　カツプ半杯

　　　アーモンド細く切つた　　　　　　　レモン・エツセンス　小匙一杯
　　　　もの　　　　　　　カツプ半杯

　　　オレンヂ・エツセンス　小匙一杯

作り方——モラセズとクリームとバタを併せて七分間絶えず混ぜながら煮て、チ
　ヨコレートを加へ五分間煮ます。のち、デーツ、胡桃、アーモンド、ベーキン
　グ・パウダーを加へて、沸騰する迄混ぜ、弱火で煮詰めて少量を冷水に落して
　それが指先で丸められる固さになつた時火より下してなめらかになる迄混ぜ
　油を塗つた平な天パンに流して冷して固め、四角に切つてキヤンデーとして
　召上るのです。

No. 311　　　CHOCOLATE CARAMELS

2 Cupfuls granulated sugar
1 Cupful light corn sirup
1 Cupful evaporated milk
1½ Cupfuls light cream
3 Squares chocolate
2 Tablespoonful butter
1 Cupful broken nut meats
1½ Teaspoonfuls vanilla

Place all the ingredients, except the vanilla and nuts, in a saucepan, and heat until the sugar is dissolved and the chocolate is melted. Cook, stirring constantly, until the mixture reaches 246 degrees F. Add the vanilla and nuts, and pour into a greased pan, nine inches square. When cold, invert the pan, turn the mixture onto a wooden board, and cut in one-inch squares. Wrap in oiled paper.

No. 312　　　ORANGE FONDANT

A delicious variety of orange bon bons may be made from an uncooked orange fondant, which is simple to prepare:

3 Tablespoons orange juice
1 Tablespoon lemon juice
Grated rind of 1 large orange
1 Egg yolk, well beaten
1 Tablespoon melted butter
Powdered sugar

Mix fruit juice, grated rind, egg yolk and butter. Add powdered sugar to make a stiff paste of fondant consistency. If desired, color a deeper orange shade, with vegetable coloring. As the different candies are made, place on waxed paper. Let stand in a cool, dry place for from 24 to 48 hours to harden.

No. 313　　　ORANGE COCOANUT CREAMS

Mix orange fondant with cocoanut. Shape into balls.

No. 314　　　ORANGE CREAM DATES

Remove stones from dates and stuff with orange fondant.

No. 315　　　ORANGE RAISIN CLUSTERS

Mix orange fondant with chopped raisins or broken nut meats. Shape into balls.

No. 311　　　　チヨコレート・キヤラメル

材料	グラニユ糖	カツプ二杯	薄色のコーン・ジロツプ(蜜)	カツプ一杯
	クリーム	カツプ二杯半	料理用ビターチヨコレート	三角
	バター	大匙二杯	細く切つた胡桃	カツプ一杯
	ヴアニラ	小匙一杯半		

作り方——ヴアニラと胡桃を除く他の材料を全部鍋に入れ、火に掛けて絶えず混ぜながら、煮て居る材料が二四六度になる迄煮詰め火より下しヴアニラと胡桃を加へ、油を塗つた天パンに流して冷します。冷えたらば板の上に取出して五分角に切ります。パラフイン紙に包むとよい。

No. 312　　　　オ レ ン ヂ ・ ボ ン ボ ン

材料	オレンヂ汁	大匙三杯	レモン汁	大匙一杯
	オレンヂの皮の卸したもの	一個分	玉子の黄味をよく混ぜたもの	一個
	溶したバター	大匙一杯	粉砂糖	

作り方——オレンヂ汁、レモン汁及び皮の卸したもの、玉子の黄味等を合せ、バターを加へてよく混ぜ、これに粉砂糖を少量づつ加へ、カツプ三杯以上入ると段々固くなりますから、多過ぎぬ様に形を保たせるに必要の分量だけを加へます。此の儘小さく丸めてキヤンデーにするか次の方法で種々のボンボン・キヤンデーを作り皿の上に並べ數時間置いて固めます。

No. 312　　　　オレンヂ・ココナツツ・クリーム

作り方——オレンヂ・ボンボンの材料に適宜にココナツツを混ぜて丸めます。　ココナツツの代りに乾葡萄、胡桃を用ひても結構です。

No 314　　　　オレンヂ・クリーム・デート

作り方——乾したデート(果實)又はプルンズの種子を取り、その中にボンボンの材料を詰めます。

No. 315　　　　オレンヂこ乾葡萄のクリーム

作り方——オレンヂ・ボンボンを作り、その中に細く切つた乾葡萄を入れ、小型の團子に丸めます。

No. 316   **BOSTON CREAM**

3 Cupfuls sugar   3 Tablespoonfuls butter
1 Cupful evaporated milk   ¾ Cupful walnut meats
1 Cupful milk   ⅛ Teaspoonful salt

Caramelize one cupful of the sugar and when lightly browned add the evaporated milk. Stir until the resultant lump is dissolved, then add the remaining sugar and milk. Stir until the sugar is dissolved, then cook to 238 degrees F. or until a little tested in cold water forms a soft ball. Remove from the fire. Add the butter and the salt. Beat until creamy, then add the nuts and when firm pour into a greased pan, 9 inches square. When cool cut into squares.

No. 317   **CHOCOLATE-COCOANUT CREAM**

1-1/3 Cupfuls condensed milk   4 Tablespoonfuls cocoa
⅛ Teaspoonful salt   Shredded cocoanut
½ Teaspoonful vanilla

Add salt and cocoa to the condensed milk and cook in heavy iron frying pan, stirring constantly for 12 minutes or until a soft ball forms when a little is dropped into water. Remove from fire and add vanilla and pour into well-greased pan. Cool. When cool, roll one teaspoon of mixture into small balls and coat with grated cocoanut.

No. 318   **CHRISTMAS PUDDING CANDY**

3 Cups sugar   1 Pound figs
1 Cup evaporated milk   1 Pound raisins
Heaping tablespoon butter   1 Pound Shredded cocoanut
1 Teaspoon vanilla   1½ Cup walnuts
1 Pound dates

Cook sugar, cream and butter to soft ball. Beat until creamy, then beat in fruit and nuts. If cocoanut is coarse, grind it. When well mixed, roll as for meat loaf. Wrap in dampened cloth, then in waxed paper and put away to ripen. Make at least two weeks before you wish to use it. When wanted, slice in squares and oblongs.

No. 316　　　ボストン・クリーム

材料　砂糖　　　　　　　カツプ三杯　　　クリーム(罐詰)　　カツプ一杯
　　　ミルク　　　　　　カツプ一杯　　　バター　　　　　　大匙三杯
　　　胡桃微塵切り　　　カツプ四分ノ三　鹽　　　　　　　　小匙八分ノ一

作り方——砂糖をカツプ一杯だけフライパンに入れ、薄い茶色になる迄混ぜなが
　　ら焦し、クリームを加へて塊が溶ける迄混ぜ、殘りの砂糖とミルクを加へ、
　　砂糖が溶ける迄混ぜ、後、靜に煮續けます。少量を水に落して、これが指先
　　で丸められる固さになつたらば火より下し、バターと鹽を加へ、滑に固まり
　　始める迄混ぜ、火より下したバタと鹽を入れ混ぜて、胡桃を加へ、油を塗つ
　　た天パンに流して冷します。冷えて固まつたらば四分角位に切ります。

No. 317　　チヨコレート・ココナツツ・クリーム

材料　コンデンス・ミルク　一罐　　　　　鹽　　　　　　　　小匙八分ノ一
　　　ヴアニラ　　　　　　小匙半杯　　　ココア　　　　　　大匙四杯
　　　ココナツツ　　　　　カツプ一杯位

作り方——ココアとコンデンス・ミルクを混合せ、鹽を加へ、フライパン又は鐵鍋
　　に入れ絶えず混ぜながら弱火で煮詰め、少量を水の中に落して指で丸められ
　　る位の固さになる迄約十二分間煮ます。火より下してヴアニラを加へ、油を
　　塗つた天パンに流して冷します。後、小匙一杯位づつ手で丸め、細く切つた
　　ココナツツの中にころがしてまぶします。

No. 318　　　クリスマス・キヤンデー

材料　砂糖　　　　　　　カツプ三杯　　　クリーム　　　　　カツプ一杯
　　　バター　　　　　　大匙山盛り一杯　ヴアニラ　　　　　小匙一杯
　　　デーツ細く切つた
　　　　　もの　　　　　一封度　　　　　乾無花果細く
　　　　　　　　　　　　　　　　　　　　切つたもの　　　　一封度
　　　乾葡萄　　　　　　一封度　　　　　ココナツツ　　　　一封度
　　　胡桃細く切つたもの　カツプ一杯半

作り方——砂糖とクリームとバターを併せて、十分位煮立たせ、少量を冷水の中
　　に落して指先で丸められる位の固さになつたらば火より下し、なめらかに固
　　まる迄よく混ぜ、他の材料を混合せ楕圓形の一塊に丸め、水にぬらしてよく
　　しぼつた布巾に包み、のち、パラフイン紙に包んで少くとも二週間程密閉し
　　て置きます。召し上る時には薄く切り四角又は三角に切つてキヤンデーとし
　　ます。

No. 319   **CANDIED GRAPEFRUIT PEEL**

Remove peel from two clean-skinned grapefruit in quarters. Cover with water to which one teaspoon salt has been added. Boil 20 minutes. Drain. Repeat process three times, omitting salt. Cut with scissors into strips. Cover with fresh water and boil until peel is tender, 20 to 30 or more minutes longer. Drain. Bring one cup sugar and cup water to boil. Add peel. Boil gently until syrup is nearly absorbed. Drain. Roll in sugar.

No. 319　　　　　　グレープ・フルーツ皮の砂糖漬

作り方――グレープ・フルーツ二個分の皮の内側の白い所を取り、他を　四ツに切り、かぶる程の水に鹽小匙一杯を入れた中で二十分間茹で、水をすてゝ新しい水で鹽を入れずに更に二十分間茹で、また水をすて、以後同樣に鹽を入れぬ水で二回茹で、水をすて皮を鋏で二分位の厚さの細長い形に切り、また水をかぶる程加へて二、三十分間皮が軟くなる迄茹でて水をすて、砂糖カツプ一杯と湯カツプ半杯を沸騰させた中に入れ、弱火で蜜が殆んど無くなる迄煮て皮を取り出し、グラニユ糖にまぶします。

No. 320   TOASTED GIBLET AND EGG SANDWICH

Cook the Giblets from one chicken in salted water until tender. Put through a food chopper together with a hard-cooked egg. Add one tablespoonful of cream or evaporated milk one half teaspoonful Worcestershire sauce, one teaspoon tomato catsup, and one half teaspoonful salt. Use as a filling for toasted sandwiches.

No. 321   PEANUT BUTTER AND BANANA SANDWICH

½ Cup peanut butter	½ Teaspoonful lemon juice
¼ Cup cream or hot water	2 Bananas

Mix the peanut butter with the cream until smooth and light in color, then combine with banana plup and lemon juice, or sliced banana over layer of peanut butter on bread.

No. 322   SANDWICH FILLING SUGGESTIONS

A. Raisins worked into cheese.

B. Chopped raisins, figs, dates or prunes, and nut meats moistened with mayonnaise dressing or lemon juice.

C. The well whipped white of an egg mixed with a cup each of chopped raisins and nut meats, seasoned with a little salt.

D. Olives, peanut butter and celery in equal quantities and moistened with mayonnaise dressing.

E. Peanut butter moistened with salad dressing and mixed with raisins, dates, figs or bananas.

F. Peanut butter mixed with chopped dill, sweet or sour pickles.

G. Creamed cheese and chopped stuffed olives.

H. Cheese and shredded pineapple between very thin slices of bread.

I. Tunafish mixed with parsley, lemon juice, seasoning and a bit of onion.

J. Ground boiled ham and chopped pickles or chopped peanuts.

K. Pimientos, cucumbers and onion, minced mixed with mayonnaise and spread on buttered entire wheat bread.

L. Green pepper, pimiento and olives with mayonnaise.

M. Boston brown bread with minced corned beef seasoned with mustard and rubbed to a paste.

N. Green tealate melted over hot water and added to creamed butter.

No. 320　　　　鷄の肝のサンドヰツチ

作り方——一羽の鷄の肝、心臓等を軟くなる迄茹で玉子一個と共に挽肉器で挽き
クリーム大匙一杯、ウイスタシヤ・ソース小匙半杯、トマト、ケチヤツプ 小
匙一杯、鹽小匙四分ノ一を加へパンの間に塗りその儘又はバターを溶したフ
ライパンの中で兩面を燒いて溫いサンドウヰツチとします。

No. 321　　　　ピーナツツ・バターとバナナ

材料　ビーナツツ・バター　　カツプ半杯　　バナナ裏漉にしたもの　二本
　　　クリーム　　　　　　カツプ四分ノ一　レモン汁　　　　　　小匙半杯

作り方——ビーナツツ・バターをクリームで滑かに延し、レモン汁と バナナを加
へてパンの間に塗るのです。

No. 322　　　　サンドヰツチ用材料いろいろ

A. 乾葡萄を細く切つて軟く煉つたチーズの中に混合せたもの

B. 微塵切りの胡桃、無花果、デーツ、プルンズ、乾葡萄等を マヨーズ・ドレツ
シング又はレモン汁で和へたもの

C. 充分泡立てた玉子の白味一個に鹽小匙四分の一と胡桃を細く切つたものカツ
プ一杯と乾葡萄を細く切つたものカツプ一杯を加へたもの

D. オリーブとピーナツツ・バターとセロリを同じ分量づつ混ぜてマヨネーズ・ド
レツシングで和へたもの

E. ビーナツツ・バターをマヨネーズ・ドレツシングで軟く延して、バナナ、デー
ツ、乾葡萄、無花果等を少し加へたもの

F. ビーナツツ・バターにビツクルスを微塵切りにして加へたもの

G. チーズを軟く煉つて、細く切つたスタツフト・オリーブを加へたもの

H. チーズを煉り、微塵切りのパイナツプルを加へたもの（これは薄い白パンの
間に用ひます）

I. 鮪の油漬に少量のパセリの微塵切りを加へ、レモン汁と玉葱汁で味を附けた
もの

J. ボイルド・ハムの挽肉に微塵切りのビーナツツとビツクルスを加へたもの

K. 微塵切りのビミエント、胡瓜、玉葱等をマヨネーズで和へたもの（これは黒
パンのサンドヰツチによい。）

L. グリン・ペパーとピミエントとオリーブの微塵切りをマヨネーズ・ドレツシン
グで和へたもの

M. コンビーフをほぐして芥子と和へたものをボストン・ブラウン・ブレツドに塗
つたもの

N. 固形緑茶を溶してバターと煉合せたもの

No. 323   **CRISP RELISH**

12 Red peppers	2 Tablespoons celery seed
12 Green peppers	2 Tablespoons mustard seed
12 Small onions	1 Quart sugar
1 Medium head cabbage	1 Quart vinegar
½ Cup salt	

Grind red and green peppers, onions and cabbage with coarse blade of food chopper. Put in a bag with one half cup of salt and drain all night. In morning add celery and mustard seeds, sugar and vinegar. Mix well and can cold. Relish stays crisp all winter.

No. 324   **PEPPER HASH**

12 Green peppers	1 Quart vinegar
12 Red peppers	3 Cups sugar
14 Medium sized onions	

Mix all together and boil for 20 minutes. Pour into jars, let cool, then cover with wax.

No. 325   **CHOPPED PICKLE**

4 Quarts sliced green tomatoes	1 Teaspoon allspice
4 Quarts sliced cabbage	2 Teaspons celery seed
4 Medium-sized onions	2 Teaspoons mustard seed
2 Red sweet peppers	2 Cups brown sugar
1½ Quarts vinegar	3 Tablespoons salt

Chop all vegetables together after measuring. Add spices, sugar and vinegar using 1 quart vinegar and 1 pint water, if vinegar is very strong.

Boil for 25, minutes or until there is just enough liquid to moisten well. Seal in sterile jars. This makes about 4 quarts of pickle.

No. 323　　　　　　キ ヤ ベ ツ 漬 物

材料　赤唐辛子　　　　　　　十二個　　　グリン・ペパー　　　　十二個
　　　小さい玉葱　　　　　　十二個　　　キャベツ　　　　　　　（中）一個
　　　鹽　　　　　　　　　　カツプ半杯　セロリ・シード（香料）　大匙二杯
　　　マスタード・シード　　　　　　　　砂糖　　　　　　　　　　カツプ四杯
　　　（芥子種子）　　　　　大匙二杯
　　　西洋酢　　　　　　　　カツプ四杯

作り方——唐辛子、グリン・ペパー、玉葱、キヤベツ等を目の荒い挽肉器で挽くか又
　　は全部微塵切りにして、袋に鹽と一緒に入れ一晩つるして置きます。朝にな
　　つたらば香料、砂糖、酢等を加へ充分混ぜ、その儘、熱湯に入れて一度煮立
　　てた貯藏瓶に入れ、密閉して置きます。これは數ケ月間保存して置き必要の
　　時に瓶から出して召し上るのです。

No. 324　　　　　　ペ パ ー ・ レ リ ツ シ ユ

材料　グリン・ペパー　　　十二個　　　赤唐辛子　　　　　　　十二個
　　　玉葱　　　　　　　　（中）十四個　砂糖　　　　　　　　　カツプ三杯
　　　酢　　　　　　　　　　カツプ四杯

作り方——全部を細く纎切りにして、砂糖と酢を加へ二十分間沸騰させ、熱湯で
　　一度煮たガラスのコツプに入れ、冷して後溶したパラフインで上を密閉して
　　置き、數ケ月間保存して置いて好みの時召し上るのです。

No. 325　　　　　　微 塵 切 リ 漬 物

材料　青トマト薄輪切り　カツプ十六杯　キヤベツ纎切り　　カツプ十六杯
　　　玉葱　　　　　　　四個　　　　　赤唐辛子　　　　　二個
　　　西洋酢　　　　　　カツプ六杯　　オール・スパイス　小匙一杯
　　　セロリ・シード　　小匙二杯　　　芥子種子　　　　　小匙二杯
　　　黑砂糖　　　　　　カツプ二杯　　鹽　　　　　　　　大匙三杯

作り方——野菜を量り、全部を細く切るか又は挽肉機で挽き、他の材料を加へま
　　す（此の場合酢が强い時は、酢カツプ四杯に水カツプ二杯用ひるとよい）。火に
　　掛けて二十五分間煮て液體がほとんど無くなりましたらば熱湯で煮沸して殺
　　菌した貯藏瓶に詰めます。

No. 326   PICKLED WATERMELON RIND

1 Pound diced watermelon rind	½ Stick cinnamon
1 Lemon thinly sliced	1 Pound sugar
1 Tablespoon whole cloves	2 Cups vinegar

Peel and slice, rather thick, rind from watermelon and cut into cubes. Let stand overnight covered with water to which one tablespoon of salt has been added for each quart. Drain. Boil the watermelon and other ingredients together until clear and thick. Seal in jars. Cantaloupe rind may be prepared in the same way.

No. 327   SPICED GRAPES

7 Pounds grapes	3 Tablespoons cinnamon
1 Pint vinegar	1 Tablespoon cloves
5 Pounds sugar	1 Tablespoon mace

Wash the grapes and pick them from the stems. Slip the pulp from the skins and cook them for a few minutes until soft. Rub the pulp through a coarse sieve to remove the seeds. Combine the pulp with the skins. Add the sugar and spices and cook the mixture until thick and clear. Pour into hot, sterile jars and seal.

No. 328   GRAPE CONSERVE

8 Pounds grapes	4 Pounds sugar
2 Oranges	1½ Pounds seedless raisins

Pulp the grapes, separating the pulp and skins. Boil the pulp and strain out the seeds. Add the pulp to the skins and cook for 15 minutes. Add the sugar and raisins and oranges, which have been put through a food chopper. Cook the entire mixture for 45 minutes. Pour into hot, sterile jars and seal.

No. 326　　　　　西 瓜 の 皮 の 漬 物

材料	西瓜の皮の賽ノ目切り	一封度	レモン薄輪切り	一個
	ホール・クローブ	大匙一杯	ニツケの枝小さく	
			折つたもの	一本
	砂糖	一封度	酢	カツプ二杯

作り方——西瓜皮を割合に厚く切り、これを五分位の賽ノ目切りにして一晩水を
　かぶせ大匙一杯の鹽を加へて置き、次の朝、水を切ります。此の賽ノ目切り
　西瓜一封度に對して他の材料を上述の様に量り、これを加へて沸騰させます。
　透明になり汁が濃くなりましたらば、熱湯で煮て殺菌した瓶に詰めます。メ
　ロンの皮も同様にして漬けます。

No. 327　　　　　葡 萄 香 料 入 リ 漬 物

材料	葡萄	七封度	酢	カツプ二杯
	砂糖	五封度	ニツケ	大匙三杯
	クローブ	大匙一杯	メース	小匙一杯

作り方——葡萄の皮と實を別々にして皮を數分間（五分位）煮て軟にし、實は裏漉
　にして柯子を取り、皮と實を併せます。これに砂糖と香料を加へ、濃く透明
　になる迄煮て、熱湯の中で煮沸して殺菌した貯藏瓶に入れ密閉します。

No. 328　　　　　葡 萄 コ ン サ ー ブ

材料	葡萄	八封度	オレンヂ	二個
	砂糖	四封度	乾葡萄	一封度半

作り方——葡萄の皮と實を別々にして實を軟く茹で、裏漉にして種子を取り、實を
　皮と併せて十五分間煮ます。オレンヂと乾葡萄を挽肉器で挽くか又は微塵切
　りにして砂糖と混ぜ、前の煮た葡萄に加へ、弱火で四十五分間煮て後、熱湯
　で煮沸殺菌した貯藏瓶に入れて密閉します。

No. 329   **SPICED CRANBERRIES**

5 Cups cranberries   2 Leaves mace

3 Cups sugar   2 Pieces of cinnamon bark

6 Whole cloves   1 Piece dried lemon peel

4 All spice berries

Wash the cranberries thoroughly and pick over. Add water to cover and simmer over low fire. Put the seasoning in a small bag and put in the stew pan with the berries. When the cranberry skins burst they are done, take out the spice bag and add the sugar and simmer for a few minutes longer, until clear. This is excellent to serve with roast turkey.

No. 330   **SWEET PICKLED PEACHES**

16 Cups peeled peaches   ¼ Cup whole cloves

7 Cups dark brown sugar   ½ Cup bark cinnamon

5 Cups vinegar

Boil sugar and vinegar three minutes. Add the spices loosely tied in a muslin bag. Add the peaches and boil gently until very tender and well glazed. Pour into jars and fill to overflowing with hot syrup.

No. 331   **ORANGE MARMALADE**

6 Oranges   1 Cup lemon juice

3 Lemons   Sugar

Wash the oranges and lemons and cut in thin slices skin and all. Add water to cover and allow to stand over night.   Next morning cook the fruit in the same water for 45 minutes and leave standing over night once more. Measure in the morning and add one and a half times as much sugar and cook 45 minutes again. Add lemon juice as you remove from the fire and seal in steralized bottles immediately and seal with parafine.

No. 329　　　　　スパイスド・クランベリー

材料　クランベリー　　　カツプ五杯　　　砂糖　　　　　　　　カツプ三杯
　　　クローブ　　　　　六個　　　　　　オール・スパイス　　四個
　　　メース　　　　　　二枚　　　　　　ニツケの枝　　　　　二本
　　　乾レモン皮　　　　一切れ

作り方――クランベリーをよく洗ひ、いたんで居るのは取除けて、水をかぶる程
　　加へて火に掛けます。クローブ、オール・スパイス、　メース、ニツケ、レモ
　　ン皮等の香料を小さな袋に入れ、クランベリーの中に沈ませて煮ます。クラ
　　ンベリーの皮がはち切れたらば煮えたのですから、香料入りの袋を取り出し
　　砂糖を加へ更に弱火で透通る迄数分間煮て火より下します。此のソースはク
　　リスマスの時七面鳥の添物としてよいものです。

No. 330　　　　　桃のスパイス（甘い香料入り漬物）

材料　桃の皮をむいたもの　カツプ十六杯位　黒砂糖（花見砂糖）　カツプ七杯
　　　西洋酢　　　　　　　カツプ五杯　　　ホール・クローブス
　　　　　　　　　　　　　　　　　　　　　　（香料）　　　　カツプ四分ノ一
　　　ニツケの皮　　　　　カツプ半杯

作り方――砂糖と酢を三分間沸騰させ、クローブとニツケを小さい袋に入れたも
　　のを加へ、桃を靜かに入れ軟くなる迄靜かに煮ます。次に桃を一度熱湯で煮
　　て貯藏瓶に入れ、沸騰して居る桃の煮汁を入れ之に加へて密閉して二週間以
　　上置きます。肉等に添える甘い漬物です。

No. 331　　　　　美味しい蜜柑マーマレード

材料　オレンヂ　　　　　六個　　　　　　レモン　　　　　　　三個
　　　・レモン汁　　　　　カツプ一杯　　　砂糖

作り方――オレンヂとレモンはよく洗つて皮ごと薄く輪切りにして、かぶる程の
　　水に入れ一晩置きます。翌朝水と果實を四十五分間煮て再び一晩置き、次の
　　朝分量を計り、その一倍半の分量の砂糖を加へ、四十五分間煮ます。之を火
　　より下しながらレモン汁を加へます。これは直に熱湯に入れて煮沸した貯藏
　　瓶又はガラスに入れパラフインで蓋を密閉して保存します。

No. 332   **WHIPPED CREAM**

Put one half cup cream in straight-sided bowl or top of small double boiler and beat until thick. Add gradually two tablespoons sugar and one fourth teaspoon vanilla and continue beating until stiff.

Whipped Evaporated Milk: Scald evaporated milk in top of double boiler 10 minutes. Chill very thoroughly. Surround with crushed ice and finish like whipped cream.

Whipped Powdered Milk: Measure six tablespoons cold water in top of double boiler, add four and half tablespoons powdered milk and beat until entirely blended an smooth. Place over hot water and scald three minutes. Chill thoroughly to 42 degrees F. and finish like whipped cream.

No. 332　　　クリームの泡立て方

<u>生クリームの場合</u>　生クリームをカツプ半杯深い器に入れ、泡立て器で混ぜながら少し固まり初めましたらば大匙二杯の砂糖と小匙四分ノ一のヴアニラを次第に泡立て續けながら加へて用ひます。

<u>クリーム(罐詰)の場合</u>　二重鍋の上部でクリームを十分間煮て沸騰させ、冷して深い器に入れ、周圍に氷を盛り、泡立て器で泡立てます。

<u>粉ミルクの場合</u>　水大匙六杯と粉ミルク大匙四杯半を混ぜて二重鍋の上部で三分間煮て後冷し、氷を周圍に盛つた器に入れ、泡立て器で泡立てます。

Table of Weights and Measures

4 Teaspoonfuls of liquid	1 Tablespoonful
4 Tablespoonfuls of liquid	1 Gill, ¼ cup, or 1 **wineglassful**
1 Tablespoonful of liquid	½ Ounce
1 Pint of liquid	1 Pound
1 Quart of flour	1 Pound
4 Cups of flour	1 Pound
1 Tablespoon of flour	½ Ounce
3 Cups of corn meal	1 Pound
1 Cup of butter	½ Pound
1 Pint of butter	1 Pound
1 Tablespoonful of butter	1 Pound
Butter the size of an **egg**	2 Ounces, or 2 tablespoons
Butter the size of a walnut	1 Ounce, or 1 tablespoon
1 Pint of chopped meat	1 Pound
10 Eggs	1 Pound
A dash of pepper	⅛ Teaspoonful, three **shakes**
25 Drops	1 Teaspoonful
2 Cups granulated sugar	1 Pound
1 Pint granulated sugar	1 Pound
2½ Cups powdered sugar	1 Pound

Brown sugar is lighter than white by 1 ounce.

Important

One pound avoirdupois = 120 momme.

Cup used in measures is the ordinary tea cup size, holding ½ pint of liquid. An ordinary water glass is the same size.

小 匙 四 杯　　　　　＝　大匙一杯

大 匙 四 杯　　　　　＝　カツプ四分の一

大匙一杯の液體　　　　＝　二分の一オンス

一パイントの液體　　　＝　一封度

一クヲートのメリケン粉　＝　一封度

カツプ四杯のメリケン粉　＝　一封度

大匙一杯のメリケン粉　　＝　二分の一オンス

カツプ三杯のコーンミール　＝　一封度

カツプ一杯のバター　　　＝　二分の一封度

一パイントのバター　　　＝　一封度

大匙一杯のバター　　　　＝　一オンス

鷄卵大のバター　　　　　＝　二オンス

胡桃大のバター　　　　　＝　一オンス

纖切肉の一パイント　　　＝　一封度

鷄 卵 十 個　　　　　＝　約一封度

胡椒の一と振り　　　　　＝　小匙八分の一

二 十 五 滴　　　　　＝　小匙一杯

カツプ二杯のグラニユ糖　＝　一封度

一パイントのグラニユ糖　＝　一封度

カツプ二杯半の粉砂糖　　＝　一封度

★黑砂糖は白砂糖より一オンスかた輕し

★一封度（常衡十六オンス）＝百二十匁

For Baking: Oven Terms

Slow Oven .... 250 to 300 degrees F.

Moderate Oven .... 300 to 350　　,,　　　　,,

Hot Oven .... 350 to 400　　,,　　　　,,

Quick Oven .... 400 to 450　　,,　　　　,,

Very Hot Oven .... 450 to 550　　,,　　　　,,

Approximate Time Needed to Prepare Oven

200 to 250 degrees F. .... 5 minutes before needed

350 to 400　　,,　　,, ... 7　　,,　　　,,　　　　,,

400 to 450　　,,　　,, ... 10　　,,　　　,,　　　　,,

450 to 550　　,,　　,, ... 12　　,,　　　,,　　　　,,

Candy Terms

Pearl .... 220 degrees

Small Thread .... 228　　,,

Large Thread .... 236　　,,

Blow .... 240　　,,

Feather .... 242　　,,

Small or Soft Ball .... 244　　,,

Large or Hard Ball .... 250　　,,

Light Crack or Brittle .... 254　　,,

Hard Crack or Snap .... 284　　,,

弱　火　の　天　火　＝　華氏二五〇乃至三〇〇度

中　火　の　天　火　＝　華氏三〇〇乃至三五〇度

強　火　の　天　火　＝　華氏四〇〇乃至四五〇度

極強火　の　天　火　＝　華氏四五〇乃至五五〇度

華氏二〇〇乃至二五〇度に天火を熱するには……約五分間

華氏三五〇乃至四〇〇度に天火を熱するには……約七分間

華氏四〇〇乃至四五〇度に天火を熱するには……約十分間

華氏四五〇乃至五五〇度に天火を熱するには……十二分間

注　意

　本書の調理法中、材料の部は左右二段に組んでありますから、左から右へ、又左に戻つて次に右へと讀んで戴きます。

不許複製
禁無斷轉載

昭和八年十二月二十六日印刷
昭和八年十二月三十日發行

編輯者　ジヤパン・アドヴアタイザー家庭欄主任　ドロシー・エドガース

發行者　右代表者　ジヤパン・アドヴアタイザー新聞社　ジエームス・アール・ヤング

印刷者　ジヤパン・アドヴアタイザー新聞社　大石米三

印刷所　ジヤパン・アドヴアタイザー新聞社

發行所　東京市麴區町内山下町一丁目一番地　ジヤパン・アドヴアタイザー新聞社　電話銀座(57)一五七一・二三三〇・四七四〇番

定價　金壹圓五拾錢

About the Author

Marjorie Young, wife of newsman and foreign correspondent, James R. Young, enjoys entertaining, especially in unusual ways.

During her six years in Japan she exchanged lessons in American table settings with silver, dishes, linens, guest chair seatings and menus, with a group of eight prominent Japanese ladies in return for proper chopstick maneuvering with various types of Japanese porcelains, lacquer trays, floor pillows and honor guest seatings for formal and informal luncheons and dinners. Recipes were exchanged and tried in their own home kitchen. Many of them are included in this volume.

While in Tokyo, *The Japan Advertiser,* an American daily newspaper managed by her husband, produced the first foreign-style cooking schools and fashion shows in that country. In this volume are tested recipes, suggested by Swiss, Italian, French, German, Japanese and American chefs in Japan at that time.

Marjorie Young served as technical advisor on the film *Behind The Rising Sun* taken from the book written by her husband.

She has written several books. Among them are *Decorating For Joyful Occasions* and *It's Time For Christmas Decorations.* She is also contributing writer for cook books of the Women's National Press Club, and the Overseas Press Club. She attended Le Cordon Rouge and Le Cordon Bleu cooking schools in Paris. She is listed in "Who's Who of American Women".